MW01089784

NEWSWRITING
EXERCISES

NEWSWRITING EXERCISES

Second Edition

Ken Metzler
University of Oregon

PRENTICE HALL, Englewood Cliffs, NJ 07632

Library of Congress Cataloging-in-Publication Data

Metzler, Ken.
     Newswriting exercises.

     Includes index.
     1. Reporters and reporting. 2. Journalism—
Authorship. I. Title.
PN4781.M46 1986   808′.06607   86-25549
ISBN 0-13-611641-8

Editorial/production supervision: Cyndy Rymer
Cover design: Yudal Kyler
Manufacturing buyer: Harry P. Baisley

© 1987, 1981 by Prentice Hall
A Paramount Communications Company
Englewood Cliffs, New Jersey 07632

Printed in the United States of America

10 9 8 7 6 5 4

ISBN 0-13-611641-8

Prentice-Hall International (UK) Limited, *London*
Prentice-Hall of Australia Pty. Limited, *Sydney*
Prentice-Hall Canada Inc., *Toronto*
Prentice-Hall Hispanoamericana, S.A., *Mexico*
Prentice-Hall of India Private Limited, *New Delhi*
Prentice-Hall of Japan, Inc., *Tokyo*
Prentice-Hall of Southeast Asia Pte. Ltd., *Singapore*
Editora Prentice-Hall do Brasil, Ltda., *Rio de Janeiro*

CONTENTS

Chapter Thirteen

USING NUMBERS 71

Chapter Fourteen

WRITING THE FEATURE STORY 77

Chapter Fifteen

THE PERSONALITY FEATURE 85

Chapter Sixteen

WRITING FROM DOCUMENTS 91

Chapter Seventeen

THE NEWS CONFERENCE 113

SPELLING

GRAMMAR EXERCISES

PUNCTUATION EXERCISES

Appendix B

ANSWER KEYS

Appendix C

CITY DIRECTORY

INDEX

PREFACE

In the first edition of this book, I suggested six ways in which I felt *Newswriting Exercises* differed from other exercise books on the market. The same six reasons prevail today, along with a seventh. Let's start with number 7, for it explains the major difference between the first and second editions.

The difference is that it has grown from an exercise book to a primary-level college textbook that not only presents a succession of journalistic exercises of increasing complexity, but also gives pointers and suggestions for how to handle them. For each category of news and feature writing, point-by-point instructions show how stories within the category should be written. Several model stories appear in the appendix to give further guidance.

Newswriting Exercises has thus become a mini-text intended to prove valuable to teachers who believe the best way to learn newswriting is to write—and then write some more until the techniques are mastered.

Experience has prompted some further tinkering with the format of the book, such as the following:

• An earlier entry into the techniques of newswriting. The language skills exercises that occupied the early chapters of the first edition have been moved to the appendix.

• New or expanded emphasis on the techniques of handling meetings, news conferences, obituaries, interviews, features, personality stories, and potentially libelous stories—along with a smoother organizational structure for handling these new elements.

• Inclusion of new exercises and improvement of old ones. Experience (mine and that of other teachers) has shown what works. The best exercises have been retained, the worst discarded, and additional ones have been devised to deal with new situations.

Those who have used the first edition will find that the elements that made it distinctive have been retained. They include the original six points:

1. Emphasis on language skills. Placement of most language skills exercises in the appendix does not mean de-emphasis. Several users have suggested this reorganization, however, so that language skills exercises don't interfere with the flow of material about newswriting techniques.

2. A structure that flows from simple to complex assignments, all the while giving helpful suggestions.

3. Continued emphasis on story lines to give students practice in understanding the long-range nature of news. The travails of several news personalities continue to thread their way through these chapters.

4. Real-world complexity. Almost all exercises are based on or adapted from actual news stories. Although exercises can never approach the complexity of the actual incident, I've declined to pre-digest material to make it easier for students to write. I've not always succeeded, however. One exercise portraying a statistical survey occupies three pages of this text; the original document on which it's based contains 175 pages—almost as many as this entire textbook.

5. A means of developing information-gathering skills. I've tried, through interview dialogues and references to documentary research methods, to show how reporters get information. The illustrations will prove useful when the student moves on to real-world newsgathering.

6. A confidence builder. *Newswriting Exercises* is designed to be used at an early stage of a student's newswriting skills development. It can be used with or without an accompanying textbook. By temporarily relieving student writers of the responsibility of getting information, it will allow them to develop news judgment and writing skills first. Then, when it comes time for students to do their own fact-gathering, they will proceed with more self-assurance, having already learned news values and story structure from this text.

If it is important to use an exercise book at one stage of development, it's equally important to stop using it at another—or to combine its use with live interviews in real news situations. I hope this book will fill a vital need at just the right time in the development of journalistic skills and then, as students progress beyond the need for it, that it will become a fondly remembered relic of the past.

A special acknowledgement. I owe a debt of gratitude to the many teachers who have passed along suggestions for the second edition—parituclarly Ron Marmarelli, Central Michigan University; Dr. Steve Pasternack, New Mexico State University; Rob Phillips, Oregon State University; Jim Lemert, and Duncan McDonald, University of Oregon.

Chapter One

LEARNING TO WRITE NEWS

This text has a simple, straightforward purpose: to teach you how to write news. To some extent you already know how to write. All of us write or speak news whether we realize it or not. When you write or call a friend, you usually relate news. Frequently you do so the same way professional journalists do—you say the most important part first, and then you elaborate with the details. Thus:

I just inherited a million dollars today!
    Uncle George died a couple of weeks ago, and today they read his will in the lawyer's office. And guess what? Ol' George left the bulk of his estate to me—"my favorite niece," as he put it in the will. . . .

A professional writer would omit the personal expressions, "Ol' George" or "guess what?" for example, but the process is remarkably similar otherwise. That is why you can master the technique of newswriting by adapting the way you regularly present news to other people. The process seems remarkably uncomplicated—you more or less blurt it out: You flunked a chemistry exam or your team won the softball tournament.

Sometimes, though, your news is indefinite, not a specific event. You're undecided, let's say, about whether to concentrate your studies on English literature or political science. How do you write that kind of

indefinite news? You probably would say something like, "So far I haven't been able to make up my mind about. . . ."

The public agencies routinely covered by the news media often face equally unresolved future prospects. And professionals write about them in just about the same way: "Should the city's police chief be asked to resign? The City Council couldn't make up its mind on that question after an hour of debate in its Monday night meeting. . . ." Or imagine a scenario in which a political faction on the council demands the chief's resignation and the chief refuses to comply.

Public issues do tend to get complicated, just as people's personal lives get complicated, but the reporting of news must somehow accommodate the complexity. Police officials have seemed particularly prone to controversy across the country in recent years. News media almost routinely recount their plight. Such an instance might produce a story like this:

POLICE CHIEF SHUNS RESIGNATION DEMAND

By Barbara Miller
Telegram Staff Writer

Fairfield Police Chief Ernest J. Hudson plans to stay on the job despite a demand for his resignation at the City Council meeting Monday night.

The demand came from the chairman of the council's Police Committee, Kenneth Wheelock. He said his three-member committee had voted 2–1 to ask for the resignation.

Hudson, interviewed after the meeting, called the demand a "personal vendetta, politically inspired," and said he would not resign.

Wheelock accused Hudson of "soft-headedness" in dealing with several street demonstrations last year. He said Hudson had failed to cope with increased violence, particularly rape, and with what Wheelock called "appallingly low morale" among the city's 100-member police force.

The allegations prompted an hour of council debate last night, but no action ensued. . . .

How, you may ask, do such stories get into the newspapers or onto broadcast news? They get there because news reporters constantly watch events of public interest. They even station watchers at the places where such events become known—police headquarters, city hall, the state legislature, the governor's office and many others. In news parlance, the watching process is called "covering a beat." As part of their coverage, reporters attend meetings of governmental agencies, such as the city council, where decisions are made on how to spend public moneys or actions are taken that affect people's lives.

So it was that reporter Barbara Miller attended last night's council meeting. As meetings go, Barbara decided, this was one of the more interesting ones. At least it contained some lively discussion and controversy—two important elements in the makeup of a good news story.

Who—you may ask—is Barbara Miller? Indeed, who is Ernest J. Hudson? A brief explanation is in order.

The characters in this book—a whole community of them—are fictional personalities created to represent the realities of professional journalism. The result is, to be sure, a simplification. But as such it's a place to begin. If you understand on the fictional level why Ernest Hudson has so many political problems in mythical Fairfield, you may more easily anticipate why real police chiefs—or city managers or county commissioners or governors or school superintendents—have similar (though probably more complex) problems. Read the daily newspapers or watch/listen to broadcast news and you will discover how frequently these occupational types become embroiled in controversy.

So this book contains the problems of a typical town—Fairfield—and its people. Here people argue over progress or lack of it, over zoning restrictions and street repair and crime, over politics and economics—in short, over a representative sample of the issues typical of American communities. Fairfield is Everytown, U.S.A. It has about 75,000 people—gentle people, progressive

people who take pride in their hometown. Fairfield is home of a small liberal arts college, Kit Carson College, named for the famous nineteenth century mountain man. The college has about 1,000 students, also a pretty fair football team and a faculty that likes to teach and conduct research. Fairfield is the seat of Lincoln County, in the approximate center of a state called Anystate. Its economic support is largely agriculture and light manufacturing. The community's largest employer is Acme Manufacturing (3,500 workers), which produces hundreds of different devices to make things a little easier for humankind, including paper products, plastics, and a large array of electronic devices from toys to cockroach zappers, from heat-sensor mousetraps to electronic babysitters.

The book also contains some problems typical of newswriting. One is the name of the city's mayor, Rodney Dmytryshyn (pronounced dim-a-TRISH-un). The name may cause you spelling problems—that, too, is a subtle touch of reality. The name of the former mayor, a grand old character named Ivan R. VanDenBosch, is scarcely better. Learn the importance of spelling names correctly at this exercise stage and you'll have a lot fewer problems later on.

This book contains 97 exercises that will help you develop your professional reporting and writing skills. They are not idle or miscellaneous exercises designed to make work. They are part of an integrated story context designed to help you learn some of the realities of professional newswriting. You won't be in professional journalism long before discovering that reality runs similar to soap opera. What *are* the powerful, mysterious forces aligned against crime fighter Ernest Hudson? Can he cope with the political machinations determined to cause his downfall?

Any reporter coming into a newsroom—you, for example—soon learns that news is not a single, isolated incident. Almost all events have both histories and futures. A reporter dropped into the middle of such a scenario as the police controversy must try to discover and understand the background.

So this is an integrated exercise book, reflecting the realities of news reporting. Characters such as Barbara Miller, the reporter, are fictional composites based on people the author knows personally. The newsmakers are likewise known. Indeed, most exercises in this book stem from factual incidents or situations reported in the news. If some of them seem strange or unbelievable, they merely reflect a reality that no fiction writer could duplicate for fear of being thought overly imaginative.

Such is the texture of reality.

So Barbara Miller is a typical reporter for the *Fairfield Telegram.* Last night she sat through an hour of sometimes-angry discussion about police problems. Nothing specific happened—the chief wasn't fired nor did he resign—but Barbara recognized it as an important story anyway, for the public has both a right and a need to know the circumstances surrounding the apparent political animosity between the police chief and at least two members of the council.

The council's discussion seemed chaotic to the untrained ear. How is one to make sense out of the vitriolic charges and counter-charges? But to a reporter like Barbara Miller, the elements of a news story emerged clearly enough. *Police committee demands resignation because of several alleged incidents of malfeasance, and chief refuses.* Barbara learned over the years to listen carefully to such discussions and seek out representative comments on either side. Doing so helps capture the essence of the issue. Transferring political chaos into a coherent news report is, after all, what a news reporter does for a living. Those who have no interest in that sort of thing seldom perform well as newswriters.

So Barbara's mind began to sort things out, point by point, almost intuitively. It wasn't intuitive at first; she had to learn the sorting process just as all beginning writers do. These points, or categories of information, would form the outline for her story. As discussion proceeded among members of the council, Barbara began to form questions.

1. What's the issue?
2. What specific points are involved? That is, what specific acts of "malfeasance" is the Police Committee talking about?
3. Who's involved?
4. Why is the issue being brought up now?
5. What are representative statements on either side of the issue?

And so forth. Barbara got most of the answers and quotations by listening to the discussion. She also interviewed the chief after the meeting. From him she picked up the comment that the affair was a political vendetta—at least from the chief's perspective.

Barbara Miller, true to her profession, doesn't take sides in such issues; she merely reports what happened, as best she can determine it through observations and interviews. The participants may express opinions; even her newspaper may do so on the "editorial page." But the editorial page is far removed from the news department where Barbara works. Barbara, through professional training and a firm belief in fair play, must remain neutral. It is not her job to pass judgment on what people do or say; she is a reporter, not a judge and jury.

That, believes Barbara, is why people will talk to her. She is a professional listener, nonjudgmental, tolerant. She has interviewed a wide variety of newsmakers—

from governors to convicted murderers and rapists—and she believes it is this diversity of personalities encountered day by day that makes her job exciting and worthwhile.

Not all stories are intensely controversial, however. That day another story appeared in the *Telegram:*

CHAMPION SWIMMER AWARDED LIFESAVING MEDAL

Linda McCormack, 17-year-old daughter of former Anystate Gov. Edward W. McCormack, received a heroine's welcome Thursday night for an "act of sheer bravery that saved the lives of two children."

McCormack received a gold-plated medal for swimming to the rescue of two children trapped in a partly submerged car at River City last October.

Another *Telegram* reporter, Fred Scott, wrote that story, based on a news release the newspaper had received a week earlier from the Red Cross. Fred had written an "advance" (a story that reports an upcoming event) and then put a note on his calendar to write a follow-up story when the event occurred.

He did not attend the meeting—the story was too minor for that. He merely telephoned the Red Cross to confirm that the event had actually occurred. He called Linda McCormack for a comment. He also checked the paper's library, which keeps indexed files of previous stories, to get background details on the rescue at River City (a nearby community).

It took Fred about twenty minutes to write the story on his video display terminal (VDT), an electronic typewriter linked to a computer. The computer will eventually drive the typesetting machinery that will set the story in type for publication. The story was routine. Another *Telegram* story, however, was more difficult to track down. Reading it in the paper, you get little hint of the problems Barbara Miller had getting the information for it, her second bylined story in that day's paper.

PAGEANT QUEEN QUITS; WON'T POSE IN BIKINI

By Barbara Miller
Telegram Staff Writer

Fairfield has no contestant in the Miss Anystate beauty pageant after "Miss Fairfield"—22-year-old Jeanne Gray—resigned in a dispute over posing in a bikini for publicity pictures.

"They told me either to pose for the pictures or get lost," Gray said today, "so I got lost. Somebody's got to draw the line on the exploitation of women."

Richard Bangor, president of the Metro Club, sponsor of the Miss Fairfield competition, declined to comment on the resignation.

Gray, a fifth-grade teacher at Frederic W. Goudy Elementary School, said the bikini pose "wasn't in my contract" and would embarrass her in her job as elementary school teacher.

Gray won the Miss Fairfield title in last week's Metro Club pageant, competing with 17 other contestants. She would have been a contestant in the state pageant next summer. The state winner will compete in the Miss America pageant in Atlantic City. . . .

If Barbara Miller had any strong feelings on this issue, she kept them to herself or would let them go no further than a few personal friends.

That's not to suggest that she was totally neutral on the question or, indeed, on any of the issues about which she writes. Having feelings about issues of the day is not a bad trait for a newswriter. As an editor once remarked, a good reporter should have a skin thin enough to be sensitive to what's going on, but thick enough to take a neutral stance in writing about it.

In short, Barbara did not find it necessary to personally approve or disapprove of the queen's actions or motives. Her professional decision to pursue the story was based primarily on what she perceived to be the public interest. She reasoned that if she felt strongly about such an issue—a person quitting the pageant rather than being forced to pose in skimpy attire—chances are others would, too. That helps to make it a story of more than routine interest. A certain public cynicism has intruded on beauty pageants in recent years, considering such scandals as a Miss America's resignation after several previously posed nude photos appeared in print. So when events deviate from ordinary pathways—a scandal or a resignation on principle—they're always more newsworthy.

Miller, in any event, had long believed that the test of professionalism in news reporting was the ability to write an accurate, balanced and fair-minded account wherein private opinions do not intrude. Even the difficulties of *getting* such a story should not intrude on the way the story is written, Barbara decided. Like many news items, this one came to a reporter's attention in the most offhand way. Barbara happened to talk with a man at a luncheon meeting. He said his wife works at a local fashion store where a beauty contestant had ordered several evening gowns and then canceled the order two days later.

"I wonder why she did that," said Miller.

"She said she wasn't going to be a queen anymore because they were asking her to pose in a bikini, and she said she wouldn't do that."

Miller called the fashion store, then the queen herself, then members of her family, then various members of the Metro Club. She made fourteen calls and got four outright refusals to talk. The Metro Club president

burned her ear with a litany of offenses he felt the media had committed in the name of press freedom. He also hinted darkly at economic repercussions, such as his company's withdrawal of advertising from the paper, should it be so foolish as to run a story about the resignation.

Through it all Miller kept her composure. She did not get angry or defensive in response to the outbursts. She understood Bangor's concern: He had hoped the issue could be resolved without publicity. People are always doing or saying outrageous things to get stories in the paper or to keep them out, and they are particularly passionate in moments of crisis or controversy. Miller took none of it personally, but she was firm—in a calm, dispassionate manner—in her belief that it was a story of legitimate public interest. Meanwhile she rather enjoyed the challenge of keeping cool under fire and piecing together a story under adverse circumstances. In a perverse way, it made the story more exciting. The more people try to cover up, the more curious and interested reporters and the public become.

After writing the story she made a note on her appointment calendar to check for a possible follow-up story. An issue such as this will have additional installments in the same manner as fictional conflict requires some kind of resolution. New developments would come forth—the queen might change her mind, or the club might, or a new choice would be announced—clearly something had to happen. It would bear watching.

And so, as the chapters unfold, we will be watching. Because most of the exercises in this book are based on real events, you may find some of them frustrating. Detail will sometimes be incomplete, and you're not allowed to make up facts (though classroom instructors may wish to supply additional details or answer students' questions). This book portrays the work of journalists like Miller and Scott in *getting* information as well as writing it. The process of doing so is seldom smooth. Rather it is filled with false starts, uncooperative sources and sometimes-contradictory information. That's reality, and it should be no less true here.

The book's intentions are honorable, however: to prepare you to gather news and to write reports and features for publication or broadcast. Before you can write for publication, you will find it helpful to go through an intermediate step: writing for practice.

Instructors in journalism are rightfully concerned about accuracy in such details as reporting names, addresses and factual details. They are just as important as the larger concepts. The instructors will be able to check your work more easily—catching the carelessness and bad habits at a benign stage—if they can see how you handle information from standardized sources.

Instructors want to make sure, for example, that students get in the habit of checking every name in the *City Directory*. Reporters have learned, sometimes the hard way, that most people are careless with names. But the media dare not be. All names must be carefully checked in the directory. Be forewarned that not every name in the notes and interviews is spelled correctly. Assume that the final authority for names and addresses is always the *City Directory* in Appendix C.

A second goal of this set of exercises is *practice*. If you want to learn to write, then write. It takes practice to learn to weave fragments of reality into a smoothly written news story. Starting with a set of exercises is a little like learning to drive a car in an empty parking lot before venturing out onto a busy boulevard.

Finally, your instructors want you to learn the techniques of getting information with a minimum of trial and error. This book can help show the techniques involved because most exercises are based on real newsgathering and newswriting experiences. How do you conduct an interview? What if the source doesn't want to talk to you? How would you approach a source on a sensitive or potentially embarrassing subject? The answers to these and similar questions are shown through such things as the sample interview dialogues. You can turn to them for help if you are ever confronted with a problem, such as interviewing a bereaved family, because they are based on real experiences—those of the author or of persons interviewed by the author—in the activity depicted.

Newswriting Exercises focuses on writing for newspapers, primarily for the sake of depth and convenience. No other medium encompasses so wide a variety of news and information writing as newspapers do. Broadcast writing tends to be briefer and less far-reaching. To achieve the broadest possible experience within the confines of an exercise book, then, the primary emphasis of this book will be on newspaper writing.

The principles are largely the same, however. Learn the principles here and you can transfer them to other media—broadcast and magazines, particularly—with scant need for retooling of skills.

One final reality that must be discussed here: *reporting and writing of news is fun.*

Some of it is dull and routine, true, though the mark of a good reporter is to be interested in everything you encounter. Few other occupations give you such a wide range of experiences or put you in contact with such a wide array of people—from heads of state to disreputable felons. A good reporter learns how to absorb the best from all of them, even the felons, and to grow as a person from the experiences. Many a reporter, for instance, has confessed to becoming a safe driver only after covering a few fatal auto wrecks and viewing mangled bodies.

Your purpose as a newswriter—telling the world about the people and circumstances that define our civilization—is truly noble and altruistic. It's like being a perennial student—a student of real life. For many, that's a rewarding experience.

Chapter Two

SPELLING, PUNCTUATION AND GRAMMAR QUIZ

A recent journalism graduate applied for an opening on a daily newspaper. To his astonishment, the editors had the audacity to ask him to take a language skills test before they'd talk seriously with him. He promptly flunked the exam, which covered spelling, punctuation and grammar. He didn't get the job.

By no means is this a rare situation. A lot of journalism graduates are woefully deficient in such basics as spelling "accommodate" or knowing whether the doctor should tell her patient to "lay down" or "lie down." What's worse, some young journalists don't even seem to care—at least until they make their first attempts to impress professional editors. By then it may seem too late.

"If I see a single misspelling or grammatical error on an employment application," says one editor, "I immediately discard that candidate." On that basis alone he discards two-thirds of the applications he reads.

Another editor remarked that if carpenters had so few skills in the basics of their craft, they'd be pounding screws with hammers, hanging bathtubs from ceilings and installing windows by nailing the panes into place with rusty spikes.

Master carpenters care for and respect their tools, suggests one language authority. "And so too must writers. Words are our tools and there is, indeed, the right word for each job. Learning grammar is learning how to choose these words and connect them with precision."[1]

Poor language skills remains the major single complaint of editors about new journalism graduates. Fortunately, it's never too late to do something about it. Journalism schools are tightening their standards. One professor gives language exams to his advanced editing students and demands A+ performance (95 percent correct). If they don't measure up, they take additional quizzes until they do. Exercise 1 is one of the quizzes he uses.

To his surprise and delight, most of his students eventually pass the quiz. They study hard for it if only to avoid the humiliation of having to take still another quiz when many of their fellow students have already passed it. Try it yourself. When finished, consult the key in the appendix. Should you score fewer than 95 correct out of the 100 possible, you'll find a bibliography of language skills manuals, reference books and spelling aids accompanying the key. Students who use such materials often find that they can improve their language skills faster than they originally expected.

You will also find in the appendix additional quizzes covering language skills, copy editing, and the Associated Press guide for style.

[1]Lauren Kessler and Duncan McDonald, *When Words Collide.* (Belmont, Calif.: Wadsworth, 1984), p. 4.

EXERCISE 1   A Self-Test

You can administer this test yourself, in private, and only you will know the result. When you have finished, score yourself from the key in Appendix B.

Spelling   *This list of spelling words comes from a file of the most often misspelled words in newswriting students' papers. Circle the correct choice in each group. Use the preferred dictionary spelling where a choice is available.*

1. accomodate, accommodate, acommodate
2. accoustics, acoustics
3. all right, alright
4. apalling, appalling, appaling
5. aweful, awful, awfull
6. beleive, believe
7. benefitted, benefited
8. cemetery, cemetary
9. consistent, consistant
10. correspondant, correspondent
11. defendant, defendent
12. definite, definate, defanite
13. deisel, diesel
14. developement, development
15. exagerrate, exaggerate, exagerate
16. firey, fiery
17. fluorescent, flourescent, flourecent
18. harassment, harrassment, harrasment
19. hemmorage, hemorrage, hemmorrhage, hemorrhage
20. hygiene, hygeine
21. innoculate, inocculate, inoculate
22. laison, liason, liaison
23. occassionally, ocasionally, ocassionally, occasionally
24. occupant, occupent, ocuppent
25. ocurred, occurred, occured
26. picnicking, picnicing, picniking

27. privelage, privilege, privelege, privilage

28. responsable, responsible, responseable

29. sacrament, sacrement

30. sattellite, satellite, sattelite

31. separate, seperate

32. sheriff, sherriff, sherrif, shariff

33. subpena, subpoena, supena

34. temperment, temperament, temporament

35. terific, terrific, terriffic

Punctuation.   *Some of the sentences below contain errors in punctuation. Some contain no errors. Please correct any errors that you find. Punctuate only; do not change the wording.*

36. A five-year old girl was injured Saturday.

37. Dr. John Messerle, father of the bride failed to show up.

38. Police said that, the suspect returned Monday night.

39. Captain Johnson asked ''Where's the guilty party?''

40. How did you like ''Tale of Two Cities?''

41. ''She was gone for only a moment,'' the childs mother said.

42. He said the city is in, ''Dire need of a financial boost.''

43. Inflation was up three percent unemployment was down four percent.

44. Police arrested two men, and a woman, for trespassing.

45. Their work finished at last the firefighters left the scene.

46. Mayor Dmytryshyn said, ''Where but in Fairfield will you find the pioneering spirit mixing with the global view?''

47. The driver his face streaming with tears said he did not see the child crossing the street.

48. ''It's a girl!'' the nurse said.

49. Jones did not heed the mayor's advice, however, he later sold the property and gained a favorable response from city hall.

50. The trees, which workers planted last spring, are dying.

51. The trees that workers planted last spring are dying.

52. ''The team has been resting on it's laurels too long,'' Coach Holloway said.

53. It was a dark, and stormy, night.

54. "I don't trust the mayor, moreover, I think he's a crook," Smith said.

55. "Will you be at work tomorrow?," he asked.

56. In tears Jane Doe told the judge, "He walked up the ramp and said, 'See you later, Sweetie," and that was the last time I saw him alive."

57. The slim long-haired defendant left by the side entrance.

58. The horse lost its saddle.

59. He said he'd be in the Hilton Hotel in Atlanta Georgia.

60. Who's raincoat is that?

61. The defendant said the raincoat was her's.

62. The childrens beds were unmade.

63. The girls names were Carol and Marsha.

64. Governor Burns could not attend the meeting because of the heavy snowfall last night.

65. Snow she said is what she loves most.

66. Police reported seeing Charles car in Circle City last week.

67. A set of well defined rules gives us a sense of order.

68. The victims were Jane Smith, 38, Boston Joe Friday, 44, New York City and Stephanie Cyphers, 19, Yonkers.

Grammar. *Select the correct word from the choices given.*

69. Police returned the gun to John and [she, her].

70. The tire chains she got for Christmas [make, makes] it easy to drive in the mountains.

71. The team of eleven boys [was, were] ready to win the game.

72. The woman, [who, whom] police believe was murdered, did not return home last night.

73. The county commissioners made little progress in [its, their] meeting last night.

74. The City Council, composed of nine members, set [its, their] meeting for Thursday.

75. Annoyed [is, are] the readers when backward run the sentences.

76. Sitting in the car [was, were] three police officers.

77. He said the reward should go to [whoever, whomever] found the treasure.

78. "Just between you and [I, me]," she said, "I prefer men."

79. The forecaster said it looked [like, as if] it might snow.

80. The witness said he felt [bad, badly] about the accident.

81. Jane, asked about her health, said she feels [fine, finely].

82. The doctor told the patient to [lay, lie] down.

83. When he [lay, laid, lied] down he fell asleep.

84. She [lay, laid] the gun on the table and surrendered.

85. Neither Jones nor Smith [have, has] the answer.

86. Neither Jones nor his daughters [have, has] the answer.

87. Governor Penfold, [who, whom] the Republicans supported for Congress, could not attend.

88. It was [he, him], Robert Redford, whom you saw in the hotel.

89. The council approved the [mayor, mayor's] taking a stand on the issue.

90. She testified that she could not imagine [him, his] shooting an innocent bystander.

91. The United Mine Workers [is, are] negotiating a new contract.

92. She [sat, set] the bomb on the porch and ran away.

93. If she [was, were] a princess she'd marry a handsome prince.

94. She looks good [as, like] a princess should.

95. All of the sand [was, were] dumped from the truck.

96. All of the dancers [was, were] aboard the ship.

97. The news media [is, are] on the job.

98. She gave the basket to John and [she, her].

99. [She and I, Her and I] will leave for Denver tomorrow.

100. Jane is taller than [I, me].

Chapter Three

WHAT IS NEWS?

As suggested in Chapter 1, most people recognize news. We use it every day in such personal statements as "I just got a new job" or "I broke my arm skiing last week." Most of us present it precisely the way professional news reporters do: first the essence ("broke my arm"), then the elaborating details. This personal level of news doesn't have much interest outside your own circle of friends. Certain circumstances could change the interest factor, however. If your "new job" were that of President of the United States, then the news of your broken arm would circulate throughout the world within minutes.

So circumstances can change the value of news. The value goes up if prominent persons or institutions are involved. It increases whenever dramatic or unusual circumstances intrude: you broke your arm when lightning struck the ski lift, snapped a cable and flung you 60 feet down a canyon. Readers will marvel at your incredible luck in breaking *only* your arm, thus boosting the news value a notch or two. The measurements of news values are never precise. They may seem capricious. If Bill Johnson, the Olympic ski champion, fell out of bed and broke his arm, a high news value derives from *both* his prominence as an internationally renowned athlete *and* from the irony of a man known for his daring on the ski

slopes hurting himself in such a routine kind of domestic mishap.

Journalists sometimes say, tongue only slightly in cheek, that gathering and writing news is like playing the slot machines in Las Vegas. When one orange shows up, you might have a minor payoff. But when *three* oranges (read: news elements) show up, you've hit a journalistic jackpot.

Consider a real example. Anyone can fall and get hurt. Not much news there, unless the person is Mary Decker Slaney, the famous Olympic distance runner. Add the fact that she falls in a highly publicized Olympic race in front of millions on television, and you have still higher news values. Add a nice twist of irony—she trips over the legs of a prime competitor, Zola Budd—and the news value zooms almost out of sight. Now add "consequence"—as a result of the fall one of America's prime contenders for Olympic Gold will have to wait four years for another try. You have a combination of news values that makes this incident in the 1984 Olympics a story of international importance, one that will be discussed for years.

Such is the capricious nature of "news." Professionals do have a set of measuring devices by which to estimate news values, however.

1. *Prominence.* The big public stories involve more famous people or institutions. Celebrity athletes are more newsworthy than ordinary people. Harvard going bankrupt would be a bigger story than East Siwash Teachers College going broke.

2. *Consequence.* The more the event or situation affects people, the bigger the news. The news value goes up if the legislature passes a law to increase the sales tax. It affects everyone in the state. News value also goes up if last night's big storm has stranded thousands of holiday travelers or caused enormous property damage.

3. *Magnitude.* You lose $20 to a thief and few people care. A bank loses a million dollars and it's major news. Similarly, news value rises with the size of the event; big stories emerge from big money, widespread violence, major disasters and so forth.

4. *Timeliness.* It's bigger news if it just happened, is about to happen or was only recently discovered.

5. *Proximity.* The closer something is to the reader or viewer, the more interest it has. This usually means geographical proximity: Tomorrow's local weather is more important to the local populace than a major storm 3,000 miles distant. But it also can mean commonality of interests. A medical doctor, for example, will find a new cancer treatment of great interest, even though the research occurred at a distant medical center. Similarly, the celebrities we see on films or TV seem "close" to us, which helps to account for the public interest in their activities.

6. *Action.* A specific, concrete action—such as resigning from a beauty pageant on principle—has more news value than a mere expression of beliefs. The more extreme or violent or unusual the action, the more newsworthy.

7. *Concreteness.* News stories are seldom abstract or academic. A concrete story is one that involves a specific, real incident or situation, with real people involved. A single body in the street—the victim of a drunk driver— has more news value than a police chief's warnings about the dangers of drunk driving.

8. *Personality or human interest.* Personification—that is, writing about the activities of real people—has more reader appeal than discussion of issues in the abstract. Writing about traffic safety in general has far less dramatic impact on readers than writing about how the Jones family lost a child to a drunk driver, and what the family is doing to prevent its happening to another child.

9. *Change.* New ideas and attitudes are more newsworthy than those that represent the status quo. Things aren't what they used to be. People are getting married at a later age than before, having fewer children and retiring at earlier ages. News reports of such change interest us, whether we approve or not.

10. *Conflict.* Issues on which people's opinions differ sharply have higher news value than those on which everyone agrees. The conflict often suggests impending change; it illustrates unsettled conditions. The public wants to know how the issues will be resolved.

11. *Rarity.* Like precious metal, the more rare the event or situation, the more newsworthy it becomes. An inch of snow in Miami, where snow rarely falls, is a bigger story than a foot of snow in Buffalo, where snow is common.

All these principles must be learned by newswriters, must be so ingrained in your thinking that they become almost intuitive. That way you react almost automatically if the inch of snow in Miami (rarity) causes massive traffic tie-ups (magnitude, consequence), including the President's limousine (prominence) enroute to a scheduled speech. Perhaps the prominence factor would dominate, so that your opening paragraph (called a "lead" in professional jargon, pronounced "leed") might run something like this: A rare snowfall struck Miami this morning, leaving President Blank among the thousands of people stranded in massive traffic jams. . . .

So what is news? News is usually a concrete action or unsettled situation involving a publicly prominent person, group or agency. It often rises from a basic philosophical issue in which the public has a stake or an interest.

It's important to distinguish the *news issue* from the *news event.* One is conceptual and long range; the other is incidental or momentary. Consider an example in your personal life. You're looking for a job.

The news issue would become your long-range job search.

The news event would be any report of progress (or lack of progress) of a specific nature. You might report such milestones as getting your résumé ready, sending it to prospective employers, receiving replies, particularly the ones that express interest. You might report a specific job interview, a turndown, a nibble and, indeed, the final success in landing a job.

The principles are no less true in news presented by professionals.

A news issue, for example, is political ferment over the need for reforming the federal tax system. It is a continuing, long-range situation that probably will be with us for a long time. A news event emerges anytime a prominent politician gives a speech about it or Congress receives a tax bill or votes on one.

We even have a couple of examples in this text. Two issues emerged in Chapter 1. A beauty queen, subscribing to certain principles (the news issue), resigns from the pageant (news event). A faction of the city council has a so-far-undefined philosophical difference with the police chief (issue) and demands his resignation (event). The chief declines to resign (another news event).

Chances are we'll hear more about these issues. It cannot be otherwise. News issues can close dramatically with one side emerging victorious after much battling.

Or they can close through negotiations and amiable compromise. News stories, focusing on events, can come at any stage. Sometimes issues just bumble on indefinitely until the public grows bored and ceases to care one way or another. That, too, could make at least a small story, if only to close the record.

EXERCISE 2 Rating the News

Let's say that the following events have occurred in the hypothetical news community of Fairfield over the last 24 hours. Write a paper about (or discuss in class) how they should be ranked in accordance with news values discussed in this chapter. Which are essential? Which could be delayed or eliminated entirely? Suggestions: Consult the City Directory *(Appendix C) for information about people not fully identified. When you have completed your ranking, turn to Appendix B to see how several professional journalists handled them.*

1. First a choice between two alternatives. **(A)** Linda McCormack, daughter of a former Anystate governor, accepted a lifesaving medal last night for her rescue of two children trapped in a car partly submerged in a river. **(B)** Linda McCormack declined to accept the medal during the ceremony in her honor last night because "I don't deserve it—a dozen people helped rescue those kids, and I feel uncomfortable being singled out as the 'heroine.' " Which is the more newsworthy?
2. The ex-beauty queen noted in Chapter 1, Jeanne Gray, 22, set a new record in Fairfield's annual Marathon Run yesterday. She completed the distance, slightly in excess of 26 miles, in a time of 2 hours 55 minutes 33 seconds. It was a new woman's record for Fairfield.
3. The President of the United States visited Fairfield unexpectedly last night.
4. Fairfield Mayor Rodney Dmytryshyn returned from a trip to Japan and announced that "there's a good chance" that a Japanese electronics firm will locate a branch manufacturing plant in Fairfield, providing about 350 new jobs.
5. Edward W. McCormack, the former governor of Anystate (he's Linda's father and a resident of Fairfield), was run down by an unidentified bicyclist three weeks ago, a fact just now revealed. No injuries resulted.
6. Ivan R. VanDenBosch, a former mayor of Fairfield, went to the hospital last night with a mild heart attack.
7. Another choice: **(A)** Two Fairfield residents, Henry S. and Samantha S. Plants, were killed in an auto accident last night. **(B)** Two Fairfield residents, Helen A. Yamashita and William F. Zbytovsky, were killed in an auto accident last night. Which is the more newsworthy?
8. Acme Manufacturing Company, Fairfield's largest industrial plant, employer of 3,500 workers, announced this morning the layoffs of 300 workers, effective in two weeks, a cutback made necessary by a poor market for some of its products, according to management.

EXERCISE 3 Ranking the Elements of a News Story

Here are some facts for a news item. Using the scale of news discussed in this chapter, identify the important elements of the story and rate them as best you can in order of descending importance. Sources: Items 1 through 8 from Richard L. Bowers, city fire chief. Items 9-13 from Klinski herself. *More about this story in Chapter 4.*

1. About ten last night the Fairfield Fire Department dispatched a truck to the residence of Elizabeth Klinski, age 67, on Market Lane.
2. She had attended a concert at Carson College and returned to her home about ten.
3. She found smoke pouring from a kitchen window and called the fire department.
4. $10,000 damage.
5. Firefighters said fire started in the kitchen, probably from a short circuit in the kitchen range.
6. Mrs. Klinski's pet cat, Streetlight, died in the fire.
7. Damage confined to kitchen area.
8. Firefighters arrived at 10:10, had the fire out by 10:20.

9. Her husband Tom died 13 years ago. She lives alone.

10. She has lived in Fairfield for 37 years.

11. She was born in a log cabin in Illinois.

12. She has three grown children, all of whom live away from home.

13. She is an avid reader of English classic novels, and particularly enjoys reading Charles Dickens, Arthur Conan Doyle and Robert Louis Stevenson.

Chapter Four

EIGHT STEPS TO WRITING NEWS

Let's write, as a starter, a brief news story about Elizabeth Klinski's house fire. You can do so in eight steps.

1. *Identify a news incident or situation*. News agencies routinely visit (often by phone) such places as police headquarters or the Fire Department to learn of incidents like the Klinski fire. Sometimes they monitor via radio scanner a community's emergency frequencies. When they learn something newsworthy, they assign a reporter to obtain the details.

2. *Gather the facts*. By contacting authorities (the Fire Department in this instance) and witnesses (Klinski herself), a reporter assembles the bits and pieces that you saw in Chapter 3.

3. *Determine the news value*. Some people claim to find great mystery in the way journalists judge news values. Perhaps they fail to realize that a lot of it derives from what people talk about. Imagine yourself walking home one evening. You pass nine houses where nothing much is happening. The tenth is on fire. What would *you* talk

about when you got home? Chances are you'd say something like "The Klinski house is on fire! There's a lot of smoke coming out the window. A fire truck's on the scene. I saw Mrs. Klinski there and she's okay—maybe a little shaken but okay."

You've just defined news and "written" a news story. This is a minor one, lacking prominence, magnitude or even rarity. But the event is timely, local, concrete and active. It even contains a tiny amount of conflict in the dramatic scene of fire crews fighting to avoid destruction. That sense of drama can be a news element, too. A community newspaper might give it a paragraph; broadcast news might give it 15 seconds. A big-city newspaper would probably ignore it unless somebody important were involved.

4. *Define the essential elements of the story.* It may be interesting to learn that Klinski was born in a log cabin in Illinois and reads the classics. But these elements don't belong in this story, which must deal strictly with the facts that made it news. Defined by the essentials, the story appears to have these elements (not necessarily in order of importance):

1. the fact of a house fire
2. the death of a pet
3. the dramatic discovery: coming home to find the house afire
4. $10,000 property damage
5. Fire Department put out the fire
6. cause: electrical short circuit in kitchen
7. no injuries
8. identity of the owner, Elizabeth Klinski
9. definition of locale
10. time of incident

5. *Apply the 5W + H formula.* You can identify the essentials through a time-honored formula for the recounting of incidents. The essentials come in five words that begin with **W** and one with **H**: *Who, What, Where, When, Why and How.* When you organize your thinking this way, you can see how each factual element has its place:

Who? Klinski and the Fire Department.

What? House discovered on fire. $10,000 damage. Fire extinguished. Cat died.

When? Last night about 10.

Where? The Klinski house, 1133 Market Lane (see *City Directory* in Appendix C for addresses and correct spelling of names).

How? How started: bad wiring. How coped with: Fire Department brought in.

Why? Don't confuse Why with How. The superficial answer to Why is via the How—the fire started because of bad wiring and was extinguished because firefighters were brought in. The Why is more complex and less well-defined. Yet ultimately it may be the most important question of all to a perceptive newswriter. Why do house fires start? Why do short circuits occur? What can be done to prevent them? This story is probably not the vehicle to answer such questions. However, the newswriter who asks them will ultimately prove to be a more perceptive reporter than one who ignores them.

6. *Rank the elements by order of importance.* When we communicate important personal news, we tend to state the essence of it first—"The Klinski house is on fire!" Then we provide the details. The news media do the same. Within the neighborhood two essentials emerge (1) a house afire and (2) identification of which house. A news agency might take a more detached view because to say "the Klinski house is on fire!" has meaning only to the neighbors who know her. An early broadcast report, coming before all the facts are known, would sound like this: "Firefighters are at the scene of a house fire on

Market Lane tonight. They were called to the home of Elizabeth Klinski around ten o'clock after Klinski returned from a concert and found smoke pouring out of a window. . . ." In short, from the wider perspective, the station considers the fact of a house fire more important than the identification of a nonprominent citizen. To neighbors, however, identification of *which* house is vital. Both are valid news judgments given the different circumstances.

Let's assume now that all the essential facts are in, as a newspaper reporter might encounter them at the Fire Department the next morning. The report can now be more complete. Here is one possible ranking of elements, from most important to least.

1. $10,000 damage
2. drama of returning to see smoke from window
3. Fire Department saves house
4. cause: faulty wiring
5. absence of injuries to humans
6. death of cat

7. *Write your lead.* The writing of the opening paragraph of a news story involves two procedures. The first is defining the most important element—the essence of the story. The second is assembling the words that represent your definition. Neither procedure is easy. Newswriters don't always agree. The traditional news pattern for a story like this one is to cite damage or injury to humans (the "concreteness" criterion) as the most important. Thus:

A fire caused about $10,000 damage to the home of Elizabeth Klinski, 67, 1133 Market Lane, last night.

Another writer might consider the drama of coming home to see your house afire (the "action" criterion) as most important. Thus:

Elizabeth Klinski, 67, returned to her home about ten last night to find her house on fire.

8. *Write the elaborating details, more or less in order of descending importance.* Follow your outline (Step 6) as you relate the remaining details. Here's the rest of Version 2, starting with Paragraph 2. Note that the story could be cut from the bottom up (a common practice) without deleting the story's essentials. The last paragraph, in other words, is the least important.

She called the Fairfield Fire Department, and the responding crew had the fire out by 10:20 p.m.

Fire Chief Richard Bowers estimated the damage at $10,000. Most damage was in the kitchen where the fire apparently started from a short circuit in the electric range.

No injuries resulted, but Klinski's pet cat, Streetlight, died in the fire.

Eight easy steps. Perhaps they are not always so easy, but they represent a distillation of the steps most news reporters go through almost instantly and intuitively once they have learned the principles. Some additional principles will prepare you for the exercises in this chapter.

Use short sentences, short words, short paragraphs. Material written to be set in narrow columns of type—designed for quick reading—should follow this rule. Sentence length should average no more than thirteen to fifteen words. (The average, however, might include a combination of longer sentences balanced by shorter sentences.) Keep the sentences simple and in regular order: subject, verb, object. Avoid sentences that start with a lengthy clause. Keep words short. The bigger the word, the less readers understand it. Newspaper articles should contan short paragraphs as in the sample story about the house fire. A good average length for paragraphs is thirty to fifty words (three to five typewritten lines). The lead paragraph should be confined to thirty words.

Attribution. Reporters don't make up facts; they gather them from sources. Statements are always attributed to these sources. Note that Fire Chief Bowers is cited as the source of the information in this example. *Always* quote a source for the information you present.

Identification. Newswriters must be sure to identify the people who appear in their stories. Typical means of identification are by age, title or occupation (*Fire Chief* Bowers), street address (Klinski *of 1133 Market Lane*) or by the role they play in the news (such as identifying a witness to an event as a *bystander* or a *passerby*).

Accuracy. Writers must be sure to verify every statement of fact. Mistakes are easy, even when working with a set of facts. Double-check the fact sheet to ensure that your story is accurate in every detail. Get in the habit of checking names and addresses in the *City Directory*.

Exercises

Following are six simple, hypothetical newswriting exercises typical of the stories a beginning reporter would write for a community newspaper. Use them for practice to perfect the principles you have learned. Imagine that you are a new reporter for the *Telegram,* an afternoon paper in Fairfield.

After you've completed Exercises 4, 5 and 6, see the model stories in Appendix B (we trust you not to peek beforehand). Exercises 7 and 8 are to be critiqued by your instructor.

In all cases, strive to keep certain already-cited principles in mind: short paragraphs, short sentences, short words, use of relevant information only, attribution of sources, identification of persons. Always check the *City Directory;* some names and addresses may deliberately be misstated just to keep you on your toes. In case of conflicting statements, assume the *Directory* is correct. Use only the facts given; do not make up facts no matter how spotty you consider the information provided here.

EXERCISE 4 A Burglary Report

The Westside Middle School was burglarized last night. From the following notes, write a brief story.

The school is in the west end of the city. About 500 students attend there. Burglary was discovered at 6:30 this morning by school's janitor, "Hermie" Melville. Entry apparently gained through a window at the principal's office on the first floor of the three-story building. Access gained by shattering the window. Principal Lowry reports that about $18 is missing from petty cash drawer, also two stereo tape recorders missing from the music room. A locked door was pried open to get into the music room. Tape recorders are valued at $300 each. [*Source:* Police Chief Ernest J. Hudson.]

Due Tuesday.

EXERCISE 5   Resignation

John A. Elwell was appointed Fairfield's head librarian three years ago. He had been assistant librarian for the previous five years. He is 47 years old, married (wife: Betty Lou) and has three children (Bruce, 15, Angie, 17 and Tom, 19). Elwell is a Republican, member of the Presbyterian Church, has a BA degree in history from the University of Nebraska and a master's degree in librarianship from the University of California at Berkeley. Today he hands you a copy of a letter he presented last night to the city Library Board.

Dear Board Members:

It is with the deepest regret that I submit to you this letter. Personal considerations, however, have forced me to reconsider my goals in life, and this has led me to the conclusion that I can no longer serve in the capacity of city librarian for Fairfield.

This, therefore, will constitute notice of my resignation, effective next June 30.

I wish to take this opportunity to thank the members of the Library Board, the Mayor, and the members of the Fairfield City Council for their support. Working together, we have increased our circulation of books by 77 percent over the past three years, and we have installed a fully computerized card catalog with the provision of telephone modem access for citizens with home computers. These accomplishments, together with many other innovations such as our writer's workshops and our children's story hour, have given me to believe that my departure comes at a high point in the library's history, not a low point. I thank you for the opportunity to be of service.

Sincerely,
John A. Elwell, City Librarian

Despite your questions, Elwell declines to discuss further his reasons for resigning. You call the chairman of the Library Board, Frank D. Parker, who produces the following additional details.

1. The board will meet at 7 next Monday night at the Library conference room to consider the resignation.

2. Parker gives this statement: ''Mr. Elwell has brought a singular spirit of service to the Library in the past three years. It would be a shame to see him go. Perhaps the board can persuade him to change his mind.''

3. If the board cannot persuade Elwell to reconsider, it will appoint an acting librarian and begin a search for a replacement.

EXERCISE 6   Water Accident

Write a brief story based on the following information. Remember to try to capture the essence; don't clutter your story with the over-abundance of detail here. The report is purposely made wordy and rambling to force you to seek out the essential news elements.

Yesterday about 4 p.m. Deputy Sheriff John A. Markvardsen was patrolling in the south end of Lincoln County near the community of Wagontire (population 550, located 30 miles south of Fairfield). A radio dis-patch sent him to Zumwalt County Park about 3 miles south of Wagontire. Upon arrival at the park, a group of people was observed, one of whom was giving mouth-to-mouth respiration to a small child. The child's mother is Dorothy Fleming of Fairfield. Child's name is Terri, age 3, female. Fleming stated in substance that she and two neighbors and their children had gone to the swimming hole at Zumwalt Park, a deep pool in Zumwalt Creek which runs through the park. Terri disappeared momentarily, and several people started looking for her. About 10–15 minutes later they found the child unconscious in the creek about 100 yards downstream from the pool. Artificial respiration immediately started. At about 4:45 an ambulance arrived and attend- ants used a respirator to attempt to revive the child. Child and mother removed to Providence Hospital in Fairfield. Child pronounced deceased upon arrival at the hospital. Body removed to Chapel of Memories. Funeral arrangements are pending. Dorothy Flemming treated for shock at hospital and released. Child was the youngest of three children belonging to Flemming and her husband, Donald. Others are Robert, 8, and James, 5. Donald Fleming was at work driving truck at time of accident. [*Source:* Lincoln County Sheriff Bud Kuykendall.]

EXERCISE 7   Writing an Advance

"Advance" means a story about an upcoming event. Next Friday night is the date of the annual meeting of the Fairfield Chamber of Commerce. From the following notes, write a story that announces the event.

Who? Fairfield Chamber of Commerce. *What?* Annual First Citizen Banquet. *When?* Friday night [insert the date] at 6:30. *Where?* Fairfield Country Club, 3345 Wellesley Drive, Fairfield. *Details:* Three prominent citizens of Fairfield have been chosen for the "First Citizen of the Year" awards. They will be identified at the banquet. Entertainment will be provided by The Jazzmen, an all-male jazz band of Kit Carson College. Main speaker for the event will be Carl Rowan, the syndicated newspaper columnist. Master of ceremonies will be Chuck Davies, a radio disc jockey in Fairfield. *Background:* This will be the 33rd consecutive First Citizen Banquet sponsored by the Chamber of Commerce. However, other organizations have sponsored the First Citizen awards since 1929. The Chamber of Commerce assumed responsibility for them 33 years ago. Since then it has selected up to three persons each year for "outstanding achievement and contributions to the community."

In the 33 years of Chamber of Commerce sponsorship, 96 persons (76 men, 20 women) have been selected for the honor. Of those, 54 continue to live in Fairfield. Eighteen have died, and the remaining 24 have moved to other regions. Earlier recipients have included former Governor Ed McCormack, Mayor Rod Dmytryshyn, former Mayor Ivan "Van" VanDenBosch, industrialist K.L. Walton of Acme Manufacturing, South High coach Pete Krewson and auto retailer Carl Crawford. Each winner receives (1) a plaque with name inscribed (2) name engraved on a large wall plaque in the lobby of the Sandy River Inn, and (3) a year of free lunches at Sourdough Jim's Restaurant. Ms. Sandy Jones manager of the Chamber of Commerce, is in charge of the event. [*Source:* Sandy Jones.]

Suggestion: A trip to the library might enable you to include some information on the guest speaker, Carl Rowan.

EXERCISE 8   Follow-up

News is seldom a once-only report. Most issues develop histories, causing a reporter to delve into the files for background information. Such is the case here. Write a story that captures the new information, but be sure to include the necessary background from the previous report (Exercise 5), which told of the resignation letter submitted (we'll say) one week ago.

The Fairfield City Library board met in "executive session" (closed to the public) last night with John Elwell. After two hours they emerged to report that Elwell had decided not to resign after all.

Here's his explanation, quoted word for word: "I had an excellent discussion with the board, and I think we are moving in some new directions that I find very exciting.

The personal considerations that I mentioned earlier were, frankly, that I was getting ulcers. I'm an innovator, but I was being frustrated by what I thought were the board's demands for a more traditional style of library management. Our discussion has cleared the air, and I now find the board most supportive of my ideas."

Comment from Mr. Parker: "We're just delighted

that John has decided to stay on. I think under his leadership that we can expect the library to become one of the best small-city libraries in the nation.''

Suggestions. Let's assume that neither man would discuss specifics at this time, despite questions you might logically ask. (What, precisely, was Elwell trying to accomplish? What innovations? How was the board getting in his way? What new ideas are in store for the future?) In other words, let's not make the story too complex at this stage. Use the comments by Elwell and Parker as direct quotes—that is, word for word. Best to extract brief statements rather than use the complete text of both.

Chapter Five

LEADS

Once you have gained some preliminary experience with organizing and writing a news story, you can begin to concentrate on and practice the most important part of the story structure—the lead.

Most journalists insist that writing the first paragraph of a news article is the hardest. The lead must capture the essence of the news, usually in a direct, no-nonsense manner. It must attract the reader to the content. And it must represent your best judgment of news value.

Most news stories employ a *summary* lead, so called because it sums up the essence of the material. It's what people use most often when relaying news in personal conversations. We don't fool around with long preambles when the news is urgent—"The Klinski house is on fire!"—and the listener or reader also appreciates the quick summation of essentials. Here is an example of a summary lead:

DILLON, Colo. (AP)—A chairlift cable at a ski resort jolted violently Saturday, throwing scores of skiers to the ground and injuring 49 people, 11 seriously, witnesses and authorities said.

In just 27 words this Associated Press story relays the most important aspects of a complex incident. Analyze it to see if you can identify the 5Ws and the H. Not all are

there. Why it happened, for example, might not be known for weeks.

Writing leads takes patience and practice. Two of the worst faults of lead writing are *misplaced emphasis* and *clutter*.

The first fault produces leads like "Police Chief Ernest Hudson delivered a speech Thursday to the Kiwanis Club." The news is not that he spoke but that he presumably said something of note. Thus the lead should concentrate on what he said, such as, "Police Chief Ernest Hudson identified Fairfield's ten most dangerous traffic hazards Thursday in a speech to the Kiwanis Club." People will read on to find out where those hazards are.

Here is an example of the second fault, clutter.

The speaker at the regular Thursday noon luncheon of the North Fairfield Rotary Club will be J. Dennis Fairbanks, an attorney from Denver, Colo., who will speak on tax regulations in an address titled "How You Can Save Tax Dollars Under the New IRS Regulations" at noon in the Sheraton Motor Inn, 800 McKinley Road.

The message comes through more clearly if you remove the clutter, thus:

A Denver tax attorney will discuss ways to save tax dollars in a talk to the North Fairfield Rotary Club Thursday noon.

J. Dennis Fairbanks will explain new federal tax regulations at the club's luncheon meeting in the Sheraton Motor Inn. . . .

Exercises in this chapter are designed to give you practice in writing leads. Here are some further suggestions.

1. Concentrate on the summary lead, at least for exercises in this chapter. Feature leads will be discussed later. Within a summary lead various elements in the 5W + H formula can be emphasized. Sometimes you'll emphasize the *Who* (Governor Hugh Penfold announced today that. . . ."), other times the *What* ("Pay raises for state employees will be delayed at least six months, Governor Hugh Penfold said. . . ."). You can probably think of times to emphasize the *When* ("Monday is the deadline for. . . .") or the *How* ("Poisoning caused the death of Jane Doe, a coroner's jury decided Friday. . . .").

2. Don't try to crowd all the W's into the first paragraph. Think of your lead as being more than a single paragraph, as in the "clutter" example about the tax attorney.

3. Use simple words and short sentences. Try to limit your leads to thirty words.

4. Use active verbs and strong nouns. Don't say "A truck carrying live turkeys en route to the morning market was hit by a train Thursday." Make it "A south-

bound freight train sliced into a truck Thursday, killing 130 turkeys. . . ."

5. Be a thinking reporter. Think through the details of a complicated event to determine just what *is* important. Strive in your research and interviewing to get a full understanding of an event because it's impossible to describe something you don't understand.

6. When dealing with a complex story, consider a chronological approach—first things first. Sometimes events are too complicated for easy summary. You could start with a lead like "Police Thursday launched an investigation into the disappearance of a Fairfield attorney whose blood-smeared car was found beside Highway 123, its engine still running." Your story can then review step by step the various complexities.

7. Remember to *attribute*. This means citing the source of the information with such phrases as "police reported" or "Governor Penfold announced." The attribution need not come in the first paragraph, but the statement of source must show up somewhere early in the story.

8. Remember that the emphasis in leads changes as news values change. The importance of a story increases with: (1) increased property damage, (2) increased number of deaths or serious injury, (3) greater prominence of people involved, (4) greater mystery, irony or abnormality, and (5) greater violence, conflict, tension or dramatic action

EXERCISE 9 PRACTICE LEADS

From the information given in each incident write a lead. Remember that the lead might be more than one paragraph. Keep the paragraphs short.

A. A squirrel climbed a transformer pole yesterday. [Note that exercise information will usually say "yesterday" or "tomorrow" because we don't know what day you're working on it. You should always change it to a specific day of the week in accordance with Associated Press style. See Appendix A for information on correct news style.] The squirrel got onto the transformer and, according to one worker, got fried "like crisp bacon" upon contact with a 7,200-volt line. As a result, about 100 homes in southwest Fairfield lost power for 17 minutes about 2 p.m. yesterday. Repair crew dispatched immediately and restored power. Affected homes were in the vicinity of West 40th Street. Transformer pole located at West 40th Street and Garfield Avenue. [*Source:* Emory Pokrzywinski, community relations director, Fairfield Power & Light Company.]

B. A 5-year-old boy was playing in the water of the Sandy River adjacent to Pioneer Park, a city park, about

3 p.m. yesterday. Boy's name: Donald Crawford. He was with his mother, Deborah P. Crawford, 33, of 111 Onyx Avenue. Donald was paddling on an air mattress. While Deborah's attention was diverted, Donald apparently paddled out toward deep water and got caught in a swift current. Boy and mattress began drifting toward Cleveland Rapids, a rocky, turbulent, dangerous part of the river about 100 yards downstream from the beach area. Boy started waving and yelling for help because he couldn't swim. Mother screamed for help when she saw Donald's plight. A young woman in a yellow dress kicked off her shoes, ran to the river, swam about 60 feet to catch up with the mattress. She pulled it safely ashore just upstream from the turbulence. Boy okay. Rescuer disappeared before anyone got her name. [*Source:* Police Chief Hudson.]

C. Clarissa Millicent McGee lives in Providence, R.I. She has spent every summer for the past 30 years visiting and studying lighthouses around the world. She is a teacher, now retired, and has written a book, *Lighthouses of the World*. The Lincoln County Historical Society has invited her to come to Fairfield because her brother, Duncan McGee, lives here. Clarissa will lecture on lighthouses at a meeting of the Historical Society. It's in the Library auditorium, 243 E. 13th St., at 7 p.m. tonight. No charge for admission. Public welcome to attend. Come one, come all! Her talk, sponsored by the society, is titled, "CASE OF THE DISAPPEARING LIGHTHOUSE AND OTHER MYSTERIES OF THE SEA." [*Source:* Amanda Burns, president of the Historical Society.]

D. The heroine who (day before yesterday, we'll say) rescued the child (Exercise 9-B) has been identified. She is Linda McCormack, 17, senior at South High School, champion swimmer, state girl's champ in the 100-yard freestyle. She won a medal for an earlier rescue last October (see Chapter 1). She's the daughter of the former governor. One of their neighbors, Chrissy Foxxe, saw a TV news account and guessed that the "girl in yellow" might be Linda. You interview Linda by phone. She says, "I just happened by on my bike and saw the situation. It looked like nobody else was going to do anything so I just decided I'd have to go at it myself. I had a terrible time catching up with him—that current is swift." Her dad, a Republican, served for four years as governor of Anystate but lost reelection to Democrat Hugh Penfold three years ago. The family lives at 1196 Onyx. [*Sources:* E.J. Hudson and Linda McCormack.]

E. When three sheriff's deputies came to work this morning, they had a few problems getting started on their regular 8 a.m. patrol. The three patrol cars had a combined total of seven flat tires. The tires had been slashed. Patrols were delayed about three hours. Case turned over to detectives division of the Sheriff's Office. No suspects named yet. [*Source:* Sheriff Bud Kuykendall.]

EXERCISE 10 REWRITING BAD LEADS

Each of the following leads suffers from one or more maladies, such as wordiness, passiveness, awkward construction, clutter or misplaced emphasis. Write a better version for each.

1. Police Chief Ernest Hudson spoke to the North Fairfield Rotary Club yesterday. He said he had just hired three new women officers and believes that women "do an astonishingly good job in police work." He said he believes Fairfield's next police chief should be a woman.

2. Nothing stands out in the City Council meeting last night except possibly the 15 letters of protest that were read to the council last night, having to do with allegedly inadequate storm sewers serving the downtown Fairfield area, by City Manager Victor M. Allen.

3. These are indeed the times that fry men's soles. Ole' Sol cut loose with the heat Sunday, proving to everyone that summer is definitely here, with Sunday's high temperature hitting a record 102 degrees, and today's high may go even higher setting still another record for Fairfield, according to the National Weather Service.

4. Last night about 11 a pickup truck, northbound on McKinley Road, carrying two adults and three children in the cab and five children in the back, ran off the road and overturned, with resultant death to one of the kids in the back and injury to six others.

5. A wise and attractive and wonderful woman died Friday night, Jane Darnell, 76, who for the last 11 years was in retirement after having worked for 40 years as a high school teacher.

EXERCISE 11 NEWS VALUES

Write lead paragraph(s) for each of the several variations on the overturned canoe theme. Remember that news values change in different circumstances.

The situation. Yesterday about 3 p.m. three persons in a canoe floated down the Sandy River past Pioneer Park. Occupants were Clark R. Mansfield, 42, of 389 College Avenue; his wife, Pauline Mansfield, a writer of mystery novels; and their daughter, Tasha, 9. As the canoe went through Cleveland Rapids, adjacent to the downstream end of Pioneer Park, it overturned and the occupants were spilled out. [*Source:* E.J. Hudson.] *Background.* The Sandy River normally runs at a 5-mph clip. At Cleveland Rapids, however, the river narrows into a rocky gorge and tumbles over and around numerous boulders at 10 to 15 mph. It is a favorite stretch of water for canoeists, kayakers and rafters. It is considered dangerous even for experienced canoeists. In the past 50 years, at least 33 persons have drowned there, according to a tally kept by the *Telegram*. The rapids are named for Elmer W. Cleveland who drowned in them in 1879. Prominent signs have been posted along the river banks above the rapids: EXTREMELY DANGEROUS RAPIDS BELOW THIS POINT. LIFE JACKETS MUST BE WORN. The City Parks and Recreation Department, which administers Pioneer Park, does not keep a lifeguard at the rapids. It does, however, keep a ring buoy, attached to 75 feet of line, on a wooden stand on the left bank of the river near the rapids. [*Source: Telegram files.*]

Version A. All three occupants, wearing life jackets, floated through the dangerous water without further mishap or injury. They reclaimed their canoe and continued downstream. [*Source of this and all subsequent versions:* E.J. Hudson.]

Version B. The two adults floated through the rapids to safety but the child caught hold of a rock in midstream. She climbed onto the rock but was apparently afraid to get off into the deep, turbulent water. A bystander threw her a ring buoy from shore. Child grabbed the buoy and bystander pulled her ashore. All occupants wore life jackets.

Version C. Same as B except that child was not wearing life jacket and bystanders, despite a frantic search, could not find the ring buoy. Child screamed for help. After five minutes she slipped from the rock into the water and disappeared. Child's body recovered downstream. Resuscitation failed: child pronounced dead on arrival at Providence Hospital. The buoy was never found. Scott Steubing, a city official, said vandals often steal the buoy.

Version D. Same as C except that a young woman wearing yellow shorts ran into the water and saved the child just as she slipped off the rock. Rescuer identified as the same Linda McCormack we encountered in Exercise 9-D.

Version E. Same as D except that when Linda returned to shore, she found that her purse with $23 in cash had been stolen.

Version F. Same as D and E except for the following details: As they entered the rapids, Clark Mansfield, in the back of the canoe, felt a sharp sensation in his right leg. This distracted him, causing him to lose control of the canoe. As he got to shore, he experienced pain in the leg and found blood coming from it. Taken to Providence Hospital, he was found to have a gunshot wound. A .22-caliber bullet was removed from the leg. Police believe a sniper fired from a brushy area on the right shore (across the river from the park). Investigating police officers found a hole in the canoe which they believe was made by the same bullet that hit Mansfield. Police continue to investigate. Mansfield released this morning from hospital in good condition.

Version G. All three persons wearing no life jackets, drowned.

Chapter Six

TYPICAL NEWSWRITING ASSIGNMENTS

Previous chapters have shown you the overall structure of a news story, and you've had some practice in writing leads. Now you will handle some typical assignments for a daily newspaper.

Here are some tips to prepare you for the assignments. You've heard some before; they're repeated here for emphasis.

1. As you write, check all names and addresses in the *City Directory*. In case of conflicts in names or addresses, assume that the *City Directory* is correct.
2. Strive for lean prose—writing stripped of excess wordiness. Keep most of your work to simple declarative sentences: subject, verb, predicate, in that order. Avoid this kind of writing:

According to Scott Steubing, city parks director, beginning at noon on Sunday in Pioneer Park, there will be a family picnic to be followed by a flag-raising ceremony.

The point of the sentence is obscured by two lengthy introductory clauses. Revise it to read:

A family picnic will be held at noon Sunday in Pioneer Park, followed by a flag-raising ceremony. [A second paragraph can credit Scott Steubing as source.]

3. Think before you write, and make an outline if necessary. Identify the most important element, followed by subsidiary elements.
4. Rewrite your lead—or all of the story, if necessary. The best reporters revise, tinker and rewrite until they are satisfied that they've done their best. This is a sign of professional strength, not weakness.
5. Use a *transitional* paragraph to connect the lead to the body of the article. Note that paragraph two in this example covers some of the details that would otherwise clutter the first paragraph.

Fairfield's next chief of police should be a woman, says Ernest J. Hudson, the current head of the city's 100-officer police force.

"Women are astonishingly good at police work," Hudson told 65 members of the North Fairfield Rotary Club in a luncheon address Thursday.

Hudson explained that women often excell in detective work and are particularly good at interviewing witnesses and suspects. . . .

6. Continue to relay the remaining details of the story more or less in order of descending importance.
7. Keep sentences and paragraphs short.
8. Attribute information to sources.

9. Identify people (by age, address, occupation, title or role played in the news incident.)

10. Use direct quotations when possible but keep them short. A direct quotation cites the speaker's words exactly and is within quote marks: "I saw the train hit the car, and it was awful," said Jane Doe, a witness.

11. Be specific and active in your writing.

12. Think through the material as you read an exercise and try to phrase the essence of it in just a few words. Exercise 12 is a good example. Can you capture the essence in a phrase? How about "jail inmates clean up roadside litter," or "sheriff puts prisoner power to work"? It helps to capsulize in that way when you are struggling to start your story.

EXERCISE 12 TRASH COLLECTION

Charles B. (Bud) Kuykendall, sheriff of Lincoln County, provides the following details about the use of prisoners from the Lincoln County Jail (located in the Fairfield) to clean up trash along the county roads. Write a news story of 250–300 words (five or six paragraphs) for this afternoon's paper, based on the details and the interview. The sheriff's answers can be used as direct quotations; try to extract a quote or two from them to work into your story. After you've finished, see the model story in Appendix B.

Details: Yesterday seven minimum-security prisoners from the jail picked up litter along McKinley Road, a route that starts in Fairfield and runs northwest 40 miles until it joins a major highway. They cleaned up a 15-mile section. Most of the trash was picked up between Fairfield city limits and the county's solid waste disposal site, a sanitary landfill (garbage dump) located four miles down the road from Fairfield. Most of the trash had fallen off vehicles headed for the dump. The inmates picked up enough trash to fill 100 plastic bags—two truckloads.

Following is a Q–A dialogue between reporter Fred Scott and Sheriff Kuykendall—a typical news interview.

Q. An interesting idea. Where did it come from?

A. We've gotten a zillion complaints from citizens about the looks of the roadways around the county dump. It's a mess, they said, and they're right. People don't follow the law. The law says you have to keep trash covered or restrained so it won't come off. We've tried to enforce that from time to time, but we don't have the personnel.

Q. So that's when you began thinking of prisoner power?

A. Yeah. I went down to the minimum security unit and said, look here, fellows, how many of you want to get out and stretch your legs and pick up a little trash? We got 15 volunteers and chose seven. We started at seven and by three had 15 miles picked up.

Q. Nobody escaped, or tried to?

A. Nope. Minimum security prisoners are pretty good about that. We call 'em trusties. We trust 'em. Not altogether I guess—we did have a security officer on the site.

Q. Did you find anything unusual out there among the litter?

A. Like what?

Q. Like money, jewelry, valuables, old love letters, anything out of the ordinary.

A. We found a wallet with three dollars and a couple of credit cards. We sent that to the owner. Mostly we just found trash. Junk food cartons. Disposable diapers. Nothing glamorous.

Q. Will you use prisoner power again for this kind of project?

A. That depends. I want to talk to the county commissioners first, and maybe the county attorney about liability. For the moment, let's just call it an interesting experiment.

Q. A successful one?

A. You bet!

Q. Do you have any final thoughts on it?

A. Only that you ought to put something in the paper about the county ordinance that says people must cover or restrain their trash when driving along county roads so it won't spill out. If you violate this ordinance, we can cite you into court, and if you're found guilty you could pay a fine of up to $500 or get 30 days in jail. Or both.

EXERCISE 13 REWRITING A NEWS RELEASE

Rewrite this news release to make it more clear, concise and accurate.

Friendly Avenue Church of God
1106 Friendly Avenue
Fairfield, Anystate

FOR IMMEDIATE RELEASE

The public is cordially invited to attend a special program, titled, "Narcotics, the Law, and Christ," to be presented this coming Sunday night at seven o'clock at the Friendly Avenue Church of God, which is located at the corner of Friendly Avenue and West 11th Street in Fairfield.

At this meeting, at which refreshments will be served, the Friendly Avenue Church of God will have Sergeant John Marks of the Fairfield Police Department speak on the topic of drug laws with particular emphasis on how they relate to our young people. A question-and-answer period will follow the talk.

There is no charge for attending this informative and interesting meeting. We will also have three or four young people from the Agape Inn which is a home where ex-drug users practice Christianity. They will discuss their experiences with drugs, and with Christ.

The program is in charge of Anne Heatherington, who for many years was the fine and distinguished director of our Choir. The Reverend Hiram Weaver is pastor of the Church, and extends a most cordial and warm welcome to any visitors who care to attend.

EXERCISE 14 COPY EDITING

The story below, written by the paper's student intern, is handed to you for checking and editing. Check it for punctuation, spelling (including proper names) sentence structure, and conformance with the AP Stylebook. Use appropriate copy-editing symbols (see Appendix B for a list of symbols). For background, see the story on Jeanne Gray in Chapter 1.

Jean Grey the beauty queen who resigned as, "Miss Fairfield," rather than pose for

photos in a bikini, has been asked to reconsider.

And, she says, she is, "Thinking about it."

She said, today, that members of the Metro Club, which sponsors Miss Fairfield

have told her they no longer would insist on the bikini pose.

Their request, last week, that she wear a bikini for publicity shots led to her with-

drawal from further participation in the forthcoming Miss Anystate pagent. She said the

bikini wasn't in her contract and she wished to draw the line against further "sexual exploi-

tation of women.

"I'm embarrassed by all the notoriety," Grey said today. "Half of my friends including my mom are mad at me. The other half, are saying that you did the right thing Jean you struck a blow against male chauvenistic pigism."

"Which is really funny," continued the former Miss Fairfield. "I don't even consider myself a feminist except maybe on questions of equal employment opportunity. I like men, strange as that may seem nowadays."

"I like being admired by men, but I don't have to get their attention by resorting to cheap stunts like going on camera wearing a bikini. Besides, what will my fifth graders think? More important, what will their parents think?"

Ms. Grey who teaches fifth grade at Gowdie Elementry School and is a distance runner of note, having been the fastest woman runner in the recent Fairfield Marathon with a winning time of 2:55:33, a women's record in the Fairfield Marathon, says she will consider the Metro Club's request over the next day or two.

EXERCISE 15 ANNOUNCEMENT

Emory Pokrzywinski is community relations director of Fairfield Power & Light. He calls you with an announcement he'd like to get in today's paper. Write a brief story.

At approximately 3 a.m. tomorrow a crew will replace a transformer with another of larger capacity to serve a section of FP&L customers in the southwest section of town. Power will be cut off for about 20 minutes. The work is being done at 3 a.m. in order to have minimum impact on customers. People should reset electric clocks, timers and so on. The power will not be off long enough to affect freezers and refrigerators. About 200 homes will be involved. They are on the north and south sides of West First Street, West Second Street and West Third Street. Houses numbered from 2600 to 4600 will be affected. The purpose of this is to provide better service for a growing section of Fairfield, says Pokrzywinski.

EXERCISE 16 NEWSBRIEF

Write a short item (150 words, 3–4 paragraphs) based on the following information. Remember that in this and all assignments the presentation of raw material is not necessarily the way it should be written in a news article. Notes are sometimes presented awkwardly just to give you practice in straightening things out. In this story, see if you can get both the forthcoming book and the illness in the lead.

You are informed by the Lincoln County Historical Society director, Amanda Burns, that George P. Hoyt, age 63, is in the hospital. He is a local historian, writer and retired teacher. He taught at South High School for 27 years until his retirement two years ago. His book, *Liar: The Truth about Ebenezer Jones,* will be published next Monday. It is about Jones, a spinner of tall tales, who died about 50 years ago, a colorful figure in Lincoln County history. Burns said Jones considered himself, as he expressed it, "the biggest damned liar in Lincoln County—if not the world."

Yesterday about 6 p.m. the Fire Department emergency unit was called to Hoyt's home on Lincoln Avenue. Mr. Hoyt complained of severe abdominal pains. At Providence Hospital he remains in intensive care this morning with what was diagnosed as a ruptured aneurysm in the abdomen. A hospital spokeswoman describes his condition as "stable."

Amanda Burns, who has been director of the historical society for the past six years, says Hoyt's book is one of seven books on Lincoln County history published by the society. Hoyt has written three previous books with other publishers: two high school history texts and a novel titled *Rogue Fever*. *Liar* will be sold in local bookstores for $14.95. An autograph party is planned when Hoyt recovers.

EXERCISE 17 APPOINTMENT

Write a story from the following details.

Sue Corning, director of community relations for the school district, calls you about a new appointment made yesterday by Superintendent Axford. He appointed Donald J. Middlesworth as principal of Caxton Elementary School.

Middlesworth was born Sept. 15, 1954 in Phoenix, Arizona. He graduated with high honors from North Phoenix High School in 1972. He was class salutatorian. He attended Stanford University and graduated with a BA in history in 1976. He received an MA degree in 1979 from the University of Washington. He taught elementary school in Flagstaff, Arizona, in 1976–77. He has taught in Fairfield since 1980, first at Kennerly School (fifth grade) then at Caxton since 1984. At Caxton he coaches the girls' softball team (they won second place in the All-City League in 1986). Alfred Middlesworth is married (wife: Sally), and they have three children, ages 18 months through 6. The family lives on Nixon Avenue.

Al Middlesworth replaces Don Houston who resigned last month to manage his father's cattle ranch in Wyoming. Middlesworth has been acting principal since Houston left. Caxton School has grades one through six. Enrollment is about 250.

EXERCISE 18 SUPPLEMENTING A NEWS RELEASE

Rewrite the following news release, incorporating the new information gained through the interview with Dr. Steinhauer. Make Steinhauer the focus of the story, putting her in the lead.

Background. Steinhauer has a Ph.D. in psychology from Yale and has taught at Carson for 12 years. Her speech begins at 1:30.

KIT CARSON COLLEGE
College News Service
111 Deady Hall
Contact: S.E. Odegard 345-7899

FOR IMMEDIATE RELEASE

Interested persons are encouraged to preregister for the one-day conference, "Women in Today's Labor Force," sponsored jointly by the Women's Bureau of the U.S. Department of Labor and the Women's Studies Department of Kit Carson College in Fairfield. The conference is to be held Wednesday [insert date] from 9:00 a.m. to 3:30 p.m. in the West Ballroom of the Sheraton Motor Inn, 800 McKinley Road, Fairfield.

The conference will provide a wide range of views on women in nontraditional occupations, defined as those employment positions in which women constitute 25 percent or less of the workers employed therein.

State Labor Commissioner Anabelle Richards will open the conference with a welcome address at 9:00 a.m.

Other speakers include George C. Castleman, assistant director of the Bureau of Labor's Apprenticeship and Training Division, to discuss "What is Apprenticeship?"; Marianne Maskery, regional administrator of the Women's Bureau, discussing "Women's Rights and the Realities of the Job Market"; and Dr. Evelyn L. Steinhauer, psychologist and associate professor of psychology, Kit Carson College, to deliver the main address, "Self-image and its Impact on Career Choices and Career Successes."

A panel of employers will discuss their perceptions of women in nontraditional occupations and the job market. Women from apprenticeship training and those holding journey-level status will comprise the final presentation of the day and will share their experiences.

Interested persons may preregister by calling the Women's Studies Department at Kit Carson College, phone 345-0089. Registrations will also be accepted at the door. The $15 registration fee includes lunch.

Here is the essence of your conversation by phone with Evelyn Steinhauer:

Q. *Dr. Steinhauer, I have a news release about your forthcoming speech, and I'd like to add some details about the speech itself. Would you mind telling me what it's about?*

A. It's based in part on some research studies we've done here at Carson. They have suggested a high positive correlation between the self-image attitudes of women and their success on the job market, both in finding jobs and in job performance.

Q. *You mean the higher the self-image, the better they do in getting and performing jobs?*

A. Yes. The essence of my remarks will be to ask women to ask themselves, "Do I feel good about myself?" To the extent that they can answer yes,

the tendency is to be more successful both in the securing of employment and on the job itself. Women seem to have a problem in this self-image area—particularly the middle-aged homemaker new to the job market, and most particularly in reference to nontraditional occupations.

Q. *Are you suggesting that women are themselves largely responsible for their own luck in finding jobs?*

A. Not entirely. Societal attitudes that preclude women from nontraditional occupations are obviously very much present. But I *am* saying that women can improve their luck by doing whatever they can to enhance their self-image.

Q. *Will your speech give specific suggestions for doing that?*

A. Yes, definitely.

Chapter Seven

USE OF QUOTATIONS

Let's examine more closely the use of quotations in news copy. Quotations are important to news articles. They can be used to capture personality, to succinctly summarize points, to lend authority to your writing, and even to dramatize certain kinds of incidents such as tense moments in a public meeting.

Quotations come in five forms:

1. Direct quotations that depict word for word what the speaker said (use quotation marks): ''Taxes are sure as the dickens going to go up next year,'' the mayor said.
2. Indirect quotations (what the speaker said, largely the way he said it, but with some modification; no quote marks used): Taxes will go up next year, the mayor said.
3. Paraphrased quotations (said in the reporter's words with no attempt to preserve the way the comment was said; no quote marks used): The mayor foresees increased taxes for next year.
4. Fragmented or partial quotations (only a small part of comment used, usually to preserve a unique wording or lend a touch of color): The mayor said taxes ''sure as the dickens'' will rise next year.
5. Dialogue (usually a small segment of a conversation):

"Mr. Mayor," asked Councilman Dorris, "what's your prediction on property taxes next year?"

"Taxes are sure as the dickens going to go up next year," Mayor Dmytryshyn said.

Here are four rules for the use of quotations in news stories:

1. Use them sparingly. They lose impact when overused. Be wary of using long stretches of direct quotation, even if you have written material available.
2. Select them with great care. Develop an ear for the succinct summary, the voice of authority, the colorful metaphor, the offhand remark, the *human* response to a situation. Humorous asides often lend color to a story, even a serious one. (A flood victim invited a reporter to his house; the floor was covered by two inches of mud. ''Be sure and wipe your feet before you come in,'' he said.)
3. Use them to begin a paragraph rather than burying them within.
4. Avoid overuse of substitutes for ''said'': *averred, sputtered, declared, exclaimed, complained, pointed out* and so on. Used sparingly they're okay, but when in doubt use ''said''; it's a quiet, hard-working word that won't get in the way of the quote itself. Never use a word such as ''smiled'' to mean said (''I'm happy,'' she smiled).

Can you revise the wording of direct quotes? In general, no. If direct quotations are to be authentic, they must depict exactly what the speaker said. Three exceptions are customarily made, however.

First, you should correct bad grammar unless it's essential to the story or unless using it for human color (don't overdo the color, but note the example below).

Second, you normally delete obscene words, depending on the paper's policy.

Third, you trim excess wordiness and unimportant meanderings. Use common sense, however; some proclamations by important people should be quoted verbatim no matter how much they wander. Here's an example of how to trim a quote. A witness to a train wreck actually said:

Well, by golly, let's see, the train was coming from the south—no, it was from the north, now that I think about it—and it was coming mighty fast, and it just, ah, like it was never gonna stop, and it hit the bus, sliced into—ah, sliced it in two like it was a watermelon.

Will anything be gained by quoting that verbatim? Clearly not; it would in fact obscure the meaning. Yet the quote does have dramatic impact that would be lost if you were to paraphrase it. Here's a cleaned-up version:

The train was coming from the north, and it was coming mighty fast like it was never going to stop, and it hit the bus—sliced it in two like it was a watermelon.

Purists might object to such phrases as ''mighty fast'' or ''like it was never going to stop.'' But remember that the language used in everyday conversation *is* informal. Quoting it lends an informal air to your writing that's hard to achieve otherwise. It also lends color and authenticity. Changing it to *as though it were never going to stop* would mean a major loss. Note the change from ''gonna'' to ''going to,'' however.

Exercises in this chapter are designed to develop two skills: (1) recognizing a usable quotation when you see or hear one, and (2) integrating such quotes into your news stories.

EXERCISE 19 SELECTING QUOTES

For each of the following comments, provide a summary paragraph that captures the essence of the speaker's message. Do it in your own words. Then select a direct quote that best supports, typifies or adds color to the essence. Keep everything short. The combination of essence should not exceed about eight typewritten lines (eighty words). The material may be in any order (quote first, essence second, or quote sandwiched between two summary paragraphs and so on). Exercise A is an example.

A. *Sgt. Liz Franklin, 11-year veteran of the detectives division, Fairfield Police Department, commenting on the place of women in detective work:* ''Oh, boy, they'll murder me down at headquarters for saying this, but I don't mind. I'll say it anyhow. I think, on the whole, that women make better detectives than men do, all things being equal. I don't mean that as a sexist slur. The irony is that women make better detectives precisely because society has subjugated them through the years, giving them the drudgery kinds of jobs: housewife, secretary, clerk, keypunch operator. Well, despite its macho myth, detective work is just like that. Women have a better tolerance for routine drudgery. We are more meticulous about detail. We don't mind pounding the pavement looking for people or talking to witnesses. We are better organized and more diligent in handling paperwork. We are better at drawing people out in interviews. Most people would rather talk to a female cop because we are less threatening. All these are what detective work is all about. The TV image of violence and gunplay is a crock. Ninety-nine percent of detective work is a housewifely or secretarial kind of routine drudgery. The other one percent is sheer terror.''

Essence: Sgt. Elizabeth Franklin believes women make better detectives than men do. She finds women more meticulous, better organized, more adept at interviewing, more diligent in paperwork. Their work, after all, is not all violence and gunplay.

Sample quotation: ''Ninety-nine percent of detective work is a housewifely or secretarial kind of routine drudgery,'' she says. ''The other one percent is sheer terror.''

B. *Roscoe W. Waffle, a local cartoonist, discussing the sailboating trip he and his wife, Edwina, took to the South Pacific last year:* ''Most people dream of a leisurely trip sailing the South Seas. It sounds so idyllic. I know because I thought so myself until last year when we actually did it. You have all those fantasies like sunbathing on the deck all the time, or romantic moonlit nights, ukeleles, beautiful native girls—ah, the adventure of it all. But the reality is totally different. Sunbathing, hell! We spent most of our time just hanging on for dear life. Those romantic fantasies say nothing of storms, of waves as high as a house, of navigational problems like when your radio has gone out and you don't have an accurate time check for a navigational fix.

And there's the constant rigging and rerigging of the sails, like about every hour day and night, it seems. In the six months we were on the seas, I never got a full night's sleep.''

C. *Ivan R. VanDenBosch, retired business executive and former mayor of Fairfield, speaking to the City Council on his idea for a new city park:* ''I've always been a dreamer. I think you could say I'm a living example of the American Dream. I came out of nowhere, a shiftless hobo from the 1930s Depression, riding into town on a freight I'd hopped in Mandan, North Dakota—or was it Pocatello, Idaho? I seem to have forgotten. Fairfield has not only tolerated me, giving me roots and a sense of security, but it has encouraged me to remain forever a dreamer. Old as I am, I still dream about drifting the Mississippi on a raft or stealing apples down by the freight yards at Hood River, Oregon. And this kind of dream is what I'd like to see in a city park. It would be a park where everybody would be a dreamer. Nobody would be grown up in my park, even though they might be 70. The chief architect for my park would be a child—no older than 11. I wonder what kind of park he'd build for our city. What would it look like? Would it be an abandoned railroad yard full of tracks and old cabooses and engines with a Hood River apple orchard nearby? Or a ghost town with tumbledown houses? Or a waterfront with old boats? Maybe it would be nothing more than a gigantic pile of scrap lumber. Whatever my architect decided, it would be heaven for kids of all ages.''

EXERCISE 20 PLANE CRASH

Write a story about the crash of a small plane that occurred around 6 a.m. today. Quote from the various witness accounts. Note the differences in their versions. That they don't agree is typical in dramatic incidents. You'll have to sort it out as best you can, using your best judgment as to which version seems the most reasonable. Or you may wish to state frankly that ''witnesses gave varying accounts'' and quote parts of each. After finishing see the model story, Appendix B.

Details. The plane was a Cessna 150, a two-place lightplane piloted by Delbert W. Thistle, age 19, who lives in Fairfield (555 Westway). He is the son of Alan R. and Alice Thistle, who also live in Fairfield. The plane crashed into a field about four miles south of Fairfield, just along U.S. Highway 139. Pilot is dead. He was alone in the plane. The plane was burned and the body was inside. The craft departed from Fairfield Airport at 5:45 a.m. The crash is still under investigation. [*Source:* Bud Kuykendall.] Here are various witness accounts:

Virginia E. Tubbs, 18, Rt. 1 Box 555, Fairfield: ''I was in the barn helping Grandpa with the milking machines when we both heard this terrible racket outside. It sounded like ten tractors on the roof. Gramps says, 'What the heck is that noise?' So I went outside and here was this plane flying real low and its motor going on and off, and it's laying one wing over kind of like it's about to turn upside down, and then—my God—it just hit the ground. He just plowed into the south field, the one where we used to grow alfalfa. I screamed at Gramps and we both ran out there, and with the fire you couldn't get near, and the guy was still in the plane and Gramps says, 'Don't look,' and I got sick.''

Henry W. Tubbs, 65, Rt. 1, Box 55 (Virginia's grandfather), a farmer and former World War II bomber pilot: ''I didn't see it until after it had crashed. I could hear a lot of racket outside the barn, and from what I heard I don't think it was engine trouble. Sounded more like some hotdog with a nervous hand on the throttle, playing around, throttling back and forward—great way to lose an engine. I'd say pilot error, but don't quote me. We got out there, Ginny and me, and I could see there wasn't much hope for anybody inside. I told Ginny to get back to the house and call the sheriff. I'd say the pilot stalled out on one of those engine shutdowns.''

Maggie Wilkins, a county commissioner who lives at Wagontire, a small community 30 miles south of Fairfield: ''It just exploded right in the air! There wasn't anything anybody could do. It was just awful. I hope I never see anything like it again. It just came down in pieces. I was driving my car along the highway into town and the little plane just exploded sort of fluttered down in burning pieces.''

Audrey Brooks, Fairfield: ''I was driving south on the highway and it was barely light at dawn, and I was quite startled to see this little airplane just skimming over the top of my car. It frightened me. Then I think it must have hit a power line with its wing. One wing was kind of dipping low, and I think it must have hit the line and then toppled over onto the ground. Kind of like a cartwheel. It burst into flames right away. I stopped my car and got out and waited for someone to get out of the plane, but they never did. Then suddenly there was an explosion and a ball of flame and I knew there was nothing anybody could do.''

Emory Pokrzywinski, FP&L: "The plane definitely hit the wire. I was out there about an hour later with a crew. There was no damage to the line, but we did have a momentary fluctuation which suggested something hit a 7.2-kilovolt line in that location at 6:01 in the morning."

EXERCISE 21 A QUEEN RETURNS

Some sources are better than others at providing quotable quotes. Some seem to have the knack for doing so, and on a slow news day editors often assign reporters to call such people just to see what newsworthy topics they might comment on. In one community where the author worked it was the zookeeper. In Fairfield, it could well be Jeanne Gray, the sometime beauty queen, who is establishing a modest reputation for candor. The news today starts with this memo from the Metro Club. From that and the telephone interview with Gray, fashion a quote-worthy news article.

STATEMENT

The Fairfield Metro Club are pleased to announce that Ms. Jeanne Gray will continue to be our entry in the Miss Anystate competition this coming summer. Last night members of the Pageant Committee of the Metro Club met with Ms. Gray and were able to iron out any differences that may have existed in the past. The Metro Club puts their full support behind Ms. Gray in her role as "Miss Fairfield" and wishes her well in the future.

Rick Bangor, President

Q. Hi, Jeanne Gray, this is Fred Scott from the Telegram. So is it true, you're back as Miss Fairfield?

A. Yes.

Q. Can you tell me what happened? This statement from the Metro Club is pretty vague.

A. Things change. Last week I told them to forget it—no way was I gonna pose for publicity shots in that bikini. It's the principle of the thing. Well, in the meeting last night they said, sure, we understand, and we don't mind that you're throwing away thirty years of tradition. So they said how about posing in a one-piece bathing suit like they do in the Miss America pageant? We kicked that around for quite a bit, like about four hours.

Q. It took four hours to decide whether to wear a swim suit?

A. There was quite a bit of lead-in conversation. I told them my mom's really mad at me for making such a fuss. She says if I'm gonna be a singer or an actress I'd better get used to this sort of thing. Well, I got pretty emotional and I said you guys probably don't want me now even if I did come back, and they said sure we want you, and I said, well, if I'm gonna be an embarrassment to you with the scandal and all that, I'd just as soon drop out and let you get somebody else, and they said, well, had I ever posed for any nude pictures, and I said good heavens, no! At least not since my baby pictures. So they said great, we'll take you. And I said okay, and we shook hands. Are you getting all that down? Am I talking too fast?

Q. I got it. So you'll pose in this modest swim suit, huh?

A. Yes, but only for a couple of still photos. On TV I get to be in an evening gown. That much I have in writing—no swim suit stuff on live TV except for the pageant itself.

Q. I'm curious, do you ever wear bikinis?

A. Yes! On the beach. But not to get my picture on TV, for heaven's sake!

Chapter Eight

WRITING OBITUARIES

The death of a prominent person is always a newsworthy event. Community newspapers also write brief obituaries for the not-so-prominent residents. The death of a celebrity, however, calls for more than a routine obit—it calls for the recapping of a varied and interesting career.

The format for writing obituaries is standard on most newspapers. The lead paragraph gives the person's name and age, then the single most important aspect of his or her life, and finally the circumstances of death, usually in that order.

The second paragraph elaborates on the first with more about the circumstances of death, particularly if it occurred under violent or unusual conditions. It may include more about the person's life.

The third and subsequent paragraphs elaborate on the person's career and life, briefly or at length, depending on the person's prominence.

The names of survivors and the time and place of funeral services usually follow. (Some newspapers prefer to list services at or near the beginning.)

Here's a hypothetical example:

John P. Jones, 94, among the last of the old-time sailing skippers, died today of a heart attack.

Jones, who retired to Fairfield after 60 years on sailing ships, collapsed at his apartment about 8 a.m. and died enroute to Providence Hospital.

Jones, born in New Bedford, Mass., went to sea at 14 on the four-masted schooner Royal Oak . . . [and so forth about his career].

Jones is survived by two daughters, Adrian McCarthy, St. Louis, and Jennifer Chapman, Pennington, N.J., four grandchildren and 11 great-grandchildren.

Rosary will be recited Tuesday at 7 p.m. at St. Mary's Catholic Church. . . .

Obits tend to come in two groups: (1) extended ones dealing with prominent, notorious, or otherwise colorful persons, and (2) short ones dealing with everyone else. The latter, by far the majority, are often the routine efforts of the least-experienced reporters. Newspapers usually get information about deaths from mortuaries, which may (1) phone with information, (2) write their own obituaries and submit them to the paper, or (3) fill out, or have survivors fill out, a questionnaire provided by the paper.

The extended obit deals with the more prominent citizens or occasionally a less-prominent person who led an unusual life, such as a former bank robber who went straight and lived to become an employee of one of the banks he robbed.

The extended obit means supplementing mortuary information with clippings of earlier stories and with interviews with persons acquainted with the subject. Many news agencies keep up-to-date biographical files on celebrities and other prominent citizens. Indeed, obits are already written for thousands of the nation's best-known citizens. Editors need only add the circumstances of death to the head of such a story to put it into print.

The term *obituary* is unfortunate, implying a tedious listing of biographical facts and survivors. They deserve that reputation, to be sure; they *are* dull. They would be less so if reporters viewed them as writing a news story—possibly even a "feature story"—about a person who died, rather than playing a funeral dirge.

The problem is usually a lack of information about the person. Funeral homes are notorious for both inaccuracy and lack of imagination. Clips from the newspaper library and interviews with relatives and acquaintances are the best sources.

Should a bereaved family be interviewed for more information? Opinions differ among professionals. It is not a question to be taken lightly. But reporters who routinely call relatives for additional information express surprise that the families are not only cooperative and helpful but usually grateful for the reporter's sensitivity in wanting to do a more complete and accurate job. This better job is as important to the family as it is to the reporter—no doubt more so. On the other hand, the public has been subjected to too many news media specta-cles in which bereaved relatives involved in major trage-dies are hounded for reactions. Reporters and editors should carefully consider questions of taste and tact. Per-haps a two-fold test could be invoked. Is the public better served by additional information available only from the family? Is the family itself better served by that added information, in your best judgment?

The call (or personal visit) should be made in a sym-pathetic but businesslike manner. If you explain promptly and politely why you need the additional information—and how it might also be in the best inter-ests of the family to have a more complete, more accu-rate job done—you'll usually gain their confidence and cooperation. At least that is the experience of reporters who have routinely contacted the families when other sources are not available. To illustrate this point, one of the forthcoming exercises includes an interview dia-logue. Remember, you are interviewing for facts and in-cidents in the dead person's life, not testimonials or eulogies—and certainly not to ask such brutal questions as "How does it feel to have your husband (wife) killed in the plane crash. . .?" In some cases you may want to learn the *consequences* of the person's death. What does the future hold for a business firm after the owner's death, for example?

EXERCISE 22 INGRAM DEATH

Write an obituary based on the obit form provided by a mortuary. When finished, see the model story, Appendix B.

Name of deceased. Mattie Lorraine Ingram
Address. 100 Eisenhower Avenue, Apt. 35 (Fairview Manor)
Date and place of birth. January 2, 1901, Paynesville, Minn.
Occupation. Retired. Was high school English teacher 1926-1966
Spouse. Never married.
Date, place, and circumstances of death. Yesterday at apartment about 5 p.m. Apparently died in sleep while taking a nap.
Education. B.A. in English from University of North Dakota in 1923. M.A. in Eng-lish, University of North Dakota 1925. Postgraduate work, University of Chicago, Stanford, UCLA, and University of London (England).
Career details. Taught high school English (literature and rhetoric) at Bismarck, N.D., 1926-29; at Eagle Pass, Texas, 1929-30; Sacramento, Calif., 1930-41; and Fairfied, Any. (South High School) 1941-1966. In 1936, 1938 and 1953 she conducted summer tours of Europe with groups of eight to ten high school students.
Honors and awards. South High "Teacher of the Year" in 1950.
Public Office. Unsuccessful candidate for City Council, Fairfield, 1954.
Survivors. One sister, Joy Ingram Brunner, Burbank, Calif. Predeceased by two brothers, Nicholas and Harold.
Services. Pending.

Additional information. Miss Ingram traveled widely during summers when school was not in session. She went frequently on study tours and had visited 49 states (all but Alaska) and 54 foreign countries.
Mortuary. Resthaven

EXERCISE 23 THOMPSON DEATH

Write an obit based on the following information provided by a mortuary.

Name of deceased. ANNA MARIE THOMPSON
Address. 100 Eisenhower Avenue, Apt. 40 (Fairview Manor)
Date and place of birth. March 1, 1886, West Branch, Iowa
Unmarried name. ANNA MARIE EVANS
Occupation. Homemaker. Mother. Rancher.
Spouse. Married Gerald E. Rogers, who died in 1925. Married Thomas C. Thompson in 1931. Mr. Thompson died in 1967.
Date, place, and circumstances of death. Died at Providence Hospital about 4 this morning. She had been ill for about a week, and was admitted to the hospital two days ago. Cause of death not immediately known.
Education. Finished 8th grade in West Branch, Iowa.
Career details. Worked in father's general store at West Branch for many years. Married Gerald Rogers, a rancher, in 1910. Moved to his ranch near Worland, Wyoming. After Mr. Rogers died, she married Mr. Thompson, a widower, who lived on a nearby ranch. Mrs. Thompson had six children, as follows:
William C. Rogers, born 1913, died 1984.
Abagail Rogers Carich, born 1915.
Jane Eleanor Rogers, born 1919, died 1925.
Charles E. Thompson (stepson), born 1926.
Addie Marie Thompson Barnett, born 1929.
Janice Eleanor Thompson Exley (adopted), born 1933, adopted 1935.
Mrs. Thompson had two brothers and four sisters, all of whom preceded her in death.
Survivors. Daughters: Addie Marie Barnett, Fairfield; Abagail Carich, Hilo, Hawaii; Janice E. Exley, Great Falls, Mont.; stepson, Charles E. Thompson, Houston, Tex. Also 11 grandchildren, 23 great-grandchildren, and 7 great-great-grandchildren.
Services. Tomorrow at 11 a.m. in chapel of Fairview Manor, 100 Eisenhower Av. Donald J. Lamb, pastor of Friends Church, officiating. Interment in Forest Lawn Cemetery.
Additional information. Mrs. Thompson lived in Fairfield since 1968. She received greetings from President Ronald Reagan on the occasion of her 100th birthday, March 1, 1986. Also greetings from many prominent people, including Anystate Gov. Hugh W. Penfold, Sen. Edward Kennedy of Massachusetts and Sen. John Glenn of Ohio. For many years Mrs. Thompson traveled annually to visit her daughter in Hawaii. She visited Japan before World War II. Until the very end Mrs. Thompson exhibited an intellectual alertness and a zest for living.
Mortuary. Chapel of Memories

Following is a clipping from the newspaper library published March 1, 1986, the occasion of her 100th birthday.

BY FRED SCOTT
STAFF WRITER

Anna Marie Thompson celebrates her 100th birthday today with a party at Fairview Manor where she plans to dance and "kick up my heels."

"I think the kids nowadays are going to live a lot longer," she said in an interview yesterday. "They're so active—dancing, running, bicycling, swimming. Exercise is what keeps you young."

Anna Thompson credits her own longevity to exercise—including hard days as a rancher's wife—and to clean living and freedom from worry.

"Some of the girls I grew up with used to chew and smoke," she said. "I never did any of those things."

As for worry, Mrs. Thompson had this advice:

"You have to forget the bad and remember the good. There is nothing better for good health than forgetting the past and looking to the future. Remember the good times. Dream about a future full of good times like the ones in the past."

Born 100 years ago in the quiet Quaker community of West Branch, Iowa, she walked the same dirt streets as young Herbert Hoover, who later became president. Though Mrs. Thompson never knew Hoover personally, their families were good friends.

Today Mrs. Thompson frequently walks to the home of her daughter, Addie Barnett, seven blocks away. Her doctor says she's in perfect health. She has never been hospitalized for an illness. She comes from a long line of Quakers noted for their creativity and longevity, she says. Her mother lived to be 96.

Until she turned 98 she traveled annually to Hawaii to visit another daughter, Abagail Carich, who is married to a minister. She also visited Japan in 1938 when Abagail was stationed there as a missionary. A Democrat, she maintains a keen interest in politics and believes Woodrow Wilson was the nation's finest president during her lifetime, followed by Teddy Roosevelt, Franklin Roosevelt and Harry Truman.

"My husbands could not abide any of those men," she said. "Oh, we used to have some dandy arguments.". . .

Another clipping in the March 2 paper shows a photo of her dancing with a great-grandson, Curtis Barnett, 17. "I think Curt did most of the dancing," she said, "but I had a good time."

EXERCISE 24 WICKHAM DEATH

Write a news story based on the mortuary report and the interview.

Name of deceased. Samuel B. Wickham

Address. 789 Ridge Drive, Fairfield.

Date and place of birth. February 11, 1917, York, England.

Occupation. Businessman, owner of Wickham's Outdoor Store. Owned real estate in Fairfield and Lincoln County. Part-owner of Lincoln Flight Service at Fairfield Airport. Captain for United Airlines from 1948 to 1977.

Spouse. Married in 1954 to the former Cheryl Breyer of Chicago.

Date, place, and circumstances of death. Died while on fishing trip. Details not available.

Education. B.S. University of Illinois, 1939.

Career details. Learned to fly while in college in 1939. Entered U.S. Army Air Corps in 1941. Served with 8th Air Force in England during World War II. Flew 25 combat missions. Joined United Airlines in 1948. Flew variety of airliners—DC-4, DC-6, DC-7, DC-8, Boeing 727, Boeing 747. Was Boeing 747 captain from 1972 until retirement in 1977. Moved to Fairview in 1977. Purchased Hawkeye Outdoor Store that year and renamed it Wickham's Outdoor Store.

Honors and awards. Distinguished Flying Cross, 1943.

Survivors. Wife, Cheryl; son, Dana, Reno, Nevada; daughter, Darla Conradi, Menlo Park, California; daughter, Irene Wickham Chilton, Miami, Florida, from a previous marriage. Two half-brothers Henry Glaser, Vancouver, B.C., and Arthur B. Glaser, New York City.

Services. Pending.

Affiliations. Rotary International, First Methodist Church, Airline Pilots Association.

Additional information. Mr. Wickham was an avid outdoorsman, hunter and fisherman. Traveled frequently to Canada and Alaska on outdoor expeditions; also made one trip to Chile and another to Africa to hunt and fish.

Mortuary. Resthaven

Following is a telephone interview dialogue with Cheryl Wickham:

Q. Mrs. Wickham, my name is Barbara Miller, a reporter for the Telegram. I'm very sorry to hear about your husband. I'm writing a story about him for today's paper but the information I have is incomplete and I want to do a good job. Would it be all right if I ask you a few questions to fill in some of the gaps?

A. Yes, I'll try to tell you what you want to know.

Q. Thank you. First I'd like to check a few details to see if the information I have is correct. You were married in 1954, you have a son and a daughter, Dana and Darla—may I ask where they are and what they're doing now? . . . [Start such interviews with nonthreatening questions. The "may I ask" approach is soft and nonthreatening, appropriate for the circumstances.] May I ask how you met Mr. Wickham?

A. I was a stewardess for United and got on one of his flights out of Chicago. We had a small problem with a DC-6 that night—an engine out and another malfunctioning, so we made an unscheduled stop in Omaha, and that's where I got to know him. After that I tried to get on all of his flights.

Q. [Rapport established through such questions, you can proceed to the business at hand.] Can you tell me how Mr. Wickham's death occurred?

A. I don't know all the details. Sam and our son, Dana, were on a fishing trip to British Columbia in Canada, and they had been out in a boat all day. When they were docking the boat, Sam felt rather violently ill and so they took him to a hospital some miles away, and, I don't know—he just died that night.

Q. I see. And you don't know the cause of death?

A. No.

Q. When and where, precisely, did this happen?

A. Night before last. Apparently he died very early yesterday morning. The lake where they had been fishing is called Shuswap Lake. I don't know the name of the town where they took him.

Q. Okay. I notice that Mr. Wickham was part owner of Lincoln Flight Service. Did he continue to fly after he retired from United?

A. Yes, for pleasure. He bought a small plane and keeps it out at the airport. It's an old World War II trainer—an antique, kind of a Red Baron thing with open cockpits. He flew it for the sheer pleasure of it, but he never did anything commercially since United. The flight center was just an investment and a means of keeping his maintenance costs low on his little plane.

Q. Can you tell me when Mr. Wickham came to America from England?

A. As an infant. His father was killed in World War I, and his mother went to New Jersey to stay with a sister. Eventually she took out citizenship. Sam was the only child from that first marriage, but she had two other sons from a second.

Q. I see that Mr. Wickham had been married before—is that correct?

A. Yes, he married in England during the war and they had a child, but I guess the marriage kind of fell apart afterward.

Q. I see. Mrs. Wickham, can you think of any other points about his life I should consider for my story?

A. You might want to consider his winning the Distinguished Flying Cross in 1943. He was flying a B-17 over Germany and it got shot up quite a bit—three engines out and half a stabilizer gone yet he somehow managed to belly land it at the base in England on just one engine. All the crew had bailed out except Sam and the tail gunner who'd been hurt and couldn't jump, so Sam decided to try to land it. He always said that was his best landing, ever. Compared to that, the emergency in Omaha was a piece of cake.

Q. Yes, I'll write that into the story. Thank you for suggesting it. And thank you for talking with me. Again, please accept my condolences. . .

EXERCISE 25: VANDENBOSCH DEATH

The former mayor of Fairfield, a man long known as one of the community's most colorful personalities, has died. This will be no ordinary obit. Look over the following material and review the items that have appeared earlier in Exercise 7 and 19-C.

Suggestions: Try to weave the three elements—alcoholic wanderer, the rise to responsible business position, the turn to civic affairs—into a coherent whole. Consider depicting his life in chronological order, or in reverse chronology (civic leadership first, hobo last). Don't hesitate to quote from the newspaper accounts. Don't be somber. Celebrate a rich and interesting life. This may be a difficult story. Rewrite if necessary.

Name of deceased. Ivan Robert VanDenBosch

Address. 104 Harris Avenue, Fairfield

Date and place of birth. July 12, 1911 in Oshkosh, Wisconsin, to Dirk and Willa VanDenBosch.

Occupation. Retired.

Spouse. Married in 1938 to the former Ida Rohdale.

Date, place, and circumstances of death. At Providence Hospital yesterday. Collapsed at his home yesterday about 3 p.m. after complaining about severe headaches. Died at hospital about 7 p.m. Cause believed to be cerebral hemorrhage. Autopsy scheduled for later today.

Education. Finished eighth grade at Oshkosh.

Career details. Started at Star Manufacturing Co. in 1938 in various positions. Became a shift supervisor in 1943.

Became production superintendent of the Battery Components Division, 1955, remained there when Acme Co. bought out Star in 1960. He retired in 1975.

Honors and awards. Fairfield "Citizen of the Year" in 1966 for his work with young people. He coached peewee baseball and counseled youths on drugs and alcoholism.

Public Office. Unsuccessful candidate for Fairfield City Council 1971. Elected to City Council in 1973. Elected mayor of Fairfield 1975. Reelected 1979. Served as Mayor January 1976 through December 1983.

Survivors. Wife, Ida; son, John H., Bismarck, N.D.; daughter, Mary Ann Boling, Seattle, Wash.; five grandchildren, two great-grandchildren; sister, Ella Rowan, Oshkosh, Wis.

Services. Memorial services will be held at City Hall council chambers at 11 A.M. tomorrow. Rev. William A. Stout of First Presbyterian Church officiating. Eulogies to be delivered by several city officials. At Mr. VanDenBosch's request, his body will be shipped by railroad boxcar to his boyhood home at Oshkosh for interment.

Mortuary. Resthaven

The newspaper library yields many clippings about the career and civic activities of former Mayor VanDenBosch. Here are some pertinent excerpts:

From a feature story, May 5, 1966 when he won the "Citizen of the Year" award:

He accepted the award with characteristic modesty. He told an applauding audience:

"It's just like the song says, 'You've come a long way from St. Louie, but, Baby, you still got a long way to go.' "

From a report of a speech to the Fairfield Rotary Club (January 3, 1976) on the topic of hoboing:

"A hobo is not a tramp—you've got to remember that," VanDenBosch said. "A tramp is a guy who has no intention of going to work. Hoboes were guys who were always on the move, out looking for jobs. We were poor in those days. We could and should have been starving to death in what we now call ghettoes. But we went on the road because that was a much more romantic way to starve to death."

During his years on the road, VanDenBosch visited some "mighty memorable places." They included Vaughan, Miss., where Casey Jones had his famous wreck; Hood River, Ore., "where we used to steal apples"; and Borie Junction "where the railroad branches and you had to make up your mind whether to take the left branch to Denver or the right to Pocatello."

VanDenBosch also taught Rotarians a new language—the jargon of the hobo. If, for example, a hobo suggests "diming up on the stem," he's talking about panhandling on Main Street. If the "joint's pretty well bulled up," you'd be well-advised not to get caught panhandling—it means there are lots of police or railroad detectives around. A hobo in a hurry might be a "bindle stiff red-balling it" meaning he's carrying his belongings in a cloth bag and riding a fast fruit train.

VanDenBosch has red-balled it and dimed up on the stem, but he's never hitchhiked.

"I've always detested hitchhiking," he said. "We used to call them rubber tramps. That's worse than begging."

Even worse are female hitchhikers, he said.

"Picking up women on the street is dangerous because they're always throwing sex at you. A baby-faced girl can shoot you with a twenty-two pistol just as easily as a man can. And if the gun don't get you, the sex will."

From a feature story, July 7, 1976:

Around City Hall, he's known as the "Hallucinatin' Hobo of Fairfield," largely in reference to his visionary ideas. Among them is an emergency services building for fire, ambulance and police, and a new sewage treatment plant that will be adequate to the year 2010.

He also talks, tongue in cheek, about the "paving of Easy Street." Although Fairfield has no Easy Street, the mayor talks as if it did.

"When we get this tax problem solved," he says, "then we'll pave Easy Street and lie in clover for the rest of our lives."

Mayor VanDenBosch admits to being an alcoholic and a hobo. He left home in Oshkosh, Wis., at the age of 14 and rode the rails through the late 1920s and early 1930s.

"I've been afflicted by two diseases in my lifetime," he says. "Alcoholism and wanderlust. I licked the first, but not the second."

He rode a freight train into Fairfield in the summer of 1937. He liked what he saw and vowed to quit drinking. He married a local girl, Ida Rohdale, and found a job as a janitor at Star Manufacturing Co. Eventually he worked his way up to production superintendent of the Battery Components Division, a job he held until retirement by which time the firm had sold out to Acme.

News story, July 18, 1976:

Fairfield's mayor did a little "diming up on the stem" this week.

The term is hobo jargon for panhandling, and that's exactly what Mayor Ivan R. VanDenBosch did.

He personally solicited contributions to help finance a youth center in Fairfield.

"I'm an expert at panhandling," said the mayor. By nightfall he had $890 in cash and pledges for another $4,200.

News story, April 1, 1982:

They're going to pave Easy Street tomorrow.

Easy Street, in case you have forgotten, is the mythical street Mayor Ivan R. VanDenBosch keeps talking about.

"When things get better," he has said repeatedly through his political career, "we'll pave Easy Street, and then we'll all lie in clover."

Last week an anonymous donor asked for permission to lay a 500-foot strip of blacktop, 10 feet wide, along the west end of Pioneer Park and paint a yellow stripe down the center. It would, he said, contain gentle curves and be called Easy Street.

Scott Steubing, city parks director, granted permission for the project.

"We figure kiddies can have tricycle races on it," said Steubing.

Work begins tomorrow and should be finished in two days.

What about the clover?

"We need another donor for that," quipped Steubing.

Editorial, December 20, 1983:

Mayor Ivan VanDenBosch will swing his gavel for the last time tonight. Next month a new regime takes over, and City Hall will never be the same again. Old Van is as priceless as a Renoir and just as rare. Here's the restless, uneducated hobo who rode the rails into Fairfield almost a half-century ago. Fairfield and Van VanDenBosch were meant for each other. Fairfield changed Van's life—for the better, he insists—and Van changed Fairfield. He rose from the humble janitor to become a top official at Acme and then, at an age when most would think of slacking off and going fishing, took on the multifarious and sometimes-Machiavellian affairs of city government.

How has he changed us? Two ways come immediately to mind.

Foremost, he taught us tolerance. It became evident that even an uneducated alcoholic drifter, given half a chance, can put down roots and become a solid citizen.

He taught us to believe again in the American Way. We watched almost in astonishment as he rose from the depths of alcoholism to become the community's First Citizen and eventually its most influential leader. It was as mayor that he impressed us with his visionary leadership. The Hallucinatin' Hobo can take a rest now, secure in the knowledge that he can count the following among his accomplishments:

1. Construction of the new sewage treatment plant. Van worked hard to secure federal support for this project, and its completion last year is a monument to his endeavors.

2. Development of the new central Emergency Services Station, now under construction.

3. Development of a city youth program that will reach fruition a year or two hence when the old fire station will be vacated and renovated for a youth center, complete with the old fire pole and a couple of antique fire engines.

4. Major expansion of the city's parks, particularly Pioneer Park with its new ball diamond, and the new arts and crafts building.

5. Sheer colorful personality. You had to love the old Hallucinatin' Hobo even when his ideas struck you as outrageous. For the first time in years, City Hall was a fun place.

6. The paving of Easy Street.

We will not soon forget the man who put us on Easy Street, with or without the clover.

Chapter Nine

SPEECHES

Reporters routinely cover speeches. When the speaker or the topic is newsworthy, the media will report it. You have to cover all kinds of speakers and speeches—from idealists to demagogues, from the well-organized deliveries to the rambling discourses.

The three examples in this chapter are typical. Working from a written source, as here, is different from hearing a speech, however. If you really want to learn the techniques of speech coverage as professionals do it, have someone read the speech to you while you take notes. *After* writing your news report then check the speech script to test your accuracy in notetaking.

Here are some suggestions for covering speeches.

1. Prepare for a speech by learning something about the speaker and the topic.
2. Get a copy of the speech if it is from a written script.
3. Listen carefully (and record in your notes) for the central theme of the speech. Most speeches have such a theme, which is supported by several main points. Each of the points is usually supported by specific evidence: facts, opinions, quotations, examples, anecdotes and other materials.
4. Take notes on the evidence used to support the points.
5. Try to get down in your notes word for word the col-orful comments, personal asides and succinct summaries that can be used as direct quotations.
6. Describe the speaker's appearance, mannerisms, gestures and so on when appropriate ("Pounding the lectern for emphasis, she said. . .").
7. Take notes on questions and answers that may come after the speech. Sometimes they are just as important as the speech itself, and often they're more interesting.
8. Seek an opportunity to interview the speaker directly after the speech, partly to check your notes if necessary, partly to supplement the speaker's remarks via answers to your questions.

Speech stories typically follow the format described below, though variations abound. It's best to learn the traditional format before trying others, however.

1. A lead that summarizes the speech or captures the most important point. Resist the temptation to lead with a direct quotation from the speaker. Try, rather, to capture the essence in your own words.
2. A second paragraph that develops the lead (perhaps with a short direct quote) and adds any minor details necessary, such as time and place of the speech, or any special circumstances worthy of note.
3. A third paragraph that provides a strong direct quotation that supports the statement made in the lead.

4. Subsequent paragraphs, as many as necessary, to convey the major points of the speech, using direct and paraphrased quotations. The essence of the material should be in your words. Save the direct quotations for emphasis or personal color or succinct summaries. Here's an example of the opening paragraphs of a typical speech story.

Incidents of police officers harassing or abusing citizens could result in lawsuits against the Police Department and Chief Ernest Hudson, Kenneth Wheelock, a City Council member, said Thursday.

"I'm thinking of filing a lawsuit myself," Wheelock told about 100 members of the Fairfield Metro Club at its weekly luncheon meeting. Wheelock, head of the council's police committee, has asked Hudson to resign.

"The only way to cope with these nefarious practices is to either go to court or get a new police chief," Wheelock said. . . .

Such a story would go on to cite Wheelock's comments, including specific instances of abuse if he gives them. (If he doesn't, they could be the topic of a post-speech interview.) In an issue so politically volatile, the reporter would also call Chief Hudson for a reply and incorporate it into the story. Thus the fourth paragraph might contain that rebuttal.

EXERCISE 26 SPEECH ON SEXUAL VIOLENCE

Write an article for the paper based on the following speech by Sergeant Anderson. When you are finished, consult the model story in Appendix B.

Background. Sgt. Kathy Anderson, juvenile division, Fairfield Police Department, is speaker at today's luncheon meeting of the Fairfield Business and Professional Women at the Fairway Hotel. Sgt. Anderson is chair of a Lincoln County organization called Women Against Rape. She is also leader of an interagency police team that investigates sex crimes. About 85 women attend this luncheon meeting. After a lunch, Anderson is introduced. Below is the essence of her remarks.

When I was a student at Kit Carson College in the 1960s, we girls used to get together in the dormitory lounge and talk about sex. Occasionally the discussion turned to rape.

I recall that there was no talk then of "what would you do if" or "should I carry a weapon" or "what are my chances of getting out alive if I screamed or tried to fight back?"

These are *exactly* what young women talk about today. I know because over the past few years I have addressed many groups of college women as well as groups like yours.

Twenty years ago we talked about rape as a thing that probably would never happen to you. Today's young women are talking about what happened to Susan, just down the dorm hall, or to Jane, who lives alone in an apartment on the edge of the campus. They are arming themselves with whistles, knives, hatpins and Mace, and they are taking karate and other self-defense courses in record numbers. They see it as a battle—a war against rape and other sexual violence. They also see it as the domestic war of the century.

Please note—I'm not talking about New York or Cleveland or Detroit. I'm talking about Fairfield. And rape is only the tip of the iceberg. We've only begun to fight on other fronts such as family violence or child abuse.

Let me first talk about rape.

Fairfield is not a major city with slums and red light districts and combat zones and gang warfare. We have our problems, but we're a small city typical of home communities across America.

Yet Fairfield is a deceptively dangerous city so far as rape is concerned.

We organized Women Against Rape in 1984 after an all-time record year for reported cases. The interagency rape team was organized two years later. In

1983 we had 186 reported cases of forcible rape in Fairfield and its suburbs, a region whose population was then about 165,000.

That gives us a crime rate for rape of 88.5. It means 88.5 rapes per 100,000 population, a uniform crime statistic that enables us to compare ourselves with other cities.

That same year New York City had a rape rate of 52 per 100,000, Philadelphia 42, Chicago 62, Washington 65.

Think about that. From a statistical view, your chances of being raped here in Fairfield were twice as great as in Philadelphia, a third greater than in Washington or Chicago, 70 percent greater than in New York.

This is what has prompted our concern. And I'm pleased to report that, although the war is far from won, we have made progress. Last year's rate was down to 44.6—about the same as Philadelphia's.

These statistics, needless to say, do not reveal the problem as a police officer sees it—the broken bodies, the often-grotesque psychological traumas that are the aftermath of an incident of rape.

But in any event we are fighting. Police Chief Hudson and the late Mayor VanDenBosch have been particularly sympathetic. With the approval of both Chief Hudson and Sheriff Kuykendall, we are seeking funds to build a shelter home in Fairfield to house victims of rape, child abuse and family violence. We hope to have such a unit available within a year, and we earnestly solicit your support and your contributions.

Rape is not the only thing that concerns us. Only 22 percent of the cases we see are rapes of sexually mature females. Society does not like to talk about the other 78 percent. Forgive me for bringing them up, but they are some of the worst cases of all. They are instances of family violence and child abuse. They are abused wives with black eyes, broken limbs and broken spirits. They are children. One child was hospitalized a few days ago with extreme dehydration because his parents would not give him food and water until he stopped wetting the bed. Last year we processed the case of a 7-year-old girl raped with such abject brutality that she had to be hospitalized for a week—raped by her own father.

This, ladies, is war. We have only begun to fight. It is an all-out war. We don't really expect to eliminate sexual violence or child abuse entirely. But we plan to put up one hell of a fight!

[Sergeant Anderson takes questions from the audience. Among them are these.]

Q.   *[Lori Smith, lab technician, Providence Hospital.] Sergeant, what is your advice for a woman who is attacked? Should she put up a fight? What are her chances of being hurt or killed?*

A.   I cannot answer that except for myself. I'd put up one heck of a fight unless, of course, I had a gun pointed at my head. So much depends on the situation. Our files are loaded with creative solutions by residents. Some women have calmly talked the attackers out of their intentions. One stuck her finger in her throat, which made her vomit, and the man left her alone. Another said she had herpes, a venereal disease. The would-be attacker couldn't leave fast enough. One told her attacker, "Honey, let's go to my apartment." She directed him to a busy intersection, and when he stopped for the light, she opened the door and walked away.

Q.   *[Kaye Zolotow, hotel manager.] What about screaming—is it a good idea?*

A.   Yes. Nothing is more attention-getting than a woman's screams. They're ten times more effective than a whistle. Another effective defense is to yell "Fire!" If you yell "Rape!" or "Help!" people think it's a domestic squabble. They don't want to get involved. "Fire!" always brings them on the run—everybody loves a good fire.

EXERCISE 27 STATE OF THE CITY ADDRESS

Following is Mayor Dmytryshyn's annual "state of the city" address, given to the City Council and an audience of about ninety members of the general public in the council chambers in City Hall last night. Write a story based on this speech.

Members of the council, citizens of Fairfield: Folks, here we go again. Another year has passed and it's time to discuss the future of Fairfield. We've had a glorious past, but our best days are just ahead.

Before we continue, we must pay our respects to our dear departed friend, the late, great Ivan R. VanDenBosch. No mayor in the history of Fairfield has ever rung up the set of accomplishments as the old Hallucinatin' Hobo, and we surely are going to miss him a lot.

Van is gone but not forgotten. The other day that marvelous young couple, Janis and Dan Jones, came to see me with a proposal. As you know, Dan teaches theater at Carson College, and Janis has her own dance studio. Next summer they want to put on an outdoor musical pageant at Pioneer Park—"Fairfield Hobo Days." It would honor the late mayor. Citizens would dress as hobos, dance in a make-believe hobo jungle, ride a freight train, and in general have a wonderful time. Would the mayor and City Hall support their efforts, they asked. And I said, *yes!* This could be the start of something big—a new and marvelously innovative tradition for Fairfield. It could put our town on the map. And so next summer—the weekend closest to July 12, which is Van's birthday—we'll be celebrating the first of what I hope will be an annual event—Fairfield Hobo Days.

Folks, this is but one example of the innovative spirit of Fairfield. I have four other items on my agenda. Please let me outline them to you.

1. Airport. If we are to accommodate the "hobos" and others who will be coming to Fairfield next summer, expansion of the Fairfield Municipal Airport terminal must be our number-one goal during the coming year. A modern airport is a critical underpinning of a diversified economy. We have a tremendous opportunity to see Fairfield as the gateway city to Central Anystate.

The cost of the terminal expansion I envision is ten million dollars. I propose a three-part strategy for raising this amount of money.

First I believe we can expect to obtain a third of this amount through additional federal or state grants. Through the work of our federal lobbyists, Fairfield was designated to receive priority consideration for additional funds from the Federal Aviation Administration.

Second, I propose that we ask airport service providers, including the airlines, to pay a larger share of the cost. We are currently discussing the project with them.

Third, I propose that the council consider an additional 3 percent tax on hotel and motel rooms, which would add to the current 3 percent tax, bringing the total to 6 percent. This is not out of line with the motel room taxes in other communities throughout the state. Almost all of that increase would be dedicated to airport expansion. A small amount would be used for tourist promotion and cultural amenities such as the Hobo Days celebration next summer. As you know, we have discussed this many times in the City Council and have agreed that it is a proposal worth considering. I propose that the council put it into effect this coming year. The room tax is a travel-related tax.

The improvements would increase the space in the airport terminal by 40 percent and relieve the problems of congestion, inefficiency and delayed baggage handling. They would provide adequate ticket counter space for the two airlines currently serving Fairfield—United and Interstate—and would also encourage other airlines to begin service here. At least two other airlines have expressed interest in serving the Fairfield market once these facilities have been completed.

2. Downtown. Our downtown has historically been a regional center of commerce, but today it is at a crossroads. As more business moves out of downtown to the shopping malls and the suburbs, a deterioration has begun which must be halted. In the coming months, I shall appoint a citizen committee—to be known as the Downtown Commission—to seek a new vision for the future of downtown. We must decide how to develop city-owned properties and must continue to recruit and retain businesses. Development of a major performing arts facility could be the key to downtown renewal. We must recognize that downtown is the heart of this community.

3. Beautification. Last year I appointed a five-member Tree Beautification Commission to seek ways of improving the entryways and develop programs for planting trees and landscaping many of the vacant city-owned properties adjacent to major streets. Operating under the impetus of this commission, the city has planted more than 2,500 trees throughout the area. It is even now making plans for further development of city parks and other properties. In the coming year I will ask the committee to expand its work. I envision specific proposals for further city beautification that will be undertaken cooperatively with private property owners. The commission has already discussed this with many of the businesses in Fairfield, including our major manufacturing installation, the Acme Company, where Ken Walton has pledged cooperation as have most of the other businesses. So in the year ahead we can anticipate seeing at least twice that many trees planted and acreages landscaped as we accomplished this past year.

4. Police. Much of the city's attention and energies have been needlessly locked on the on-going debate between the police committee and the Fairfield Police Department. Lest there be any doubt on where I stand as your mayor, let me make this perfectly clear—I stand squarely on the side of the police chief. I believe that Chief Hudson has come into a difficult situation and has worked hard to make this a department that we can look upon with great pride. He has dragged us—not without the proverbial kicking and screaming—into the modern computer age. It has been costly. Some do not like what it is costing us, both in dollars and in political animosity. But I believe that the forward-looking philosophies of Mr. Hudson have built our police force into a model for other small cities to follow—and follow they have. Many police departments have imitated the Hudson style in such matters as greater employment of civilian personnel, greater study of crime patterns through computers, and greater emphasis on crime prevention. I have no quarrel with this philosophy and believe the money is well spent.

Before I close I ask you to look ten years to the future. What will Fairfield be like at that time? Will it find us—as the late Mayor VanDenBosch was so fond of saying—all lying in the clover of Easy Street?

Well, maybe it won't be clover but merely the shade of the ten or twenty thousand trees and shrubs we will have planted by then. Or the newer, more lively downtown that I envision for our city. Or the creative Hobo Days celebration that Dan and Janis will be organizing for us. Or the revitalized economy that the airport expansion will bring. Working hand in hand toward that goal, we can and will leave a finer, more economically viable heritage for our children. Fairfield is on the move!

EXERCISE 28 A PROFILE OF MURDER

*Here is an impromptu speech delivered to the Fairfield Metro Club's noon luncheon to-
day. If it seems to ramble it's because it was not a prepared speech. Reporters must learn
to sort things out and to write coherent accounts of semicoherent commentary. Write a
story based on this information.*

Background. Let's assume here that the scheduled speaker (Ken Walton of Acme Manufacturing) failed to arrive because of missed airline connections. So the eighty-odd members lunching at the Sandy River Inn were asked to volunteer comments on something of public interest. Police Chief Ernest Hudson said a few words about murder. The Metro Club is composed of leading men and women from the Fairfield business, government and educational community. Hudson, 47, has been chief in Fairfield for five years, and previously worked as a homicide detective in Los Angeles. He was born in Fairfield (his widowed mother, Olivia, still lives on the family farm outside town), and has a master's degree in criminology from Michigan State University.

I'd like to say a few words about murder. If I had a title for these remarks it would be something like "Will you be murdered tonight?"

And the answer is probably not. I can just about guarantee it, at least for members of this group.

Murder is definitely *not* one of Fairfield's major industries. Last year our murder rate was 4.2 murders per 100,000 population, which is a good deal lower than the rate in L.A. when I was there—14.3. Years ago Dr. Julia Nathan, who teaches in the sociology department at Carson College, happened on an interesting statistic. She compared crime rates to climate and discovered a high negative correlation coefficient between snow and murder. That is, where it snowed the most, your chances of getting murdered were the least.

In fact, she even worked out a statistical profile of the class of person *least* likely to be murdered—an elderly married woman, Caucasian, living in a small, snowy community in New England.

I know you're wondering what are *your* chances of being murdered so I'd like to share a few of the studies that have been done on the subject over the years.

The person *most* likely to be murdered is young, unmarried, nonwhite, not too well-educated, living in a southern state. It's noteworthy that the murder rate for New England is one and a half per 100,000 people, whereas in the South Atlantic States it's something like six times greater—about nine or ten as I recall. The rate for nonwhites is nine or ten times greater than for whites.

If you were murdered tonight—and please bear in mind this is just a statistical profile—it's probably gonna be in your home or your killer's. Another common locale—in the case of one man killing another—is a public place, such as a street or alley or a tavern. When a man kills a woman, it will probably be in the bedroom. If a woman kills a man—a rare circumstance, by the way—the scene will probably be the kitchen, and she'll probably use a kitchen utensil, likely a butcher knife.

Even now you probably know your killer. The most common cause of murder is a violent argument over some trivial thing—a chance remark or some slight or insult, often not even intentional. It's astonishing what people kill each other for. In a tavern in Los Angeles a guy tried to buy a woman a drink. Her boyfriend came over and started a fight and seven minutes later the boyfriend had a cracked skull and the other guy was dead. Another time a dog got in a neighbor's yard and dug up some flowers, and the neighbor came over and shot the dog and when the owner came out to protest, he, too, was shot and killed.

In this case both men had been drinking. That's typical. The murder weapon is usually an explosive device, most commonly a gun. Your murder will probably happen on a weekend between 8 p.m. and 2 a.m.

It will not necessarily be a dark and stormy night. We have no evidence that specific weather conditions affect violent crime. A study in Houston once tried to correlate weather conditions with the times that murders occurred. They compared murder times with wind direction, rain, fog, thunderstorms, high and low barometric pressures and so on, and no connections were found. Other studies have even tried to compare murder with phases of the moon, and no connections were found. So I don't think your killer will necessarily strike in the full of the moon.

Well, these as I say are just a few random thoughts. I suppose the main point of it is that murder—contrary to the TV mystery image—tends to be pretty low caste, the passionate, emotion-of-the-moment kind of thing. Based on some of Julia Nathan's research, we find—strangely enough—that most murderers are a decent lot, not the psychotic, cold-blooded killer or the equally psychotic, sex-crazed serial killer stalking prostitutes in a big city. The media sensationalize those kinds of murder but tell you little or nothing about the typical garden variety of murder that emerges from a statistical profile.

Your typical murderer is polite, deferential, helpful, full of remorse about what happened. Studies show him to be a little more frustrated about life than most people and less able to handle the frustrations than most, but—as Julie Nathan likes to say—you'd feel safe buying a used car from your typical murderer, strange as that may sound.

And, incidentally, most murderers are caught and convicted.

And as for you ladies and gentlemen of the Metro Club—relax. You don't fit the statistical profile of the typical murder victim. The best I can say for you folks is that if you're gonna get murdered it will probably be negligent homicide—you'll get run over by a drunk driver. In fact, you have a far better chance of being killed in an auto accident than by any other means—but even there you can beat the odds. Just be sure to wear your seat belt. Don't drink while driving. If people followed those two rules, we could cut auto fatalities in half.

Chapter Ten

MEETINGS AND OTHER COMPLEX STORIES

A complex story involves several sources of information rather than just one. The sources may contradict one another in what they tell you or they may represent widely diverse points of view. Out of such bits and pieces of information you must fashion a coherent report. Of the exercises presented so far in this text, only two approximate the complexity of most major news accounts. One was the airplane crash (Exercise 20), which contained conflicting witness accounts. The other was the death of Ivan VanDenBosch (Exercise 25), which utilized numerous background clippings. Complex stories are what reporters write most of the time. You'd soon grow bored by the lack of challenge if all your stories were simple.

Meetings rank among the best examples of complex stories. Where a well-prepared speech has a theme and a clear set of supporting points, the discussion at, say, the meeting of a public agency accommodates a diverse set of viewpoints, most of them unrehearsed and therefore usually delivered in an offhand, rambling manner. Not only do people contradict each other, but they often contradict themselves as debate progresses and people change their minds. Somehow the newswriter must sort it all out and present a coherent story.

Here are some suggestions for handling such stories.

1. Learn to see the overall picture rather than getting hung up on the bits and pieces. A baseball game is a bunch of fragments—this pitch, that hit, that attempt to steal second, this strikeout. It's complicated, yet the writer makes overall sense of it with the report that the Yankees beat the Red Sox 7 to 4. The writer then goes on to cite some of the reasons why. You can do the same with a meeting. You identify and report the major developments or the standoffs or whatever you perceive to be the essence of the meeting. You then go on to cite the reasons why.

2. Look for ways to combine items. Suppose you are writing about several traffic accidents. An accident on Fifth Street injures five persons and kills one. Another on Tenth Street injures seven. A third on Fifteenth Street kills a pedestrian. Consider combining them into an omnibus lead such as this. "Two persons died and 12 others were injured in three separate accidents in Fairfield Thursday, police reported."

3. Learn the "flashby" technique, particularly in writing leads. A flashby uses parallel structure to allow you to cope with several facets of a complex event quickly and efficiently. Note the italicized portion of this hypothetical lead. "Tornadoes followed by heavy rain swept

through several plains states Sunday, *injuring 60 persons, causing $4 million property damage, and bringing floods to three rivers.*'' The injuries, the damages, the floods are flashed quickly in the opening and will, of course, gain further attention later in the story.

4. Don't try to crowd everything in the opening paragraph.

5. Use a chronological organization when possible. In a complex crime story you could start with a summary lead, then write a transitional paragraph such as "Police gave this account of the incident." You then would go back to the beginning and retrace the details in chronological order.

Consider an example of a complex story situation. You attended a school board meeting last night where several events occurred. The board:

1. Raised the per-diem allowance for school district personnel traveling outside Lincoln County from $42.50 to $56.50.

2. Granted unpaid leaves of absence to four teachers.

3. Accepted the bid of Zenith Bakery to supply bread to schools at 75 cents per 1.5-pound loaf, up from last year's contract of 66 cents.

4. Accepted the bid of Lincoln County Dairy Products to supply half-pints of milk at 15.65 cents, up from last year's contract of 13.2 cents.

5. Raised the price of school lunches from 35¢ to 50¢ for elementary school students and from 60¢ to 80¢ for junior high and senior high school students, effective next fall.

6. Passed a resolution to prohibit students from wearing

''suggestive'' T-shirts on school grounds (''suggestive'' defined as bearing inscriptions that promote drugs, alcohol or sex, or containing double meanings of a sexual nature).

The actions are only the beginning. No doubt the meeting contained discussion on these and other issues that also should be reported. But for now, just consider how those six items could be reported. Step one is to eliminate the unimportant (unpaid leaves could be dropped). Step two is to select the most important (the increase in school lunches more directly affects the public than any other; the suggestive T-shirts is probably the most controversial). Step three is to spot any points of commonality. Do you see anything? (How about the fact that *lots* of prices are going up?)

Here is one approach to the story lead:

> School lunches will cost Fairfield students 15 to 20 cents more next year, the Fairfield School Board decided last night.
>
> The board also moved to prohibit students from wearing ''suggestive'' T-shirts to school—the kind that contain sexual innuendoes or promote drugs, alcohol or sex.
>
> And three other board actions reflected inflationary cost increases. The cost of bread supplied to the district is up 14 percent, milk up 19 percent and the daily allowance for travel up 33 percent.

The body of the story would elaborate on these lead items. Note how numbers can be converted into percentages to allow comparisons and promote easy understanding. For more on the use of numbers in newswriting, see Chapter 12.

EXERCISE 29 COMPLEX LEADS

From the fragments of information provided in each paragraph, fashion a lead that pulls the diverse elements together.

A. Assume that today is Monday and that the State Highway Patrol reports the following accidents, all within Lincoln County. (1) Saturday night a motorcycle skidded on gravel on McKinley Road on the north end of Fairfield and upset. Driver Ralph N. Thompson is in critical condition at Providence Hospital. (2) A pickup truck flipped over Sunday morning as a result of a tire blowout on Highway 138 four miles south of Fairfield. An 11-year-old boy, Ernest Chalmers, 2234 E. 32nd, was killed instantly when the vehicle rolled over on him. (3) A head-on collision on Highway 55, 17 miles west of Fairfield, killed one passenger, Olivia McGee, and injured her husband, Duncan McGee. All are Fairfield residents. [*Source:* Sgt. Bill Anderson.]

B. Contract negotiations between the Retail Clerks Union, Local 676, of Lincoln County, and grocery store companies in Lincoln County will begin tomorrow. Current entry level wage for grocery clerks is $4.15. Journeyman clerks get $7.53. Negotiations for a two-year contract will begin tomorrow at 6 a.m. There are 900 clerks involved. They work at 55 groceries throughout the county. The union is asking for $8.90 an hour for journeyman clerks for the first year and $9.89 for the second. Also for $4.33 for entry-level clerks for the first year and $4.90 for the second. The grocers have offered $7.90 and $8.33 respectively and have not stated an offer for entry positions. The union's current contract expires in 30 days. [*Sources:* Irv Miller for the union, Jim Isaacs acting as spokesman for grocers.]

C. A major snowstorm hit Fairfield last night. Twelve inches of snow fell in 12 hours. The airport is closed. Interstate Airlines and United Airlines flights (16 a day to and from Fairfield) have been canceled today and to-morrow. Traffic is at a virtuál standstill. Snow removal equipment is working and it is expected that major routes in and through Fairfield will be cleared by 3 p.m. today. National Weather Service expects more snow starting again tonight—about 3 to 5 inches more. Helicopter runs by Sheriff's Office rescued about 20 people from cars stranded on U.S. Highway 56, U.S. 139, and from some country roads. Hospital says two fatalities occurred this morning as result of sudden heart attacks while shoveling snow. In addition one man was found dead in a stranded auto on Highway 55 about seven miles east of Fairfield. He had kept the engine running and apparently died of carbon monoxide from defective muffler, according to Bud Kuykendall. One house burned down about 4 this morning; fire equipment delayed 15 minutes because of snow-clogged streets. No injuries.

EXERCISE 30 PLANNING COMMISSION MEETING

The Fairfield Planning Commission, composed of five citizens (see City Directory), meets twice monthly. Write a story based on last night's meeting. (Model story, Appendix B.)

Background. The Planning Commission holds public hearings and makes recommendations to the City Council on the physical development of the city. These include the zoning of real estate for varied uses: residential, retail commercial, light industrial and so on. The idea is to prevent an industrial plant from locating next to residential structures and vice versa. On tonight's meeting agenda is a request for permission to operate a home for unwed mothers in a residence at 880 East 11th Street, a district zoned for "high density" residential use, meaning multiple-dwelling apartments and boarding houses. Tonight the commission, chaired by Ms. Kelly Estelle, holds a public hearing on the question of the "conditional use permit" requested by Hosanna Children's Center. Here, in essence, is the discussion.

Ms. Estelle. Is there anyone who wishes to be heard on the matter of the conditional use permit requested by Hosanna Children's Center?

Mr. Lindley. Madam Chairman, my name is Cal Lindley and I live at 895 East 11th Street, just down the street from the proposed center. I certainly would like to raise a strong objection to this center for unwed mothers. The area around east 11th Street is among the most historic and picturesque in the city. I know there has been talk within the City Council about changing the zoning of that district from high density to medium density. If the center for unwed mothers is permissible under high density, it would not be under low density, and I object to it on that grounds. If you permit them to move in there, I think you can kiss the historic preservation factor goodbye as it would simply be a first step toward the deterioration of the neighborhood. We would lose any chance we have of getting the area rezoned for medium density. I also would object on the further ground that the neighborhood runs the risk that things might go astray at the center. These are highly charged and emotional young girls, and anything can happen. I think there is a real fear within our neighborhood that these girls might go beserk and create a crisis that the counselors in the center can't handle.

Ms. Anderson. I am Priscilla Anderson, and my husband and I live on East 11th right next door to Mr. Lindley. Yes, I certainly support Cal's comments here. I mean we are dealing with a highly undesirable element here, maybe not the girls themselves, you know, but their boyfriends are gonna be hanging around and there is a real danger of trouble in what has up to now been a very quiet neighborhood. I mean these young children that go and get themselves pregnant, why they are just the most undesirable element of our society, I mean, I'm not a bigot or anything, but I just think if there's gonna be a lot of noise and coming and going by boys on motorcycles, and we're just not prepared to handle that kind of confusion out on East 11th.

Mr. Zweig. My name is Paul Zweig, and I am a semi-retired gentleman who has taken on the task of organizing the shelter home we propose for the unwed mothers. I am manager of a nonprofit, interdenominational church agency known as the

Hosanna Center, presently headquartered down on Eisenhower Avenue. May I say that the type of home we are looking at is always needed—but unfortunately it's always needed in someone *else's* neighborhood. What we are attempting to do here is present an alternative to abortion. I personally detest the idea of abortion, most particularly when we know of the countless childless couples who are desperately seeking babies to adopt. We believe that when life is conceived, the unborn child thereby earns the God-given right to life, and we want to do what we can to preserve that life. I assure you that we are not the kind of people who would throw bombs at abortion clinics—we merely go quietly about our business and are careful not to intrude on anyone else's affairs. We would anticipate having anywhere from six to ten girls in the home at any given time. These girls are mostly ages 13 to 16 and referred to us either by the state Children's Services Division or by the local school districts. We are chartered by the state of Anystate to operate such a home, and we submit to periodic inspections by the Children's Services Division. At our present location we can only take in two girls at most, and we need the room to meet the demand. There will be three live-in staff counselors, all women, and in addition we will have tutors and additional counselors on call if and when needed. These girls are fine people no matter what you may think. They are not troublemakers. They do not appeal to boys on motorcycles. This type of girl is not going to be out on the street looking for trouble. She's got enough trouble as it is. Thank you.

Commissioner Zolotow. I'm pretty much convinced that the center will perform a useful service and will not cause undue hardship to the neighborhood. I want to propose two stipulations, however. One, only unwed mothers are to be housed there. We do not want to see sick girls there or kids on drugs. Two, that this commission review the permit after one year's time. Mr. Zweig, would you have any objection to those conditions?

Zweig. None whatever.

[Following the hearing the five-member commission votes 5–0 to approve the application for a "conditional use permit," including the two stipulations proposed by Ms. Zolotow.]

EXERCISE 31 COUNCIL MEETING

At the end of last night's meeting of the Fairfield City Council, the following discussion took place. Write a story based on that discussion. Try to capture the essence of what occurred and quote comments from either side, but don't get too bogged down in the extravagant charges. The persons named below are members of the City Council plus Chief Hudson. Members of the Police Committee are Wheelock (chair), Beatty and Hixon.

Wheelock. Before we adjourn may I comment on a recurring problem?

Mayor. Of course.

Wheelock. Some weeks ago we discussed with the chief of police some problems with officers within the Police Department abusing citizens. Mr. Hudson then assured the council that the problem was being taken care of. Since then we have had two meetings of the Police Committee, and frankly this problem is not going to disappear.

Mayor. Well, I'm certainly sorry to hear that. I keep yearning for a little tranquility around City Hall, Mr. Wheelock.

Wheelock. Just in the last few weeks I've had many people come to me and complain about the conduct of the police. I ask them, do you want me to take it to the chief? And they say, "No, no—why bother? They'll just whitewash the whole thing?" Just yesterday the committee tried to meet with Mr. Hudson, but we failed to achieve one iota of cooperation.

Mayor. Do you have any particulars?

Wheelock. Here's one case of a teen-age girl, stopped *twice,* two evenings in a row, for equipment checks on her car, even though the car is only six months old. She came to me half terrified. I don't think that's a legal action for an officer to take.

McPherson. I think I'd like to hear the the other side of that story, from the officer. Mr. Wheelock's anti-police biases are well known by us.

Wheelock. A 17-year-old boy came to me and said the police just walked right into his home and began questioning him without even telling him why. And another kid was stopped at a road block and saw several cops crouched behind their cars pointing guns at him. My lord! Surely this is not a necessary police action!

Beatty. I can cite another experience or two. My neighbor's son was treated roughly by an officer who stopped his van and kept saying things like "Nice van—I'll bet it goes *real* fast"—the implication being that "I've got my eye on you, kid!" And then I had a teen girl come to me and say that she'd been picked up by a cop late at night and when he got her into his squad car he *touched* her. . . uh, *improperly*!

McPherson. I especially want to hear both sides of that one.

Estelle. Mr. Mayor, I'm as enthralled by this gossip as anyone, but I fail to see the point of discussing it here. Surely the department has formal procedures for handling complaints of this type. If they don't, then let's suggest that they do. Let's not reduce the council to discussion of whether a police officer has improperly touched a young girl. I'm sorry Mr. Wheelock, but I just lack the patience for this kind of trivia.

Mayor. I see Chief Hudson is in the audience tonight. Since we seem to be on the record already with these complaints, I think Ernest should have a right of rebuttal.

Hudson. Our department has a standard procedure for complaints which are handled on a case-by-case basis. All a citizen has to do is file a complaint with me or my assistant and we make a complete investigation. There is no whitewash. We ask a lot of hard questions. I have not heard of the complaints you speak of. I can't act without a specific complaint in hand. I can't go on hearsay. Cops operate on the basis of solid factual evidence. If a young lady claims to have been improperly handled by an officer, let her or her parents come forth with the details.

Wheelock. We may see this case in court. Frankly I'd hoped to head this sort of thing off before it got to the courts and gave the city a black eye with all the media vultures around.

Hudson. I run an honest department, out in the open. We're not perfect, but we work hard and have nothing to hide. If we've erred, I'd prefer to make a clean admission of our mistake, learn from it, and look to the future.

Mayor. Perhaps our best procedure will be to have the Police Committee prepare some kind of specific material, a kind of dossier.

Wheelock. We would be happy to do that, Mr. Mayor. Naturally we would expect this to be a confidential report to the council, not a public document that's going to be smeared all over by the media vultures.

Mayor. I'd like to think the kind of secrecy you yearn for went out with King Henry VIII. Today we like to think the public's business can be conducted out in the open.

Hudson. The department would welcome public scrutiny. We're scrutinized plenty already, and if you can't stand the heat, as Harry Truman used to say, get off the range.

McPherson. I think we should propose a citizen's advisory committee for the consideration of the chief and the department.

Mayor. Mr. Wheelock, can your committee prepare such a proposal and report back to the council in, say, three or four weeks?

Wheelock. Indeed we can.

[Following is dialogue from two brief interviews held after the meeting by several reporters in an impromptu news conference. The first is with Wheelock.]

Q. *Do you have other complaints beyond those you mentioned?*

A. [Wheelock.] Yes. I didn't want to embarrass the chief.

Q. *Such as what?*

A. The media is gonna hear about it soon enough.

Q. *Will they be cases of physical abuse, brutality or more the verbal intimidation type you cited at the meeting?*

A. I'm not going to try the case in the media. A full report will be forthcoming.

Q. *Will that be the proposal for a citizen's advisory committee that the mayor asked for?*

A. Yes, we will do that.

Q. *Will you also specify the charges against the department in this report?*

A. We will have specifics. If not in this report, then in another.

Q. *How do you respond to McPherson's allegations of anti-police bias on your part?*

A. If being in favor of honest, clean government is an anti-police bias, then I plead guilty. I stand behind honest, open government and I want a first-rate police department.

[Police Chief Hudson also talk to reporters.]

Q. *Chief, how do you feel about Mr. Wheelock's remarks?*

A. [Hudson.] It's a free country—he can say what he wants.

Q. *Are any of his complaints justified?*

A. I have a little trouble responding to hearsay and rumors. So far that's all we have. Let's wait and see what evidence comes in. Very few citizen complaints about police abuse have come to my attention in the past year other than Wheelock's innuendoes.

Q. *Do you feel Wheelock has an anti-police bias?*

A. More like an anti-Hudson bias.

Q. *How do you feel about the formation of a citizen's advisory committee?*

A. We'd welcome it.

EXERCISE 32 POLICE DELEGATION

About thirty citizens have come to the meeting to talk about Chief Hudson and about the ongoing controversy over alleged police abuse. Mayor Dmytryshyn opens the meeting by asking the citizens to come forward and speak their minds. Here is the essence of the comments by ten of the speakers. (The council does not respond to the citizen comments; members, including Wheelock, merely listen. Chief Hudson is not present.) Write a story based on their comments.

Thomas K. Savage. Frankly, I think the council is on a ludicrous witch hunt. I've been in the military police for 18 years, just retired a couple of years ago, and I can tell you being a cop is no easy task in this day and age. You're damned if you do and damned if you don't. You have a labor dispute with picketing and people are ready to kill each other. Well, just let a city police officer show up and suddenly it's the police who are at fault—it's like *they* caused the strike and the rioting. I say let's get off Ernie Hudson's back and let him do his job. Stop this petty bickering. It does not become us as grown-up citizens.

Barbara A. Bradford. When my apartment was burglarized a few months ago, two officers came to my door, and I thought they were very courteous and nice. I could tell that they thought I was a silly fool for leaving my door unlocked all weekend, but they were nice about it.

Herman Melville. I'll say this—the cops is there when you need 'em. I got no complaints.

Bob Diekhoff. I don't think we can sweep all this under the rug. I've had a run-in or two with cops and I can tell you there's nothing courteous about them—they hate teenagers, especially. A couple of years ago I was stopped, my car was stopped and the cops were all over the place brandishing their pistols and I was treated very rudely and never told why I was stopped. To this day I don't know.

Stormy B. Marks. My husband is a police officer, and I just want to say I know the dedication of these men. We have a very honest, vital bunch of men and women, and I don't understand the complaining I keep hearing.

Carl Crawford. I'm a businessman in this town, and I can remember the days when cops were on the take. If you wanted a ticket fixed, no problem. Just slap a few dollars into the right cop's hand. I can remember when some parts of town were nothing but red light districts and boozy clip joints. Well Ernie Hudson rode like a tall man in the saddle about five years ago, and he changed all that. He's enforcing the laws. He's gotten rid of some shady cops. He's enforcing the laws equally—the wealthy and connected people aren't any better off today than the impoverished. And that's the way it should be. So I say the council should give Ernie Hudson a medal instead of a kick in the pants. He's an honest, diligent cop—and if you don't believe that, just try slapping a twenty-dollar bill in his hand to fix a ticket and see where that gets you!

Walt Valentine. Ernest Hudson is something of a fascist ramrod, and I mean that as a compliment. It takes a strong man to come in here and make some sorely needed changes in the department, turn it around 180 degrees. It's a good department and getting better. If the council has nothing better to do than engage in a witch hunt, why not attack the street department? The potholes in the street in front of my house have been there for a year, and nothing's been done.

Conrad A. Wrzaszczak. Have you tried calling the police?

Debbie Winningham. All this fancy talk amongst all the swells in this town is a crock—I think it's time we got down and dirty. Let me tell you about a friend of mine. She was raped one night. I was down at headquarters with her all night long. I can't believe the hell they put her through. I mean, they were laughing and having a ball. It was like, "Hey, Sergeant, come here and hear this broad's weird story!" And it was like, "Bet you really enjoyed it, huh, honey?" She told the story a hundred times, and it didn't stop with police headquarters. Then it was the lawyers, then it was the courts, and it got to the point where she told me, Deb, if some guy rapes you, just take a gun and shoot the s.o.b. because that's the only way you're gonna get justice. Think of that before you hang a medal around Ernest Hudson's neck.

Dr. Ken Aasen. Let us not forget that ten or twelve years ago we thought we had a problem with slightly shady dealings in the police department. When it came time to hire a new chief of police, the council appointed a search committee composed of members of the council and concerned citizens. I know, because I was on that committee. We specifically sought applications from a new breed of police officer who would turn us around from the mistakes of the past. We wanted a man of integrity, well-educated, effective with the public. We wanted a man who would give emphasis to things like crime prevention, education—not just knocking heads like in the past. I think we have just that sort of man—a gentleman cop—in Ernest Hudson, and I'm dumbfounded that he seems to be so little understood among certain factions in the council. However, no matter what happens, I can't help but think this discussion is salutary—truth and falsehood grappling on the open forum, if you will—and I think that years from now, when we look back upon this episode, we'll find in Mr. Hudson the most visionary and effective peace officer this town has ever had.

EXERCISE 33 YEARBOOK CONTROVERSY

Write a story based on a segment of the monthly meeting of the District 4J School Board. During last night's meeting a delegation of thirty citizens attended. About ten addressed the board; the following comments typify the thrust of the session.

Tillinghast (chair). Is there a spokesperson for the delegation?

Weaver. Yes, I would like to say a few words if it please the board. My name is Hiram Weaver, and I'm a local pastor. I wish to call attention to the cover of the South High School yearbook which reached my hands just a few days ago. We all know that the nickname of the South High School athletic teams has for the past 75 years been the "Blue Devils," something we have had to live with though I personally would like to see the name changed to "Blue Angels." All of us want to protest in the *most vigorous manner possible* the use of the likeness of the devil on the cover of the high school yearbook. [Holds up copy of yearbook; see the accompanying illustration.] This despicable example of man's satanic nature was called to my attention by our church's youth group who complained bitterly that our tax moneys are going to this symbolic worship of the devil. We cannot have this kind of symbolism in our schools; we cannot have our young people depicted symbolically as worshipers of the devil, of Satan, and I respectfully request that all copies of this yearbook be confiscated and destroyed! As you all know, the word devil or Satan has been used in the Good Book no fewer than one hundred and seventy times, and at all times he is pictured as an enemy of God and of mankind. He is pictured therein as a personage to be feared and avoided at all costs.

Stacey Perrin. I think the board should change the name of the South athletic teams from Blue Devils to Blue Angels, like the reverend says.

Al Kirkwood. When I look at that cover, I see a picture not of a Blue Devil, depicting the athletic teams, but of the devil himself. The symbols of the hands upraised are right out of Satanic worship.

Herman Melville. Folks get worked up over this kind of thing. I don't like the cover; I'd rather see a picture of a mountain or a waterfall. But kids have got to explore and exercise their skills. Let's not lose our heads. It don't make no difference in the long run. I bet they won't do another worship-the-devil cover for another thirty or forty years.

Ellery Quick, high school student and yearbook editor (son of Floyd Quick). When we got together and designed this cover, I guess we just didn't reckon with the consequences. To me, the only symbolism was just the support of our team, the Blue Devils. They need all the support they can get. And I guess we wanted a cover that was kind of different, something that would be remembered. I don't think it ever occurred to us that anybody would interpret it any other way. I guess we'd design it a different way if we were doing it for the Reverend Mr. Weaver, but we did it for the students, not for the clergy. Most of the kids in school loved it. It's too late to confiscate the books, however—they've already gone out, and they may become collector's items if there's a big controversy over them.

Tillinghast. Thank you all—and especially you, Reverend Weaver, for this enlightening session. I can assure you that the board will look into the matter, at the very least for the purpose of seeing that offensive publications do not come out of our schools in the future. We certainly need to keep in mind that South High and the other schools are part of a larger community and we should not willfully offend the sensibility of the general citizenry.

Chapter Eleven

WRITING FROM INTERVIEWS

The interview is the primary tool of the reporter. Here are some suggestions for conducting news interviews, followed by some exercises that demonstrate interviewing techniques.

1. Prepare for an important interview by learning as much as you can about the topic or person involved.
2. Make your identity and the purpose of your interview clear from the beginning. Haziness or deceit invite guarded responses.
3. Prepare a set of topics to be covered in the interview, but leave room for flexibility—often a good interview will dip into worthy subjects that could not have been anticipated at the beginning.
4. Keep your questions short. Ask follow-up questions. Often the important questions are the ones you didn't know you were going to ask. They are follow-up questions stimulated by the answers you get.

5. Listen carefully to the answers. Show that you are listening by eye contact, alert body posture and even by responses like "Uh-huh." Prefacing new questions with phrases like "You said earlier that. . ." also shows that you are listening.
6. Take notes but don't try to be a stenographer. Listen for the essence of what is said and listen for supporting data.
7. Integrate your notetaking with the conversation. It is perfectly proper to slow the conversation down by a comment such as "I really like what you just said—would you give me a moment to get that in my notes?"
8. Encourage people to just be themselves. You can best do that by relaxing and being *yourself*. People often tend to talk to news interviewers in formal, guarded tones, whereas the best interviews are the ones that acquire candid observations and anecdotal materials.

EXERCISE 34 LINDA MCCORMACK'S STORY

Sometimes a story from a national wire service involves someone from the local circulation area. In such instances the story must be revised to emphasize the role of the local person or to include detail or background not available in the wire story. Let's assume that it's summer and you receive the following story from the national wire. This inspires you to call Linda McCormack to conduct a telephone interview about her many heroic exploits. Write a story based on this material.

LEWISTON, Idaho (AP)—Authorities here credit the daughter of a former Anystate governor with saving the life of a child who had fallen into the Clearwater River [yesterday].

Linda McCormack, 17, daughter of former Anystate Gov. Edward W. McCormack, swam 30 yards to rescue a child who had fallen off a passing motorboat. She then administered mouth-to-mouth resuscitation to the unconscious child until an ambulance arrived.

The child, Theresa Massey, 3, of Lewiston, was recovering at a local hospital.

Linda, touring the Pacific Northwest with her family, is a championship member of a high school swimming team at Fairfield, Any.

Background. Review the previous stories about Linda, Chapter 1 and Exercise 9-B&D and 11-D (which we'll assume is the "true" story in the lead-writing exercise in Chapter 5). Assume it's now sometime in August. Assume the Idaho rescue occurred yesterday, the Mansfield rescue (Exercise 11-D) the middle of last July, the Crawford rescue (9-B&D) in early July, the River City rescue in October of last year. The River City children are Debbie Parsons, 6, and Everette Parsons, 9; their mother is Laura Parsons, 34, of River City, which is a city of 100,000 located 100 miles north of Fairfield. Linda is state champion in the high school girls 100-yard freestyle sprints with a time of 51.8 seconds. She also is part of a four-swimmer South High School relay team that won a state championship in the girls 400-yard relay with a winning time of 3:57.58. Next spring she will participate in a national swimming competition at Mission del Viejo, California.

You reach Linda at a resort on the Oregon coast where her family is vacationing, and the following conversation occurs.

Q. *Linda, my name is Barbara Miller from the Telegram in Fairfield. I wonder if you'd mind talking with me on the phone for a few minutes for a story I want to write about your numerous water rescues. We just got a report that you rescued a child in Idaho. How many times has it been now—at least four rescues?*

A. I'm flattered. Did you run out of things to write

about? I lost track of rescues. Do you count the one three years ago at Niagara Falls?

Q. *Another one? You rescued somebody from the falls?*

A. No, just the swimming pool at the motel. This baby fell into the pool and I pulled him out. No great heroics or anything. I was 14 then and I just happened to be there.

Q. *Okay, let's see—there's the River City Rescue for which you won the medal. Then two in the Sandy River. Then Idaho. Plus Niagara. That figures out to five rescues of six children. Any others?*

A. No, that's it.

Q. *Tell me which of the rescues was the most dangerous or difficult.*

A. The two kids at River City.

Q. *Can you tell me about that rescue?*

A. Okay. I was visiting this girlfriend in River City, and we were riding bikes along the highway beside the Chickahominy River. It was October and there'd been a little rain. The river was high and muddy.

Q. *Uh-huh. . .*

A. This car suddenly skids on the wet pavement. It's so unreal! I mean, it just spins off the road and overturns and then it's in the water. And when we get up there, here's this lady, drenched in mud, blood all over her face, and she's screaming, "My god, my god, get my babies!"

Q. *That's when you learned that children were trapped in the car?*

A. Yeah. The car was upside down, maybe 30 feet out, its bottom sticking out of the water and the wheels still spinning. By now there's maybe three or four people around. I remember saying something like "Let's *do* something," and some guy goes, "That water's cold—and I can't swim."

Q. *So you went in yourself?*

A. I thought I could just wade out. I didn't think it was that deep. Boy, was I wrong!

Q. *How deep was it?*

A. Waist deep maybe. I'm not sure. The problem was the current was so swift I couldn't stay on my feet. So I came back and took my clothes off—well, not *all* of them—but I figured I'm not going to go out there in that kind of current without some leg-power. So I took my jeans off. God, how freaky, now that I think back. People are drowning and here's this goofy girl taking her clothes off.

Q. *How did you get the kids out?*

A. They were thrashing around inside, but they had about a foot of air at the top. I just plucked them out one by one through an open door. By the time I got them out and sitting on the car, someone was there throwing a rope, which I tied to the axle. They came out and helped us back. And then I suddenly got very cold. That was the first I realized how cold the water was. God, was it cold! I thought I'd die—freeze to death. Funny I never noticed the cold until then. In a few minutes the ambulance was there with blankets. Can I tell you something freaky?

Q. *Yes.*

A. Months later some cop comes up to me one day and congratulates me for the medal but then tells me *never* do that again—swim out to an overturned car in the river. You never know when the car will turn over in the current and trap you, he says. You've got to wait until somebody gets a rope on it. Well, I didn't know that!

Q. *At the time you probably thought it was a matter of life and death—*

A. I still do. I'm not sure how long the kids would have lasted in the cold water.

Q. *How does it happen that you're on the scene of so many emergencies?*

A. Just sheer dumb luck, I guess.

Q. *Your other rescues—I gather they weren't as dangerous or difficult.*

A. Well, they were in summer and at least the water wasn't freezing. I didn't think they were difficult. You just dive in and do what you can.

Q. *What about swimming in Cleveland Rapids to save the Mansfield girl?*

A. I swim in rapids all the time. Diving into the rapids is like diving into a glass of champagne—I love the bubbles.

Q. *Linda, can I ask what your goals are? Career goals?*

A. Go to college. Maybe get into a college that has a great women's swimming team, maybe even get an athletic scholarship. I'm a fair swimmer, so I might have a chance.

Q. *And beyond that? What will you study?*

A. Good question. My father says I'm smart enough to do anything I want. Well, you know how fathers are. I love sports. Maybe I'll be a football coach at Notre Dame.

EXERCISE 35 REPORT TO THE COUNCIL

Reporters often play hunches in pursuit of news articles, not always quite sure what they will get into. This exercise is a case in point. Let's say that three weeks have elapsed since the meeting depicted in Exercise 31. With another council meeting coming up next Monday night, it's time to find out what happened to that report the Police Committee had been asked to prepare. Will it be on the meeting agenda next Monday night? A call to Mr. Wheelock yields the following. Write a story.

Q. *[On phone] Mr. Wheelock, this is Fred Scott at the Telegram. I'm planning to write an article about the problems of the Police Department and I wondered if I might ask you a few questions about your report to the council.*

A. Go ahead.

Q. *Is the report finished yet?*

A. Yes.

Q. *Will it be presented to the council next Monday night?*

A. Yes, it's on the agenda.

Q. *Would it be possible to obtain a copy?*

A. No. This is really a private matter with the council, and I would be precluded from providing a copy to the media.

Q. *I see. I suppose the council might not be considered*

a private agency, though. With its public meetings and all, it would be hard to imagine this really being a private matter.

A. Be that as it may, this is the procedure by which I and the Police Committee plan to operate.

Q. *Okay. Can you tell me the essence of the report?*

A. No—I just said that I would not be providing any information in advance of the council meeting, so don't ask those kinds of questions. After all, the report might be rejected by the council.

Q. *Does the report contain instances of police abuse or is it the proposal for a civilian review board?*

A. Both.

Q. *Can you suggest the nature of the complaints it contains about police abuse?*

A. No, I said I will not be answering those kinds of questions.

Q. *Can you tell me how long the report is?*

A. It's a *long* report.

Q. *Does it contain the details and case histories that Chief Hudson has asked for?*

A. Mr. Scott, if you'll excuse me, I have work to do, so I'll have to cut this short. Please understand that there is little I can say about it at this stage. Good day. [Hangs up.]

[Reporters shouldn't take the petulance of news sources personally. What one official doesn't tell you, another might. You call the other members of the Police Committee. Hixon declines to talk, but Beatty agrees to answer questions on "procedural matters."]

Q. *Did Wheelock prepare the report himself, or did you and Hixon also work on it?*

A. [Beatty] We had several meetings at which we pooled information that we had gathered from some complaining citizens. Ken wrote three drafts in all, and we approved the final draft last night.

Q. *Did you interview citizens or what?*

A. Each of us has been talking down through the past few months with citizens who have had complaints about the police. We had letters and notes on file.

Q. *And from those you fashioned the report?*

A. Yes.

Q. *Did you talk with anyone other than complaining citizens? The police chief, perhaps, or other officers?*

A. No, it was not our role to represent the police view. We wanted to represent the citizen-taxpayer view as a basis for further discussions in the council.

Q. *How long is the report?*

A. About 50 pages, typewritten, single spaced.

Q. *Does it contain the factual information, case-by-case, that Hudson is looking for?*

A. I'm not at liberty to talk about content.

Q. *Okay. Does it contain any specific recommendations for change?*

A. I'm sorry—I don't really want to say until the council sees it.

Q. *I understand—but I do have to ask one more question. Does it contain a recommendation for forming a citizen's advisory committee?*

A. I can't comment on that.

[Mayor Dmytryshyn tells you that he put the report on the agenda for Monday's meeting. Chief Hudson has not seen the report but answers your questions.]

Q. *You've never attended any meetings of the Police Committee?*

A. [Hudson.] No, not in recent weeks. I was never invited.

Q. *Did any member of the committee talk to you?*

A. Not in recent weeks.

Q. *Did the committee talk with anyone in the department?*

A. Not that I'm aware of.

Q. *So you're as ignorant of the matter as the rest of us?*

A. Probably more so.

Q. *How does that make you feel?*

A. When I was a young cop, I recall walking into a burning building with my gun drawn one time. There were supposed to be three highly volatile drums of gasoline somewhere inside, plus three fugitives supposedly holed up in the building, and they were armed and dangerous. The fire department couldn't fight the fire for fear of being shot by these lunatics. I don't recall being as nervous then as I am right now. Does that answer the question?

Q. *It does!*

A. Well, the end of the story is that nobody was in the building, and the drums of gasoline turned out to be vats of pickle juice. The fire was mostly smoke and it probably would have fizzled out even without the firemen there. I learned a lesson from that.

Q. *Which is what—to stop worrying?*

A. It's that where there's smoke there may be nothing but pickle juice.

EXERCISE 36 ECONOMIC UNCERTAINTIES

Write a story based on this interview with Ken Walton, the founder, president and chief executive officer of Acme Manufacturing Company, Fairfield's largest employer. Topic of the interview is rumors of a downturn in the market for Acme's products. Following are some documents consulted before starting the interview.

From the Annual Report. Acme was founded in 1956 by Ken Walton and Howard Venture in the back shop of Venture's radio, TV and appliance shop in downtown Fairfield. They started producing mechanical and electrical toys, radio devices and paper products. Howard Venture eventually sold his interest and moved to Mexico to retire. Under Walton's leadership, Acme has grown to a major manufacturing firm with $200 million annual sales, 3,500 employees, producing some 300 paper and electronics products. Today it has five major divisions: (1) electronic toys, (2) electronic devices for the home, such as burglar and smoke alarms, automatic plant waterers, electronic babysitters and telephone peripherals, (3) battery components and specialty products, (4) paper products, including writing bond, packaging papers, industrial filters, and automotive oil and air filters, and (5) electronics components such as miniature cathode ray tubes, integrated circuits and computer peripherals.

From a newspaper account two years ago of Ken Walton. Walton once wrote a high school autobiography for his English class. He got an A grade, and he's kept the paper for 40 years. Here's an excerpt:

"After finishing high school I plan to establish my own business and go further into the study of radio. I want to learn everything possible about radio. There is so much to know; I think any day we shall be transmitting and receiving radio waves to and from distant planets, from Mars and Jupiter, and radio is the means by which we shall bind our planet together so that communication can be instantaneous. I will probably carry on many experiments in this field and also possibly some other branches of science. If I do all that I hope to do, I shall probably make some inventions. I have several ideas for inventions which if put to use would be of great benefit to peoples of the world. I believe that the possibilities of radio are unlimited and that most people have almost no idea of what radio can offer in the way of benefits to mankind."

In the next 40 years he would acquire no fewer than 47 patents for products ranging from an electronic cockroach zapper to the electronic babysitter which sounds an alarm whenever a child wanders beyond a specified distance.

His net worth is said to be in the $90- to $100-million range, yet he retains a modest, unassuming demeanor. . . .

Q. *Mr. Walton we've heard rumors at the paper that Acme may be in for tough times because of a soft market for its products. Can you comment on those stories? Is there a possibility of layoffs?*

A. I'm happy to have an opportunity to set the record straight. I was not aware that such rumors were afield, though there is little doubt that the market for certain electronic and paper products is rather on the tentative side at this time. To make one thing clear—no, we do not find it necessary to plan for any layoffs at Acme. However, our corporate directors will shortly be studying the current economic situation, and I think it is safe to say that we shall be cutting our workforce by about three to five percent.

Q.   *How many workers would that involve?*

A.   Let's say between 100 and 200 workers. We believe we will be able to do this without resorting to involuntary layoffs. Our normal turnover amounts to 300 annually, and so our plan is simply not to replace most of the workers who will be leaving through normal attrition—that is through retirements, resignations and unpaid leaves. We have already circulated information to our employees to this effect. We have also encouraged early retirement by offering $5,000 to $30,000 cash bonuses to any who leave before the mandatory retirement age. Some 15 or 20 workers will be taking advantage of that offer.

Q.   *What divisions will be affected?*

A.   None more than any other. That is, the attrition will take place throughout the five divisions of Acme.

Q.   *And the reason is a soft market for your products?*

A.   I'd call it an uncertain market. Some of our products are doing well—better than expected. Sales of our electronic babysitters are at least 40 percent over predicted sales. Unfortunately, some of our other products have not reached their quotas. Battery components and paper filter components have been well below expectations.

Q.   *Does this mean you'll be expanding some divisions and shrinking others?*

A.   Unquestionably yes. We have transferred many valued workers out of paper and retrained them in electronics, particularly the production of the babysitter units.

Q.   *Why are babysitters doing so well?*

A.   I think it's because for anywhere from $49.95 to $99.50—retail prices for our various models—parents can enjoy great peace of mind. These units place a tiny electronic transmitter around the child's neck. If the parent's receiving unit fails to receive the signal—either because the child has wandered out of range or has fallen into the swimming pool—an alarm sounds and the parent knows something is amiss. We have hundreds of letters suggesting how this unit has saved children from great harm.

Q.   *How many of those have you produced and sold?*

A.   Thousands! I can't give you a specific figure but it would be upward of 100,000 units in the last twelve months and we're six months behind in our orders. It's our best-selling product.

Q.   *Is the downturn in the market for your other products a temporary thing in your view?*

A.   It's always difficult to predict. Our best guess is that a year or two may elapse before things pick up. We at Acme are girding for a continuation of an uneasy market for both our paper and electronic products.

Q.   *What is the trimming of the workforce likely to cost the community in lost payroll?*

A.   We're talking about $3 million annually, I think. Maybe a little more.

Q.   *Do you anticipate that workers may have to take pay cuts just to keep their jobs, as has happened in other industries?*

A.   We're hoping that won't happen. Acme is unique in that most of our workers are also among our major stockholders. Our own workers own some 30 to 35 percent of the company's stock. This is why we have enjoyed fine labor relations over the years. This is why we're unlikely to take any actions that are not in the best interests of our own workers and our own community. Profitability is important but it is not the sole criterion that guides us.

Q.   *Can you identify other products that are doing particularly well?*

A.   Yes, our electronic cockroach zappers are doing well in selected markets—New York, Cleveland, New Orleans, Miami and Honolulu.

Q.   *Have you new product lines coming up?*

A.   Lots, though I can't publicly reveal them now for obvious reasons. And we've had a failure or two.

Q.   *You've had failures?*

A.   Our biggest failure was the Howard Cosell Zapper the research department was trying to develop some years ago. The idea was that we would develop a minicomputer that could read voice patterns. We could program it to read Cosell's voice. The moment it picked up that familiar Cosell pattern it would turn down the sound on your TV and keep it down as long as the voice persisted. We developed a prototype that actually worked. Unfortunately the cost was high. We never got it under $900 per unit, so we had to give up. Too bad. At $29.95 we could have sold thousands. Cosell retired a few years later, so it ceased to matter.

Chapter Twelve

EDITING

Exercises in this chapter will help you focus on typical writing problems. Among them are wordiness, passiveness, awkward sentence construction and lack of organization. Chances are you will find the problems more easily in someone else's writing than in your own, authorship having its blind spots. Please remember, however, that the problems you see here could well blemish your own work. Try to apply the same ruthless objectivity to your writing that you apply to these exercises.

EXERCISE 37 PARALLEL CONSTRUCTION

Revise the following sentences to conform with the principles of parallel construction. (For an explanation of parallelism and additional exercises, see Exercise 89 in Appendix A.)

1. Barbara Justice is a novelist who enjoys revising her manuscripts as well as doing research, and she even likes to read reviews of her books.
2. The Langtrys have three children: 4-year-old Jamie, Teresa, who is 3, and little Timmy is not quite 26 months.
3. During their trip abroad, the Katsuyuki Sakamoto family enjoyed skiing in the Swiss Alps, though they had an equally pleasant time scuba diving in Bermuda, while the tour of Pearl Harbor proved to be another highlight of the trip.
4. Gen. Gordon Taylor is a man who hates politicians, though he loves the smell of a good political battle, even though he despises the arrogance of the victors.
5. Japanese cooking, Charlie Barnett believes, is simple, and he feels it is exotic as well, and in addition there is much pleasure to be derived from it.

EXERCISE 38 PASSIVE WRITING

Passive voice means overuse of weak verbs, particularly those derived from the verb "to be." Examples:

Passive: The life saving medal *was accepted* by Linda McCormack.

Active: Linda McCormack *accepted* the life saving medal.

Passive: Jane Doe *was arrested* last night by police for trespassing.

Active: Police *arrested* Jane Doe last night for trespassing.

Passive: There *was* a smile on Jeanne Gray's face as she accepted the roses.

Active: Jeanne Gray *smiled* as she accepted the roses.

Rewrite the following sentences to eliminate passive voice.

1. The ball was slammed out of the park by shortstop Ricky Blitz.

Rewrite the following sentences to eliminate passive voice

1. The ball was slammed out of the park by shortstop Ricky Blitz.
2. There were dark clouds on the horizon.
3. There was a tall, dark stranger who came to Tanya's house yesterday.
4. An angry tirade was delivered to the council last night by Mayor Dmytryshyn.
5. There was much concern showing on the faces of the council members as they were listening to the mayor's angry outburst.
6. Finally there was a pall that settled on the council chambers; there was almost the deathly silence of a mortuary slumber room.
7. The jury's verdict was announced by a stern-faced Judge Carl Wimberly today—and thus it was that Jane Doe was declared guilty of murder in the first degree.
8. The girls on the South High swimming team were both laughing and crying—and the crowd was cheering their victory—as their winning time was announced: 3:57.58 for the 400-yard relay; it was a new state record.

EXERCISE 39: ELIMINATING WORDINESS

Rewrite the sentences below to eliminate unnecessary words and to repair awkward sentence constructions.

Example: There is another factor contributing to the county deficit, and that is the cost of fuel.

Revised: The cost of fuel also contributes to the county deficit.

1. Jane is a niece of Richard's.
2. Reigning over the 44th annual Pioneer Day Parade will be Queen Cindy Valentine.
3. What the council is attempting to do is to get the citizens to work on the energy problem themselves.
4. There is one thing that anyone who has ever eaten at Sourdough Jim's Restaurant will agree on, and that is the fact that Jim really knows how to cook.
5. There was this one man, whose name was Herman C.

Melville, and he gave a whole pile of clothes to those who had lost theirs in the tornado.
6. Collecting and restoring old furniture is a hobby that Betty Jane loves.
7. Parents who don't watch their children, people who take merchandise off one shelf and replace it on another, and the kind of person who visits in the middle of the aisle and shows no consideration for others who would like to get past are Cheryl's, a grocery clerk, pet peeves.
8. Men are the best shoppers, Cheryl says, who usually have a list and buy only what's on it. [Note the ambiguity here. Does Cheryl mean *all* men who come to shop or only the men who have lists? Assume the former.]

EXERCISE 40 CLARITY AND CONCISENESS

Each of the following items contains needless information and wordy, roundabout sentence structure. Examine the following:

Wordy: Mayor Dmytryshyn cautioned the city's citizens about their being too hasty in making a judgment

about the tax issue.

Revised: Mayor Dmytryshyn cautioned residents to avoid a hasty judgment on the tax issue.

Or: Don't judge the tax issue too soon, Mayor Dmytryshyn cautioned residents.

Edit or rewrite the following paragraphs to make them simple and concise. Eliminate useless words and make sentences short, simple and direct. Check names and addresses in the City Directory.

A. Property owners in Fairfield will be getting their property tax bills in the mail next week, according to a statement from the Lincoln County tax assessor, Jayne D'Arcy.

B. For anyone interested in learning how to square dance, lessons will be starting this coming Thursday evening at the Fairfield Community Center in Pioneer Park. The lessons will begin promptly at 7:30 p.m.

C. The River Avenue Market, on River Avenue, caught on fire last night and burned with about 25 percent of the building lost in the flames, according to a report this morning from the Fairfield fire chief, Richard L. Bowers.

D. An outdated, dilapidated and crumbling structure may soon feel the unmerciful blows of destruction as demolition begins next week on the old North High School athletic stadium in preparation for the construction of a new structure, a stadium, scheduled to be built in time to be available for the first fall football game three years from now.

E. According to a report from th city police, a 53-year-old Fairfield man, Allen L. Kirkwood, 501 Jefferson Ave., is reported dead of an industrial accident. He was the night janitor at Acme Manufacturing Co., and his body was found early this morning by arriving workers. Cause of death was not officially determined, but the police theory is that Kirkland fell approximately 30 feet from a scaffolding above.

EXERCISE 41 EDITING AND REWRITING FOR CLARITY

The following stories need extensive editing or rewriting for clarity, proper news emphasis and brevity. Try also to eliminate passive construction (overuse of variations of the verb *to be*, especially "there was, there is," and so on.) Verify accuracy of names and addresses; check for spelling, grammar and AP style.

A. Announcing his decision after a field of 95 candidates was narrowed down to three, City Manager Victor Allen was able to report that James Bacon, who lives in Phoenix, Ariz., has been appointed the new assistant city engineer for the City of Fairfield.

There was no opposition to the appointment of Bacon from the City Council at last night's meeting. In fact, what there was, was a scattering of applause from members of the council.

Bacon is a home-town lad and was born and raised in Fairfield and attended Gowdie Elementary School, South High School (Class of '77), and Kit Carson College (Class of '81).

B. According to a spokesman for Providance Hospital, there was a report of a man falling from an apple tree in front of his house in the western section of Fairfield.

John Graves, who age is given as 79 years, and whose address is listed as 777 Grant Aven., suffered the fall about 3 p.m. yesterday afternoon while attempting to trim the very uppermost branches of an apple tree in the front yard of his home, according to the spokesman for the hospital.

He is presently recovering at the hospital after falling a distance of approximately 20 feet from the tree to the ground, according to spokesman. It was reliably reported that Mr. Graves sustained several broken ribs in the accidental fall, one of which punctured a lung and causing it, thereby, to collapse. He is presently in the intensive care ward on the third floor of providance hospital, according to spokesman, where the doctor says he will probably be for at least an additional 24 hours or even 36.

Mrs. Graves says the family want to express their appreciation to the Fairfield Fire Department rescue crew for their extraordinarily fine service rended in the line of duty, and to all their neighbors for their assistance. Were it not for the careful and expert handling of these individuals, Mrs. Greves told the Telegram, the injuries sustained by the unfortunant Mr. Groves would be or at lease might have been vastly more seveer.

Mr. Graves used to be the Fairfield city librarian, a position he held for 27 years until his retirement 15 years ago.

BULLETIN! Another call to the hospital very late this morning reveals no change in Mr. Grives condition, according to spokesman.

C. Assume the same story as above, except the ''Bulletin'' reads: ''Another call to the hospital very late this morning reveals that Mr. Graves passed away at 11:35 a.m. today, according to spokesman.'' Rewrite the story.

Chapter Thirteen

USING NUMBERS

Newswriters find it essential to use numbers effectively. Much news, after all, comes from statistical tables, budgets, crime statistics, research projects, tax assessment tables, annual reports—the list goes on. The reporter who can glean useful insights from statistical tables will produce more interesting and worthy articles than one ignorant of numbers.

Moreover, the news itself tends to come in numerical tallies rather than in black and white. We hear of an 80 percent chance of rain, a 17 percent decline in violent crime, a 1.1 percent increase in the cost of living, a 20 percent shortfall in city tax collections.

Reporters who are comfortable with numbers can make their reports simpler and more precise, often more graphic. Instead of merely saying the community had a "bad" winter, you can cite supporting data: temperatures averaging 10 degrees below normal or snowfall 30 percent above normal.

When numbers complicate a story needlessly, a reporter at ease with arithmetic can find ways to simplify. Consider an example:

With 345 of the county's 431 precincts reporting, the election stands at 63,665 votes for Candidate A and 61,547 for Candidate B.

A couple of readings may be necessary to glean the significance of those figures—that approximately 2,500 votes separate the two candidates. Broadcast news makes it even harder—if listeners miss the figures, they may get hopelessly lost. Converting to percentages can help:

With 80 percent of the county's 431 precincts reporting, Candidate A leads Candidate B by 51 percent to 49 percent.

Trend stories can also benefit from the work of a number-savvy writer. To say a city's population has increased from 1,309,276 to 1,453,296 in twelve months is awkward and confusing. Simpler to say that the city's population has "grown by 11 percent to almost 1.5 million."

Often a reporter can make numbers more graphic and dramatic by using a few calculations. Instead of saying traffic accidents kill 50,000 people a year in the U.S., why not say that "every 10.5 minutes, on the average, an American dies in a traffic accident"?

You can also dramatize figures by making comparisons. To dramatize the meanderings of the Mississippi River, "one of the crookedest rivers in the world," Mark Twain said the river takes 1,300 miles to cover a distance a crow could fly in 675. To show the immense power of the four jet engines on the Boeing 747, an AP writer said their 174,000 pounds of thrust matched the power of 87 diesel locomotives.

The exercises in this chapter will give you practice with numbers, starting with a simple test.

EXERCISE 42 A QUIZ ON NUMBERS

The following problems involving numbers are typical of those facing newswriters. (Most of them come from real news reports.) Do the calculations required in each problem.

Example: The City Council approved raising the sewer fee from $4 to $5 for each household in the city. What's the percentage of increase?

Answer: To figure the percentage, subtract $4 from $5 and divide the result by $4. Thus, a 25 percent increase.

1. The retail clerk's union demands an increase in pay from $5.50 to $7.20 an hour, a _____ percent increase.

2. Ricky Blitz, the baseball player, has been at bat 77 times this season and has gotten 24 hits. What's his batting average?

3. In an election to pass a tax levy, voters in a community cast 301 yes votes and 286 no votes. What percentage voted yes?

4. If the community in Question 3 has 2,110 registered voters, what percentage of them voted in the tax election?

5. County Commissioner Janice Taylor is critical of the county's budget for dog control. "If people divide the 850 dogs handled last year into the budget of $101,000, they're going to think that's an outlandish amount of money for each dog," she says. How expensive is it per dog?

6. The ages of 11 members of a college class are 17, 18, 19, 20, 20, 20, 21, 22, 22, 30 and 45. What is the average age? What is the median (mid-point) age?

7. A city with a population of 1,207,070 had 17 murders last year. What is its crime rate for murder (that is, the number of murders per 100,000 people)?

8. The population of a community has declined from 456,880 to 428,990. What is the percentage of decline?

9. A total of 397 boys and 180 girls attend a private school. What is the ratio of boys to girls?

10. In physics classes at Carson College last semester, 101 students received A's out of 678 students enrolled. In the entire college there were 1,107 A's out of 7,250 grades. Did physics give a higher, lower, or about the same percentage of A's as the college generally?

11. A labor union has tallied the records of four members of Congress concerning their votes on labor issues. Smith voted pro-labor 18 of the 33 times he confronted labor issues. Jones voted pro-labor 24 of 29 times. Johnson voted pro-labor 28 of 36 times. Brown voted pro-labor 11 of 21 times. Rank the four in order of their pro-labor voting record: the most favorable first, least favorable last.

12. Labor negotiations are in progress, and the following comparisons for part-time employees are made:

Name of Firm	Hours Worked Per Week	Gross Weekly Pay
Acme	20	$148.60
Bijou	15	90.60
Carleton	13	112.06
Dalton	18	115.20

Rank them according to their hourly rates of pay, highest to lowest.

13. Kennerly Elementary School has 400 students and 14 teachers. Caxton School has 286 students and 10.5 teachers (one half-time). Cheltenham School has 123 students and 5 teachers. Which school has the best (lowest) student-teacher ratio?

14. A company manager says only a "fraction" of her employees are from racial minority groups. She has 66 white, 8 black, 7 Hispanic and 3 Oriental employees. What, precisely, is that fraction?

EXERCISE 43 COUNCIL ATTENDANCE

Write a brief story about members of the Fairfield City Council. A political watchdog group called Citizens for Good Government (Margaret Christianson, chair) has tallied the attendance of members of the City Council. Convert the figures to percentages as a basis of comparison. Consider ranking the council, from best attendance record to worst. (After completion, see model story, Appendix B.)

Mayor Dmytryshyn: Has not missed a single meeting in the four years (104 meetings) he has served as mayor.

Eleanor McPherson: Has missed 7 meetings in 7 ½ years (of the 187 meetings that were held during that period).

Ben Dorris: Has missed 33 meetings in 3 years on the council (75 meetings held during that period).

Kelly Estelle: Has been on the council only seven months; 14 meetings were held during that period, and she's missed only one of them.

Eleanor Beatty: On the council for 13 years. In that time 330 meetings were held, and she has missed 44 of them.

Charles Johnson: In the 5 years, four months he has served on the council, during which time 139 council meetings were held, Charles Johnson has missed 17 of them.

Kenneth Wheelock: An old-timer on the council, he has missed 23 meetings during the 17-year period he's been on the council, during which time there were 444 meetings of the council.

Doug Hixon: Doug is new on the council and has missed only one of the 17 meetings the council has held during his eight months in office.

EXERCISE 44 A COMMUNITY OPINION SURVEY

Write a news article based on a statistical study made by the research department of Quick, Browne and Foxxe advertising agency. QB&F was commissioned by the City Council to determine the attitudes of residents toward services provided by the city. Below is the essence of a report delivered by Christina Foxxe, senior partner and research director for the agency. Copies of her report have been distributed to city officials and council members, and it is on the agenda for discussion at next Monday night's council meeting, to be held in the council chambers of City Hall at 8 p.m.

PURPOSE OF THE STUDY: This study has been designed to obtain a measurement of the level of satisfaction/dissatisfaction with the quality of services currently being provided by the City of Fairfield.

HOW THE STUDY WAS CONDUCTED: An approved four-page questionnaire was mailed to a representative sample of 1,500 Fairfield residents. Names were drawn on every *nth* basis from the current telephone directory. Of 1,500 questionnaires mailed, 15 were returned for invalid addresses, leaving a total of 1,485 received by residents. By closing date, 697 had been received, representing a return rate of 46.9%. The data are accurate to within a 3% margin of error. The following table shows how the sample group rated Fairfield's current provision of services.

Service:	Excellent %	Good %	Adequate %	Poor %	Bad %	Don't Know %
Street Repair	0	10	44	29	16	1
Street Sweeping	2	17	36	24	15	6
Street Lighting	6	25	43	21	5	0
Landscaping/Maint.	4	32	43	14	3	4
Traffic Control	9	48	34	7	2	0
Traffic Law Enforcmnt	11	27	42	11	4	5
Anti-Crime Programs	26	41	22	8	1	2
Animal Control	1	6	22	33	37	1
Storm Drain Maint.	2	21	42	15	8	12
Munic/Traffic Court	2	15	27	2	1	53
Fire Protection	33	44	20	1	1	1
Public Library	25	40	20	4	2	9
Sewer Maintenance	3	28	37	2	1	29
Bldg Permits/Inspect	2	11	29	10	5	43
Planning for growth	1	12	32	25	16	14
City Information	3	23	35	15	5	19
Social Services	3	13	30	12	4	38
Response to Citizens	2	12	25	22	12	27

As the above table shows, fire protection, library services and anticrime programs enjoy the highest number of excellent ratings. Animal control, street repair and planning for the city's growth have the highest number of bad ratings.

Any true ranking of residents' views on service performance requires more than an examination of strongly held good or bad opinions. The majority of opinion resides in the areas between very high and very low, it is important to examine the *cumulative* response of all the respondents calculated within the context of *all* the rating options.

To this end, we have generated a table of *Cumulative Response* representing the total of all ratings for a given service weighted according to the following formula:

Excellent = 4 points
Good = 3 points
Adequate = 2 points
Poor = 1 point
Bad or "Don't Know" = no points.

Thus a perfect "Cume," as it is called, would be 400, meaning all ratings were "excellent" in that service. A zero Cume would mean all ratings were in the "bad" or "don't know" categories. The following table shows rankings on the Cumulative scale.

Service:	Cumulative Score
Fire Protection	305
Anti-Crime Programs	273
Public Library	264
Traffic Control	255
Traffic Law Enforcmnt	220
Landscape/Maint.	212
Street Lighting	206
Sewer Maintenance	172
Storm Drain Maint.	170
City Information	166
Street Sweeping	155
Street Repair	149
Planning for Growth	129
Social Services	123
Response to Citizens	116
Bldg Permits/Inspect	109
Munic/Traffic Court	109
Animal Control	99

Cumulative Scores of 200 or more represent good or superior performance, while a score of 150 to 200 is generally indicative of an adequate level of service. Scores below 150 are felt to represent below-average service, as viewed by the respondents.

As shown here, respondents consider the level of service to be good or excellent in such essentials as fire and police protection and library services. They are rated good on street lighting, landscaping and general maintenance. Below-average scores were accorded to animal control, street repair, planning for the community's growth, and the city's response to citizens. It should be noted that low cumulative scores from courts, building permits/inspections and social services result from a higher-than-average number of "don't know" ratings rather than "poor" or "bad" ratings.

Christina Foxxe
Senior Partner
QUICK, BROWNE & FOXXE

EXERCISE 45 FUN WITH NUMBERS

Gregory Jackson teaches journalism classes at Carson College and has been experimenting over the years with a whimsical project—"on-going research," he calls it, tongue slightly in cheek. For five years he has administered a "fear inventory" to his college journalism students. Write a brief story based on this material. Try to keep the tone lighthearted.

Background details. Jackson discovered a 100-item "fear inventory" being used in a study of people's phobias by a major research hospital. It is a simple checklist that cites 100 fears, such as fear of thunderstorms, cemeteries, snakes, spiders, members of the opposite sex, flying, losing a job, dead people, darkness, untimely death, strange dogs and so forth. People were asked to check any about which they felt "a definite fear or anxiety."

Jackson gave the inventory to 377 of his students over the years, 201 men and 176 women. They were students in his classes in reporting, magazine writing, mass media and society and newspaper editing.

The table shows the top ten fears of the 377 students who completed the checklist.

Number and Percent of Journalism Students Checking Specific Fear Categories

Fear of:	Total		Men		Women	
	N	%	N	%	N	%
1. Speaking in public	126	33.4	75	37.3%	51	29.0%
2. Spiders	117	31.0	50	24.9	67	38.1
3. Illness, injury to a loved one	116	30.8	34	16.9	82	46.6
4. Suffocation	114	30.2	56	27.9	58	33.0
5. Failure	112	29.7	53	26.4	59	33.5
6. Death of a loved one	109	28.9	34	16.9	75	42.6
7. Heights	101	26.8	50	24.9	51	29.0
8. Being criticized	92	24.4	25	12.4	67	38.1
9. Falling	90	23.9	42	20.9	48	27.3
10. Auto accidents	90	23.9	44	21.9	46	26.1

Source: Questionnaires administered to 377 Journalism Students at Carson College
Note: "N" means the number of students who checked that fear in the 100-fear inventory sheet. "%" means the percentage of the total who checked it. For example, 126 persons checked "speaking in public" as one of the fears, which is 33.4% of the 377 who participated. Of 201 men, 75 checked "speaking in public," which is 37.3% of the men. Note that only 29% of the women checked it.

Q. Professor Jackson, why did you give this questionnaire to your students?

A. Sheer journalistic curiosity. I ran across the fear checklist in *The New York Times*, and I couldn't resist giving it to the students. I also wanted to give the newswriting students an exercise that would give them practice in handling numbers in their stories. I had them write up the results in news story form.

Q. How well did they do writing about numbers?

A. Terrible! Journalism students on the whole are terrified of numbers. I think it's a national scandal. Their performance on most number stories never fails to confirm my own worst fears, which are that they'll be totally inept in citing numbers or that they'll avoid using them altogether. I once gave a fifth grade arithmetic exam to my students, one I'd borrowed from an elementary school teacher. There were three or four simple proportion questions and a handful of percentage questions. Out of 17 students in that class, only two could pass the exam. And I'm talking about *fifth grade arithmetic!* Then I asked them to calculate what percentage of the total class those two represented; I thought they could at least figure out what percentage of my class could pass a fifth-grade arithmetic exam. Well, 8 of the 17 couldn't even figure *that* out—which means that 47 percent of those students were imbeciles in arithmetic.

Q. Was fear of numbers on your checklist?

A. No. Had it been, I'm sure it would have ranked number one.

Q. *So what do you make of the results you got on the tally itself?*

A. For one thing, "speaking in public" as the number-one fear among the 100 is consistent with other studies. Speaking in public has consistently rated in study after study as the number-one category of fear or anxiety of the American public.

Q. *So journalism students aren't much different than others?*

A. True. As for spiders being number two—that's funny. This whole thing should not be taken too seriously. It's all for fun. Journalism students work hard, so it's good to give them a break occasionally.

Q. *As I understand it, the procedure here was to give students the checksheet and simply have them check off the items about which they had a pronounced anxiety.*

A. Right. I gave as an example, "If you had to walk through a cemetery tonight, would you have a definite fear or anxiety about it? If so, check that item."

Q. *How many items did they check, on the average?*

A. Out of the 100 total, men checked an average of 8.6 fears, women 11.7.

Chapter Fourteen

WRITING THE FEATURE STORY

The feature story defies a precise definition because it varies so widely—from the so-called "feature bright," which is usually a brief humorous anecdote, to the full-blown series of investigative reports. In the hands of a good writer, straight news often contains feature-like attributes—touches of humor or irony or drama. The distinction between news and feature stories has thus become blurred. Treating them here as a separate entity comes largely for the purpose of description and discussion.

The key to a good feature story is good information, for reporters are seldom better than their material. Interviewing skills and substantial research—with perhaps an ear for the unusual—are the essential ingredients. A typical feature story has five elements:

1. It is like dramatic literature in depicting character, action, tension (suspense) and often even irony (an unexpected occurrence). The best features resemble short fiction stories, even though they are factual.
2. It resembles an essay in that it has a structural unity with a clear theme. The writer strives to make a specific point, and buttresses the point with supporting data. The point is not an opinion necessarily; it is more often a special view or insight that the writer has gained about the subject through research and interviewing.

3. It is like a factual report in that it deals with reality: factual matters of public interest.
4. It identifies quickly with reader interests, problems and concerns, even intimately personal concerns. It often focuses on (a) people, (b) human relationships, (c) mystery, (d) conflict, especially personal conflict such as one might encounter in fiction, (e) adventure, (f) romance, (g) suspense, (h) irony and (i) reader self-interest (material through which readers can learn more about themselves or apply the information directly to their lives).
5. It is written informally with an emphasis on dramatizing the incidents and anecdotes that show human character.

Here are eight suggestions for writing features:

1. Write deeply on a narrow topic rather than superficially on a broad topic. That is, don't write abstractly about swimming; write about how Linda McCormack won the state championship or rescued a drowning child.
2. Do a good job of research and interviewing with careful attention to anecdotal material—specific episodes that can be used as examples to *show* character traits, not just tell about them. Use plenty of concrete examples to support your generalizations.

3. Look for humor and irony in everyday situations. The more you look for them, the more you find.

4. Focus on people and their activities. Show them "acting out" the situations you describe. This requires observation and careful interviewing for detail. Don't make up material; get it through informal conversations with the people who have experienced the situation you're discussing. If you are depicting alcoholism, for example, use case histories and anecdotes gained from real alcoholics; don't rely merely on the testimony of doctors and counselors. Magazine editors have a term for the latter: "mushball journalism." A good writer practices hardball journalism.

5. Use direct quotations sparingly. Use them for emphasis, human color, succinct summaries. Tell the basic story in your own words.

6. Structure for tension. Keep your reader wondering what will happen next. If you introduce Jane Doe, alcoholic, in the opening paragraphs of your story, keep the reader guessing about what happened to her. The more unexpected occurrences—surprises—the better. Life is full of surprises.

7. Rewrite. Much of the creativity in good feature writing comes after the first draft has been roughed out and the writer can relax and tinker with the story until a clean, crisp, exciting story emerges.

8. Use narrative whenever possible. The more a feature resembles a short story the better, so long as it remains factual. Start at the beginning and take the reader through a tense situation such as a police officer entering a burning building containing an armed and dangerous fugitive. Let the reader worry a little wondering what happens next.

EXERCISE 46 WRITING A BRIGHT

A "bright" is a tiny human interest anecdote, usually written in narrative style. It often ends with a punch line: a surprise or a twist of irony. Here are random notes for three brights. Make your articles brief and snappy.

A. Harvey Underwood, manager of Frederick & Frank Department Store, thinks the paper might be interested in the following letter, unsigned, bearing a Boston postmark and containing two $100 bills. It arrived in this morning's mail. Underwood says the money will be donated to the scholarship fund at Kit Carson College.

Dear F&F:

37 years ago when I was a foolish high school girl, I shoplifted some merchandize from your store. I've always regreted this dum act. There were times, years later, when I literaly couldn't sleep thinking about it.

I wasn't poor, my parents had money, I could have all the clothes I wanted. I did it for the thrill I guess. I have no idea of the value of the merchandize stolen. Maybe $40 or $50? Please accept the enclosed $200 which I hope will cover the cost of merchandize, interest & inflation. I know I'll sleep beter tonite.

You should watch more carefully when girls go into the dressing rooms. I stole most of the stuff by wearing it out of the dressing rooms under my regular cloths.

B. Rumor has it that last night Police Chief Hudson gave a traffic ticket to his own mother. Hudson, responding to your call, suggests you call his mother, Olivia Hudson, age 67. Here's part of the dialogue:

Q. Can it really be true. . . ?

A. Yes, and I'm afraid Ernest is dreadfully embarrassed. I think it's hilarious. Poor Ernest seems to have no sense of humor. Where did we go wrong as parents, I wonder.

Q. Can you tell me what happened?

A. I was going along River Avenue around nine-thirty last night when the flashing lights came along behind me. I pulled over and here was this *dashing* young man in the blue blazer, and it's Ernest. He's *most* flabbergasted. I guess he hadn't recognized my car in the dark. He said something like, "Mother, how could you do this? Do you realize you were going 50 in a 25 zone?" And I said, yes, Ernest, and now you have no choice but to give me a ticket—I won't have it any other way. I wanted to ask him if he was eating properly—he looks so thin. So he wrote the ticket and this morning I went down and paid the $35. Ernest has always been an honest boy. He doesn't play favorites.

Q. *It seems strange that a chief of police is handing out tickets.*

A. He said he rides with the officers from time to time, just to get the feel of the officer on patrol. So last night he was out with another officer, Bob Graham. It was worth the $35 just to see Ernest on the job. He's *most* efficient and courteous, I must say. He called this morning and offered to pay the fine for me, but I wouldn't hear of it. He's such a thoughtful boy.

C. John Day, advertising manager for the *Telegram*, shows you a copy of an advertisement scheduled for this afternoon's paper.

CINDY O'CALLAGHAN IS
40 YEARS OLD TODAY!

HAPPY BIRTHDAY CUTES!

You call Thomas J. O'Callaghan, office manager at Overland Motor Freight and he confesses everything: "Yes, I'm the guilty party, exposing X-rated secrets. For two years Cindy kept saying how she dreaded reaching forty. And for two years I've had this advertise-ment in mind. Originally I was gonna rent a billboard, but I couldn't afford the $500. I took out the two-column ad in the paper—it cost me only $63.50 and darned well worth it." Mr. O'Callaghan says he won't be troubled if you call his wife, even before the ad runs. "Just don't tell her who did it." You dial her number.

[*Additional details:* They've been married 14 years and have one child, Sheila, 11. Cindy O'Callaghan is office manager for the Fairfield School district.]

Q. *Is there any truth to the rumor that you're 40 to-day?*

A. Where on earth did you hear an ugly thing like that?

Q. *[You read the ad to her.] I was told not to say who done it.*

A. No need. It has Tom's fine hand written all over it. Oh, those impetuous Irishmen!

Q. *So it's true—being 40, I mean.*

A. You're making me feel like a celebrity. Why don't you just say she refuses to confirm or deny?

Q. *Okay, but if you were 40, how would you feel about it?*

A. Terrible. No, I'm only kidding. If I ever get to be 40 I'll feel about the same as I do now at 29 or whatever. Why don't you pick on Tom? He's 44! I guess being 40 won't be too bad when you're married to a sweet Irishman.

EXERCISE 47 A NEWS FEATURE

Some news incidents call for feature treatment rather than as straight news. They are low in significance but high in reader appeal. Write a story based on the following informa-tion.

Sheriff's Office report: Fairfield PD advised at 1520 hours [yesterday] that 2 per-sons were stranded on a small island ("Smuggler's Island") approx ¼ mi. down-stream from Cleveland Rapids in Sandy R. Arrvd at scene at 1536 hours. Used inflatable raft to remove same from island.

    Contacted:
1. James Henry Walling [age 16] 735 E. 14th St, a junior at South HS
2. Karen W. Walling, mother, same address (Father: deceased)
3. Cynthia Louise Johnson [age 15] 767 E. 17th St, soph at South HS
4. Charles Howard Johnson, father, same address
5. Mary Anne Johnson, mother, same address

    Details. WALLING states that he and Johnson floated down Sandy River in a rubber raft. Raft capsized at Cleveland Rapids and occupants floated in life jack-ets about ¼ mi. to Smuggler's Island. WALLING further states that while on the island he observed several items of clothing and $1,150 in paper currency.

Evidence.
1. $1,150 in currency
2. 1 green down jacket, medium size, possible bloodstain thereon
3. 1 pr blue corduroy pants
4. 1 yellow T-shirt w/ inscription: "Bankers do it with interest"

Supplementary interview with Bud Kuykendall:

Q. *Bud, what can you tell me about this case?*

A. It's a strange one. We don't know quite what to make of it. We have no reports of missing currency. The kids have turned it over to us. The law says if the money is not claimed in six months, it will revert to the finders. It must be a legitimate claim. There are certain identifying characteristics that the owner must specify to establish a claim.

Supplementary interview with James Walling:

Q. *How about starting at the beginning and telling what happened?*

A. We skipped school because it was such a fine day. Cindy had never been on a river raft before, and she'd been bugging me about it, and yesterday morning she goes, "Let's do the river today." So I thought, why not?

Q. *So you started down the Sandy River?*

A. We'd been on the river an hour or so and were going through Cleveland Rapids. I'd been through those rapids 20 times before and never had any trouble. But this time Cindy gets all excited and jumps up and waves at some girl on shore, and that's when we spilled. We came to this island, y'know, and like I'm trying to scout for firewood and that's when we found the clothing and the money. We were so excited that I never even thought about the boat. I guess it just drifted down the river. Now my mom's mad at me for skipping school, and Cindy's mom won't let her see me anymore, and I'm kind of depressed, y'know?

Supplementary interview with Cynthia Johnson:

Q. *Can you tell me what happened?*

A. Golly, it was exiting! I mean *exciting!* Here we were going through all this foamy water, and I see my friend on shore, except she really wasn't my friend, I think, because I didn't have my contacts in, and Jimmy's got one paddle and I got the other, and I'm waving at Suzie only it's not Suzie, and Jimmy goes, "Watch Out!" and suddenly we're in the water. It's *Exciting!*

EXERCISE 48 A SIDEBAR

A sidebar is a feature story that accompanies a main news story, such as interviews of witnesses to a train wreck or a terrorist bombing. Here is a case where a woman was taken hostage by two escaped convicts and held for two hours. When writing it, consider using a summary lead or perhaps a narrative that will introduce a tense moment. Be sure to include background from the news story. Consider writing the body of the story more or less in chronological order. Here is the original story from the wire service:

RIVER CITY (AP)—Two convicts were captured here early today after escaping from the Anystate Penitentiary and holding a woman hostage for two hours yesterday.

Dale Kingsman, 41, and Ralph Kluge, 29, were armed but surrendered without incident about 4 a.m. today after police telephoned their room at the Riverside Motel and told them the building was surrounded.

The pair escaped the penitentiary at Middleton yesterday by hiding in a departing laundry truck. They stole a car and drove north to Fairfield. Abandoning the car, they abducted Audrey Brooks, 40, a Fairfield secretary. They commandeered her car and forced her to drive them 100 miles north to River City.

Police said they pushed her out of the moving car at River City after inflicting minor knife wounds. She was treated at a hospital and released.

Authorities said both men were serving life sentences: Kingsman for parole violation, negligent homicide and first-degree murder, and Kluge for rape, kidnapping and assault with intent to kill.

Authorities today filed additional charges of escape and first-degree kidnapping against the two men. . . .

Assume the state penitentiary is located in the town of Middleton, population 46,800, located 100 miles south of Fairfield. All three cities, Middleton, Fairfield and River City, are linked by U.S. Highway 139 which runs north-south.

Note in the following interview how the reporter strives to gain detailed information that will fit into a narrative account. The interviewer seeks not only general impressions of terror but also details that can be dramatized. The interview, done on the phone, proceeds through the preliminary conversational amenities and the explanation of what the reporter wants to know. Then it gets down to business:

Q. *Ms. Brooks, would you mind telling me when you first noticed that you were about to be abducted?*

A. It came totally without warning. It's truly a miracle that I ever came out alive.

Q. *Without warning? Just what happened?*

A. It's hard to sort out. I remember loading groceries into my car at McKay's Market. It was during the noon hour, and I was off from my job at the bank about a block away. Suddenly everything went topsy turvy. The next thing I knew I was in the back of the car, face down on the floor, and a gruff voice saying "Baby, this is a *very* sharp knife—one word out of you and I'll slit your throat from ear to ear and the blood will be very messy".

Q. *Sounds scary.*

A. I was terrified. He had his knee in my back, and this other man—I hadn't noticed until then there were two—took my keys and started the car. Off we went, all three of us.

Q. *The wire report said you were driving. Is that in error?*

A. That was later, after I threw up.

Q. *You got sick?*

A. *Very* sick.

Q. *What happened?*

A. We were driving along the highway and I managed to blurt out that I'm sick—stop the car, *please!* They yelled at me that I was a dirty little so-and-so, and the car lurched to a stop and they let me out. I told them, "just take the car, please. Just let me die in this ditch." Then I threw up.

Q. *But instead they forced you to drive?*

A. Yeah. They kept saying things like "Baby, you look like death warmed over." They kept calling me "Baby." Baby this, Baby that. "Hey, Baby, *you* drive this blankety-blank wreck."

Q. *Where were you at this point?*

A. On the highway to River City. I just started driving.

Q. *Was anything else said?*

A. I talked a blue streak. I tend to jabber when I get nervous. I started talking about my kids. That actually seemed to relax them, strangely enough. They were so hyper at first, I thought they were gonna jump out of their skin. But the more I talked, the more they relaxed—at least until I made the mistake of asking a question. They got very hyper again. By this time we were in River City and they were saying, "Stop the car." Now I'm really terrified. We're in a deserted section of town, and I'm thinking this is the end of me. All I could think of was my kids. And I said, "Look, if you're gonna kill me, at least let me write a note to my kids." That turned out to be another mistake. The young guy just goes bonkers. He slapped me, he's carrying this knife and he cut me on the arm—just nicks, really. By now the car is stopped and this older guy gets in the driver's seat and I'm in the middle, and off we go, tires screeching, and I'm saying, "Oh, god, I'm gonna be sick again!" Well, they slammed the brakes on, and the young guy is saying something like "We're gonna get rid of this broad," and I'm waiting for the knife to go in. They open the door and the next thing I know I'm sitting in the street gutter feeling numb all over. But I was glad to be alive. I just sat there looking dumb until a car came along and two men—two *nice* guys, not the convicts—came along and asked if I was hurt. I told them to call the police, and they took me to the hospital.

Q. *What was it you were saying about your kids earlier that seemed to relax them?*

A. Just mother talk. I told them how Jennifer was visited by the tooth fairy last night, and all the clever things kids say.

Q. *Such as what?*

A. Well, like David woke up from his nap one time and said, "Oh, heck, now I lost my place in my dream!"

Q. *What did you ask them later that made them so angry?*

A. Just whether they had kids and where they were from. They got very surly and obscene, so I switched back to kiddie talk.

Q. *Did you ever ask them who they were or why they were doing this to you?*

A. Once or twice I asked what they wanted of me—

did they want the car or money or what? I kept saying why don't they just take the car and what money I have and let me go?

Q. *How did they respond?*

A. In a very agitated way, with lots of four-letter obscenities.

Q. *Did they molest you in any way other than you described?*

A. You mean sexually? Well, if they had any such notions, my getting sick probably took care of that.

Q. *Going back to the beginning—do you recall if you were grabbed from behind or what?*

A. I remember putting a bag of groceries in the back seat of the car. The back door was open and I was leaning in with the bag. Suddenly I was on the floor and a ton of bricks seemed to be on top of me. I could feel the knife against the side of my neck. He cut me a little. At that point, I couldn't see either one, but I could smell them.

Q. *What did they smell like?*

A. A cross between a brewery and a barnyard.

Q. *Had they been drinking?*

A. They were on *something*. They were so hyper I thought they might explode from spontaneous combustion.

Q. *When you got to River City, you literally thought you might be killed?*

A. I was sure of it. I thought I'd never see my kids again.

Q. *Could I clear up a few details—names and ages of your kids, your husband's name?*

A. Jennifer is 6, David 9, and my husband, Oscar, is a dispatcher at the trucking company.

Q. *And what was the time lapse, from abduction to release?*

A. I think it was about 12:30 at McKay's. It must have been two hours later at River City when they handed me back my life.

EXERCISE 49 USING CONTEXT AND BACKGROUND

Write a story about this incident involving Linda McCormack. But think a moment before you start. On the surface the incident might be considered trivial to all but the victim and her family. Just another purse-snatching incident. But if you know something about Linda McCormack, the possibilities begin to expand. The fact that she is the daughter of the state's former governor certainly increases the news value. But even more important is the touch of irony as the perennial rescuer becomes a victim herself and in need of rescue. A story that dramatizes that aspect would have more than routine interest. Thus an important reality of newswriting emerges—the more you know about a person or situation, the more feature possibilities you discover.

Police Report #46-12078. Aggravated Assault. Victim: Linda McCormack, Age 17, 1196 Onyx Street. Parents: Edward W. and Dorothy McCormick, same address.

Vict. states that she was accosted on the bicycle pathway that runs through Pioneer Park at 3:20 p.m. [yesterday]. Vict. states assailant blocked her way and she fell off the bike. She states that assailant struck her twice on the head with fist and ran with purse containing $50. Vict. transported to Providence Hospital Emergency. Treated for minor abrasions & released.

Witness: Terrence L. Diamond, age 20, 104 University Ave. Witness states that he gave chase of fleeing susp. & tackled same, recovering purse. Susp. departed scene on foot headed west.

Susp. described as white male, 25-30, 6', 150–160 lbs, brown hair, reddish beard, brown corderoy pants, brown leather jacket.

Robert W. Graham #228

Here is a segment of your interview by telephone this morning with Linda McCormack:

Q. How are you feeling?

A. Fine except for my black eye, my skinned knee, my skinned elbow and my aching shoulder.

Q. Can you tell me what happened?

A. I'm riding my bike to Wendy's to meet some friends after school, and this weirdo rushes out in front of me, and I take a gigantic dive onto the pavement to keep from hitting him. So I'm lying there all bloody, and this guy is reaching for me, and I'm thinking, great, he's really sorry for what he did, but instead he's trying to steal my purse! I'm screaming at him and I'm hanging on for dear life because the $50 is for shoes, which is crazy—the hanging on is crazy, I mean. He punches me a couple of times and runs off with the purse when along comes this big guy, and he's running after the weirdo. Pretty soon he comes back with my purse—the big guy, I mean, the nice guy, and the $50 is still there.

Q. Well, Linda, I guess this is quite a switch for you—being the rescuee instead of the rescuer this time.

A. Yuck. I don't like it one bit. It's awfully hard work and it hurts a lot. I'd rather be the rescuer.

Here is a segment of your interview by telephone this morning with Terrence Diamond, who is a defensive tackle for the Carson College football team.

Q. That was quite a rescue yesterday—can you tell me what happened?

A. I was sitting by the river by myself feeling sorry for myself because my girlfriend dropped me, and all of a sudden I heard these screams. This guy was hitting this girl, and I yelled at him and he took off running. She was yelling that the guy had her purse. I took off after him and it was like the Si-wash game all over again. I tackled him at about the five-yard-line and he fumbled the purse and I recovered. He got away, but at least I got the purse, which I took back to her. She's real cute, but I never found out her name because the cops came and took her away before I could ask.

Chapter Fifteen

THE PERSONALITY FEATURE

Many journalists find the personality feature the most difficult of articles. It requires you to come to grips with a complex personality in the brief time usually allotted to interviews. It also requires condensing your story into a short space, seldom more than 1,000 words, often less. For some, a strong like or dislike for the subject can also intrude on the objectivity required of the task. So can the unfortunate tendency among the young to judge people—"He's a bore"; "she's stuck up"—and, as a consequence, failing to listen to the other person's point of view. The problem is by no means confined to the young. But it is they who are most able to perceive the problem and to make appropriate changes in their own professional demeanor. The best personality writers are those able to adjust to a wide variety of personalities and to find merit in the words of even the most despicable of humans—a convicted rapist or child molester, for example. The more writers understand about child molesters the more useful their articles will be in helping society cope with the problem.

Fortunate, indeed, is the journalist who writes about a flawed character. The statement may seem strange to the fledgling writer. College writing teachers report, however, that when they ask students to write about someone they like, the themes invariably resort to platitudes. The result is deadly dull. But ask them to write about someone they *hate,* and it's a different picture.

The difference centers on the wealth of detail offered in the "hate" themes. When writing about someone they dislike, students usually cite in detail all the things about that person they can't stand, often in case history form. In a sense, then, they let the characters speak for themselves.

And that is the key to success in the good personality feature. Let the characters speak for themselves. Show them in action. Use quotes—but sparingly—especially the quotes that reveal character. Don't just say the character mangles his rhetoric with mixed metaphors (if such is the case); quote a few of them in your story. Don't say she loves to tell fanciful stories drawn from her imagination; *show* them.

Here are some other suggestions.

1. Write about a narrow aspect of the personality—an aspect that is most newsworthy about that person. Narrow and deep is interesting; broad and superficial is dull. Avoid the scattergun approach—"everything you wanted to know about Jane Doe." It can't be done at short newsfeature lengths.

2. Focus on what you perceive to be one central aspect

of the character. A person might have several attributes: successful career woman, outspoken community leader, active opponent of pornography, author of children's books, part-time painter of outdoor scenes, avid mountain climber and so forth. Choose *one* to focus on and "flash" (a writer's term meaning to briefly mention) the others. Often a news event will dictate which one: She has recently nursed an anti-pornography ordinance through the city council, so you concentrate on community leadership using the pornography work as a case in point.

3. Interview those who know the person well—family, friends, coworkers, even opponents (*especially* opponents if the person is controversial). They are especially good in providing humorous or ironic anecdotes, forever suggesting ideas like: "Ask her about the time she ran into the police car." A few minutes on the phone with each of a half-dozen acquaintances will give you more insight into your character than you can get in an interview.

4. Look for "crossroads" and "learning experiences." Crossroads are those fateful decisions people often make about their lives, and sometimes they can be dramatic and revealing of character—a woman's choice to become a mother, homemaker and community leader instead of pursuing a business career, for instance. Learning experiences are the insights a person gains from events and circumstances, particularly those that aren't obvious—a police officer learns that the *question* is a vastly more powerful weapon for law enforcement than the gun, for instance.

EXERCISE 50 A PERSONALITY FEATURE

Write a personality feature based on the material presented here.

Background and suggestions. This exercise reflects some of the principles cited above. Among them is the question of liking or disliking Jeanne Gray. Does it really matter to a professional?

In this instance, let's assume that the Miss Anystate pageant comes up in just a week. The editor of the paper's "People Today" section wants a feature story of 800 to 900 words on Jeanne Gray, the Miss Fairfield contestant.

Let's also assume for the sake of the feature that Jeanne Gray has become a minor celebrity of late. Her outspoken commentary seems to have triggered a good deal of media interest. She has appeared on numerous TV and radio talk shows in Fairfield and nearby communities. She has given talks to about twenty civic and educational groups, such as Rotary, Business and Professional Women, the Goudy School Parent-Teacher-Student Association. In such sessions, she talks about the bikini incident, her goal of becoming an actress, her work with fifth graders. She also discusses the lives and times of beauty contestants, Miss America in particular. She frequently denies being a staunch feminist except on matters of equal opportunity for employment and equal pay. She has explained the bikini incident as a demand thrust upon her unexpectedly, and she confesses that among her concerns is that of antagonizing the school board and maybe losing her teaching job if she parades in public in scanty attire.

The focus of the story, the editor says, "Should be her unique and independent views and commentary. How have they made her into a minor celebrity? Let's try to go beneath the surface. Talk with her friends, her family, even her school kids. Try to get a more intimate picture. What's she really like? People hate her or love her, but at least she's interesting."

Interview Reports

The following paragraphs depict the essence of several preliminary interviews conducted with people who know Jeanne Gray.

Bob Gray, Jr., Jeanne's older brother, 26, a hydraulics engineer: "Jeanne was a charmer right from the start. She could be mean. She'd fight with the neighbor kids. When she was 12 or 13 she was a little butterball, real fat. I left for college then, so I never knew her during her heyday, the high school prom queen and all-around athlete and showgirl, and all that. I remember being astounded when I got back from college one summer and found how slim and stunningly gorgeous she'd become. I detest this insane beauty pageant mentality, and it's hard for me to think of her as anything but a kid sister with freckles across her nose."

Rachel Gray, mother: "She was a high-spirited child. She was into everything. She started dancing lessons at 3, piano at 6, vocal at 9. She was what we used to call a tomboy—a little roughneck. She'd play with the neighborhood boys and come home all scratched and bleeding, caked with dirt. She hated dresses. She wasn't much of a student—she just got by. She was in all the class plays. She was in the choral group, the stage band, the debate team, the color guard, the yearbook committee, student senate—*Everything!* She was prom queen her

```
┌─────────────────────────────────────────────────────────────────────────┐
│                         Personal Data Sheet                               │
│                                                                           │
│   Name in full        Jeanne Eleanor Gray                                 │
│                                                                           │
│   Age                 22                                                  │
│                                                                           │
│   Address             555 Westway Avenue, Apartment 14, Fairfield         │
│                                                                           │
│   Place of birth      Fairfield                                           │
│                                                                           │
│   Names of Parents    Robert and Rachel Gray                             │
│                                                                           │
│   Talents             Acting, dancing, singing                           │
│                                                                           │
│   Favorite hobbies    Reading, fantasizing, camping                      │
│                                                                           │
│   Favorite sports     Running, swimming, hiking, softball, volleyball,   │
│                       touch football                                      │
│                                                                           │
│   Measurements        5'6", Weight 115, Measurements 34-23-35            │
│                                                                           │
│                       Dress size: 7–8, shoe size 7A, glove 7½, hair      │
│                       brown, eyes brown, complexion medium                │
│                                                                           │
│   Education           South High School, Kit Carson College (B.A.)       │
│                                                                           │
│   Occupation          Teacher                                             │
│                                                                           │
│   Additional          Special training includes five years of piano,    │
│                       five years of tap and ballet, six years of         │
│                       dramatics. Played roles in 19 stage plays in        │
│                       high school, college, and community thea-           │
│                       ter. Leading role in six stage plays at Carson      │
│                       College, including How to Succeed in Business       │
│                       Without Really Trying, Carousel, Fiddler on the      │
│                       Roof, and West Side Story. First-place woman         │
│                       runner, Fairfield Marathon; time 2:55:33.           │
└─────────────────────────────────────────────────────────────────────────┘
```

junior year, the girl most likely to succeed her senior year, the outstanding girl vocalist, the thespian of the year, the girl of the month. She was on the girl's track team and ran the mile. She was also a cutup. I remember being called by the high school principal. Seems our beautiful daughter had humiliated the entire school one night in the class play. This boy was supposed to drink poisoned tea and then die. They said it was Jeanne who substituted whiskey for the tea. The poor boy coughed and sputtered for 10 minutes before he remembered to die. Jeanne is a go-getter, stubborn, temperamental. She's had lots of boyfriends but never seems to get serious about anyone.''

Kenny DeHaviland, fifth-grader (member of Gray's class at Goudy): ''Miss Gray is okay, I guess, but I think my mom's prettier. Miss Gray is too skinny. She's fun to tease. Like one time we saw her kissing her boyfriend when she thought nobody was looking. She turns red and gets really mad whenever we bring it up in class, like, you know, Miss Gray, who were you with yesterday in the supply room?''

Janis McKenzie, another fifth grader: ''Jeanne Gray is the funniest teacher I ever had. She tells stories in class, and they're *weird!* She's always going off in space. Sometimes we play softball, and it's boys against girls, and when Miss Gray plays on the girl's side we sometimes win. Yesterday she hit a home run. She can run faster than any boy.''

Robert Gray, Jeanne's father: ''I'd call Jeanne a lovable eccentric. She never did nobody any harm. She's just full of innocent pranks and eccentricities. I never seen anybody so absent-minded. One time she made dates with three boys for the same evening. She was in high school at the time. Just before supper it strikes her that any minute now these boys are gonna come calling. So she phones up three girls and makes blind dates for the boys and then she calls each boy and tells him she's sick with bronchial pneumonia or something.''

Wendell Gray (second brother, age 24, student at Harvard Law School, interviewed by telephone): ''Jeanne has just one intimate confidant—me. When I was home we used to talk for hours. She still calls me at least once a week. She was actually jealous when I started getting serious about Jill, my wife. Jeanne's greatest goal in life is just to be loved. Boy, does that sound syrupy and melodramatic. But it's true. A lot of people hate her, especially girls. When she was in middle school, a group of girls formed the HJGC—''Hate Jeanne Gray Club.'' Jeanne cried for a week when she found out about it. Then she got angry. She began to fight back. She slimmed down and became gorgeous and sexy. She got into school activities. She found a new and charming personality. She struck back at her tormenters with the weapons at her command, personality and sex appeal. Having won a skirmish or two on that battleground, she had a third reaction—she ceased to care what anybody thought. At least that was the facade. Jeanne had become one of the most dangerous girls at South High. She could devastate any girl just by stealing her boyfriend. Everybody knew she could do it, so it ceased to be important. I doubt if Jeanne ever stole anybody's boyfriend, at least not intentionally. Jeanne's relationships with men have tended to be pretty casual. She used to say, ''Men are like streetcars—there's always another one coming along.'' I find Jeanne one of the most lovable, vulnerable people I know. She's just my scraggly, freckle-faced kid sister, but I still get a thrill out of being seen walking down the street with her.''

The Interview

Following is the interview with Gray, conducted by Barbara Miller. It takes place in Gray's apartment, which overlooks the Sandy River. It starts with small talk, focusing on several wall posters—giant color photos of a waterfall, a pristine lake backed by soaring mountain peaks, and a forest scene with shafts of sunlight slanting through giant trees.

Q. *The posters remind me of a vacation trip to Colorado.*

A. They're my fantasy posters. I look at them and imagine that I'm tripping through the woods arm-in-arm with wood nymphs, leprechauns and fairies. I have a flower in my hair. I ask this wizened leprechaun where the pot of gold is, but he just pops out of my hand and disappears behind a rock. [The conversation continues in this vein for a few minutes, then gets to the point of the interview.]

Q. *May I take a moment to explain the kind of story I want to write?*

A. Yes.

Q. *I've seen and heard you a lot on radio and TV lately. I've listened to your strong views on health, beauty, love, men, women and even beauty pag-*

eants. Now, with the help of you and your family, I'd like to write a story about the real person behind the media facade. What's she really like down deep? What motivates her? Are you really the ''lovable eccentric'' that your father describes? Or the ''scraggly kid sister'' your brother Wendy speaks of? So I'd like to ask some personal questions.

A. Scraggly kid sister? I love it! Wendy loves to tease. He gets it right back, too. You should see *him* in his scraggly beard; he looks like the phantom of the Paris sewers. But please ask me anything you like so long as you don't mind candid answers. People have been asking me personal questions all my life. Nothing shocks me anymore except maybe the answers I give.

Q. *What kinds of questions are you being asked?*

A. *Everything!* Face it—I've become a media freak. They love getting me on live television and throwing crazy questions at me. And I hit 'em right back, too—I'm the Reggie Jackson of the media games. Sometimes I strike out; sometimes I hit a home run.

Q. *What would be an example of the questions you get pitched at you?*

A. So you want to hear a typical question-answer dialogue? *Question: What are my life's goals?* Answer: To always do right. Nobody will believe it. *Question: What kind of men do I like?* Answer: Men who wear pants. *What kind of men do I dislike?* Men who wear dresses. *What do I think of Tom Selleck?* Um, nice, sensitive, but maybe just a little too excitable for my tastes. *Don Johnson?* Too flashy. Two days growth of beard—yech! *Sylvester Stallone?* Get serious! *Then who?* How about Mel Gibson? Great face! Great eyes! I'd even take him without a shave. But who can stand those Mad Max movies! *What do I usually have for breakfast?* Dry toast. *Do I believe in marriage?* Yes. *Motherhood?* Some of my best friends are mothers. *Premarital sex?* Well, gee, that kind of depends, doesn't it? What do *you* think? *Abortion?* Well, not for me—I love children. So how am I doing as a media interviewer?

Q. *Terrific!*

A. Okay, now I'm a *male* interviewer. [Gruff, mocking voice.] *Do I sleep in the nude?* No. *Do I sleep alone?* No. *Really!* I sleep with Ginger, my favorite stuffed panda bear. *Ginger? Does that mean you're a Lesbian?* You gotta be kidding! *Do I have a boyfriend?* I know a few guys. *Anybody special* *in your life?* No. *So whatsa matter, Sweetheart—nobody good enough for you?* I just haven't found the right guy yet. *So what makes you think you're so hot, Sweetheart?* Please, sir, I'm just a poor working girl—don't be cruel.

Q. *Wow! Are you serious? I don't recall any of the male reporters around our office coming on that strong.*

A. So, okay, I'm coloring things a little. But arrogance does seem to be a common trait with a lot of male interviewers. Then, too, I think you remember one or two obnoxious questions better than you remember a hundred gentle, sensitive ones. I've become very media savvy of late. It's a real kick, learning what turns media people on.

Q. *What does?*

A. A juicy quote, that's what. They want to catch you saying something outrageous. It's fun seeing what gets quoted and what doesn't. Being interviewed is like sitting on the limb of a tree with a pack of hungry dogs leaping and yelping beneath you. Every so often you throw them a juicy bone. They gobble that up and come back yelping for more. Sometimes they cajole you, nag you, attack you, or irritate you, just to get that quote.

Q. *How many times have you been interviewed?*

A. Maybe 30 since the bikini incident.

Q. *Are you finding this to your ultimate advantage? I mean, you enjoy it so much—are you manipulating or exploiting the media rather than the other way around?*

A. *Manipulating?* It's more like a wayward love affair. Believe me, we desperately need each other, like two lovers kissing in the dark.

Q. *In what ways do you need the media?*

A. Well, face it—I'm a showoff. I admit it! I'm very theatrical. So in the media we play silly games for our mutual enjoyment.

Q. *Silly?*

A. They make it a game, on TV especially. Not so much in print. Print is too serious and stern, like they have no sense of humor. But TV! Oh, boy. It works like this. They tell you beforehand some of the questions they'll ask. How do I feel about marriage, apple pie and motherhood? You're suddenly on the air and, sure enough, they do ask those questions. Then comes a curve ball, a question not previously mentioned. Something kind of sexy or naughty but not so naughty the sheriff will come and throw them off the air. At first the questions bothered me, but now I've learned to handle them.

Q. *How? What would be an example?*

A. Okay, we're on live TV. They're throwing curved-ball questions, and I'm just being myself. Since I'm so outrageous I make them a little nervous. So you can see the standoff. They're deceitful; I'm outrageously candid and keep putting my foot in my mouth. It's nothing short of a delicate balance of terror.

Q. *Sounds like fun.*

A. One guy asked me on live TV if I had an ugly scar and that's why I won't show off in a bikini. I said I'm the original bionic woman. Where my belly button used to be is an array of switches and gauges. I don't dare show off! Another time in River City this guy asks me, "If you got it, Sweetheart, why not flaunt it? I'll bet you just don't got it!" Well, I was ready for that one. I pretended to get *very* angry. I stood up. I fumbled with a button on my blouse. I said I was prepared to take my clothes off right here—live and in color! He got very flustered—he thought I was serious. He said, no, no, but could he have my phone number and he'd call me later!

Q. *What if he hadn't stopped you?*

A. Oh, boy, I never thought of that! Don't they bleep out that kind of stuff? No, seriously—it's all bluff. It's theater. I don't want to get fired again from my queenship and I'm terrified of losing my teaching job. But I'm such a ham at heart—I can throw a scare into them sometimes.

Q. *Given your feminist principles, do you think the queen business was a good idea?*

A. *What* feminist principles? The media just hung that on me; I never said I was a feminist. I may have talked a little in that direction. And certainly I wasn't keen about being taken advantage of in the bikini business. Nobody ever told me I had to pose for bikini shots. I mean, I'm an elementary school teacher, for heaven's sake—I can't go around posing in public half naked. So, anyway, I'm not hardcore anything, unless you could call me a hardcore opportunist.

Q. *Opportunist? What do you mean?*

A. Trying out for Miss America is an incredible opportunity for someone like me. Don't let anybody fool you. If you make State and go to Atlantic City—win or lose, it's a once-in-a-lifetime opportunity to get noticed, to get your talents out before an audience on national TV. As for feminism, I hate labels. Why do I have to join some kind of sisterhood? Why can't I just be me?

Q. *Do you consider yourself a loner?*

A. Loner? I *love* crowds! I consider myself independent. Particularly with regard to women's groups. Women don't like me very much. That's okay—I'd rather be hated than ignored. Men are more fun. You can say outrageous things to them and nobody gets hurt.

Q. *Do you like to flirt with men?*

A. Doesn't everybody?

Q. *I was thinking that perhaps it inflates men's egos to have a beautiful woman saying outrageous things to them because they sense that she's teasing, whereas women—*

A. Right, right. There's no payoff with women, just eternal animosity.

Q. *Do you remember the "Hate Jeanne Gray Club."*

A. God, yes!

Q. *Your brother, Wendell, told me about that. He said the Hate Gray Club carried some emotional scars.*

A. I'm sure he's right. Wendy doesn't miss much. He'll probably tell you that I have to work extra hard to make people like me—he thinks it's an obsession with me. I'm not smart enough to see precisely what he means but I'm sure he's right. I think he means I should be nicer to women.

Q. *Your dad calls you a lovable eccentric. Does that fit your self-image?*

A. Oh, sure. Fathers are very supportive.

Q. *And your mother says you served whiskey in place of tea in the high school stage play—could that be true?*

A. Guilty! Did she also tell you a bunch of us finished the bottle backstage later that night? And how I got sick? My first and last experience with being drunk! Since then I've been the world's cheapest date— a glass of wine will last me all evening long. Whoops—off the record, please. No wine. Make it

diet Pepsi; I don't want to get fired. Anyhow, the point is, I'd rather be out dancing.

Q. *I have a few more random questions to ask—first, what are your chances of winning the state beauty pageant next week?*

A. Slim. I don't see me as all that great looking. In the mirror I see a kind of cutesy-pie face with too many freckles. I think I might do all right in talent. But we have a taped interview to go through, and I know I'll blow it. I always do. I think I'm not dignified enough to be a Miss America or a Miss anything.

Q. *In retrospect, was the bikini decision a good idea or bad?*

A. Good! I've had tremendous support, even from women. It's gotten me onto TV and the newspapers, and I get to be a ham.

Q. *You list "fantasizing" as one of your hobbies. How interesting!*

A. I've always had an overactive imagination. I never grew up. My bionic circuitry allows me to pick up light and radio waves from other planets. The other day I was tuning in some planets and there was a message for me. Seems I'm not an earthling at all. I am a princess from this other planet where war and hate and violence were outlawed centuries ago. In fact, everyone had forgotten what hatred is like. So they sent me here to find out and report back. Yesterday I told them by radio that I'd learned all I needed to know about bigotry and please send the spaceship down to pick me up.

Q. *Does that mean you won't go through with the pageant?*

A. Not if the spaceship gets here first.

Q. *Will you wear a bikini there?*

A. I'm not sure whether people even wear clothes there. Maybe a gossamer gown in the evening if it gets chilly.

Chapter Sixteen

WRITING FROM DOCUMENTS

The documents regularly encountered in a reporter's work range from letters of public interest to complex technical studies. You'll find tax records, agency budgets, court documents, wills, annual reports, ordinances, petitions, committee reports, police records and countless others.

This chapter will introduce you to a few of the common ones in an attempt to show you a taste of reality. But, frankly, they are not typical. They are short. Some may not *seem* short. But reporters regularly encounter reports that run 500 pages or more—about three times the size of this entire exercise book. In working with such items, you may find the following suggestions helpful.

1. In complex documents, the kind that run 500 pages or more, look first for a section called "Summary and Conclusions," "Recommendations," or similar titles. These will help put the rest of the document in perspective, allowing you to read more selectively and perceptively.

2. Avoid using long quotations from the documents. That's an alluring trap that allows you to get the job done easily, but the result will confuse the readers—or, worse, bore them. You can say it better—that is, more clearly, with less jargon—in your own words.

3. Always seek the meanings. What will it cost? What will it accomplish? What does it mean to a community's citizens? Will it raise or lower taxes? Who will be helped or hurt by it? Will it ruin business or topple political empires? (Clearly not all documents have such ominous implications.) In seeking the meanings, you may wish to interview the people in positions to interpret for you. These are questions for them to answer, not you.

4. Don't use the jargon of a particular document. Instead, learn what it means and put that information into your own words.

5. Try to relate complicated documents to the lives of the citizens. One reporter handled a hydraulic engineering study by pointing out that citizens would be replacing faucet washers a lot less in the future because of decreased pressure in the city's water mains.

6. Don't hesitate to ask questions to cover points or terms you don't understand. Officials are usually delighted to help—they want an accurate report as much as you do.

7. Get background information when needed. You have to ask the questions that will place the document in context. Where did the need for this document begin and how has it developed?

EXERCISE 51 A WILL

Write a story based on Mr. VanDenBosch's will.

Background. Among the documents frequently seen in the courthouse are wills placed on the public record in a legal process known as filing for probate. That is, the will is filed with the Circuit Court of Lincoln County on behalf of the estate of the person who died. Here is the last will and testament of the late Ivan R. VanDenBosch who died (six months ago, we'll say) in Exercise 25. Wills have news interest when the person is prominent, where large sums of money or property are involved or when the will itself is unusual (such as leaving an entire estate to a beloved pet).

Here is some additional information. Frank Parker, Mr. VanDenBosch's attorney, says the estate has not yet been appraised but that a partial inventory suggests the value of the estate is "in excess of $500,000." At current market value, shares of common stock in Acme are 67.50 each. Huck Finn Island is a barren, rocky island, one acre in size, located in Wyman Lake, which is within Pioneer Park in Fairfield. It is a favorite rendezvous point for kids swimming, boating or inner-tubing in the lake, but it has not been developed.

Last Will and Testament

KNOW ALL MEN, That I, Ivan Robert VanDenBosch, a resident of and domiciled at 104 Harris Avenue, City of Fairfield, County of Lincoln, and State of Anystate, being of sound and disposing mind and memory, and not acting under duress, menace, fraud, or undue influence of any person whomsoever, do make, publish, and declare this my last will and testament in manner and form following, to-wit:

FIRST, I direct that all my just and unsecured debts and funeral expenses be duly paid and satisfied as soon as conveniently can be done after my decease.

SECOND, I appoint my wife, Ida VanDenBosch, to be Executrix of this, my will, and the personal representative of my estate, and to serve without bond. If my wife shall fail to qualify, or having qualified, shall die, resign, or cease to act as Executrix, I appoint my son, John H. VanDenBosch, as Executor in her place.

THIRD, I give, devise, and bequeath certain of my goods, chattels, possessions, and real property as follows, to-wit:

1. I give 400 shares of the common stock of Acme Manufacturing Company to the Department of Parks and Recreation of the City of Fairfield, County of Lincoln, for the following purposes and under the following conditions:

   a. One-fifth to be used for general improvement of parks and playgrounds within the City of Fairfield as the Director of Parks and Recreation shall deem appropriate.
   b. Four-fifths to be used for general improvement of Pioneer Park in the City of Fairfield, including, but not limited to, the development of Huck Finn Island, an island located within Wyman Lake in the aforementioned Pioneer Park, such improvements to include development of a boat dock for canoes and rowboats and construction upon the island of a fortress or some other imaginatively primitive improvement that may strike the fancy of the young. It is my wish that three boys and three girls, each of them not over the age of 11 years, be asked to provide assistance and supervision in the planning and construction of the aforementioned fortress or other developments upon the island.

2. I give 200 shares of the common stock of Acme Manufacturing Company to the Board of Trustees of Kit Carson College, a private college located within the City of Fairfield, to be used at the discretion of the Board for the following purposes and under the following conditions:

a. One-half to be used for scholarships for students in attendance at Kit Carson College.
b. One-half to be used for awards, prizes, special remuneration, or other recognition to individual members of the faculty for excellence in teaching as determined by the Board of Trustees.

3. I give 200 shares of the common stock of Acme Manufacturing Company to the Salvation Army, located within the City of Fairfield, for the following purposes and under the following conditions:

a. Four-fifths to be used to assist the Salvation Army in performing its mission of providing shelter and food for indigent persons.
b. One-fifth to be used at the discretion of the Commanding Officer to purchase transportation by bus or train for persons requiring same under emergency conditions.

4. I give my antique 1924 Model-T Ford automobile and my collection of model trains, together with the model railroad layouts, to my beloved friend, Ernest J. Hudson, if he shall survive me.

5. I give all of the real property owned by me in Fairfield, Anystate, at 104 Harris Avenue, together with all improvements thereon, all appurtenances thereto, and all related insurance policies, to my beloved wife, Ida, if she shall survive me.

6. I give the sum of five thousand dollars ($5,000) to my beloved sister, Ella VanDenBosch Rowan, of Oshkosh, Wisconsin, if she shall survive me.

7. I give the sum of two thousand five hundred dollars ($2,500) to the Alcoholics Anonymous Chapter in Fairfield, Anystate.

LASTLY, I give and bequeath the residue at my estate to my beloved wife, Ida VanDenBosch, if she shall survive me. If my wife, Ida, predeceases me, I give said property, in equal shares, to my two children, John H. VanDenBosch and Mary Ann VanDenBosch Boling.

IN WITNESS WHEREOF, I have hereunto set my hand on this 21st day of October in the year of our Lord One Thousand Nine Hundred and Seventy Five.

/s/ Ivan Robert VanDenBosch

The said Ivan Robert VanDenBosch declared the foregoing instrument to be his last will and testament and acknowledged aloud to each of the undersigned in the hearing of each that the signature previously made on said will was his, whereupon each of the undersigned at his request and in his presence attested said will by signing our respective names thereto as witnesses.

/s/ Lana H. Dmytryshyn
1151 Cherry Drive, Fairfield, Any.

/s/ Jon W. Penrose
1333 Onyx Avenue, Fairfield, Any.

EXERCISE 52 TEACHERS AS COACHES

Write a story about this petition from some of the city's high school teachers.

Background. Should a high school teacher have to be an athletic coach as well? Let's assume that the petition, a copy of which you received this morning, is on the agenda for the next school board meeting, scheduled for Monday (7:30 p.m. in the faculty conference room, South High School).

Here are some details. Mr. Axford tells you that of the 490 teachers working at both North and South High, about 120 have duties as coaches or activities directors. He says the district has no written policy on hiring practices as related to qualifications for coaching.

Two teachers are the leaders of the petition movement. One of them, Pete Westerman, teaches English at North. The other, Lyle Wilkins, teaches social studies at South. Neither man coaches. "The big problem," Lyle Wilkins tells you, "is the expansion of athletics in Fairfield, particularly girls' athletics. It's getting so bad around here that you can't get a teaching job unless you're a qualified coach. The first question the district asks you now is, 'Can you coach?' If you happen to be able to teach, fine, that's an added advantage. This used to be a problem confined to male teachers, but no more. Now the women teachers have got to be able to coach. Well, this petition encourages the board to turn that around and look for teachers who are looking for a job but don't want to coach. The district simply won't take them. So what you've got here is a classic case of the tail wagging the dog."

Both Wilkins and Westerman tell you that they will attend Monday's meeting and will speak in support of the petition.

A PETITION
To Members of the Board of Directors,
Fairfield School District 4-J

We the undersigned are members of the teaching faculties at North High School and South High School. We respectfully address the board on a matter of urgent concern to us, a matter that we feel is in the best interests of the faculty, the students, and the community at large.

Our concern is related to the board's hiring practices and policies. Specifically we refer to the hiring of teachers on the basis of their coaching and activities advising rather than on their ability to teach specific subject matter.

With the expansion of girls' athletics and with the increased participation in boys' athletics and in extracurricular programs, the need for activities advisers and particularly for coaches has become acute. As a result the district is hiring teachers with activities and coaching assignments in mind. This practice threatens academic quality and creates a potentially destructive conflict between athletics and the classroom.

Good teaching takes time. Teachers have lab exercises, lessons, and exams to prepare and grade; student essays to evaluate; classes, conferences and meetings to attend; books to read; and students to be helped before and after school.

Good coaching also takes time. Although they do not wish to be identified, several coaches suggest that even when a coach teaches an academic course, he/she must put coaching first. Two of these persons have left coaching for that reason, and a third has requested and received a lighter subject-matter class load. Coaches also testify that preparation for the classroom inevitably gives way before the inflexible schedules of practices and athletic meets. Moreover, attention given to athletic events by students, the community, and news media is so intense that a dedicated coach may find it impossible to maintain normal attention to classroom duties.

Many of the best teachers in our two high schools are not coaches and would not have been hired if coaching had been required. Similarly many current applicants for teaching positions are either unwilling or unqualified to coach a sport. To eliminate these candidates would seriously weaken our ability to select the most qualified classroom teachers. Although some teachers may find their assignments compatible with extracurricular duty, many experienced teachers have found that for them classroom teaching is a full-time job incompatible with a coaching assignment.

Good teaching and good coaching are important to the educational program in Fairfield, but they must complement, not harm, each other. Therefore we respectfully request that the Board of Directors adopt the following resolution:

1. That new teachers be hired solely for their qualifications as classroom teachers unless a teaching and a coaching assignment are closely related: English/Drama or P.E./Athletics for example.

2. That nonrelated extra-duty assignments not be mentioned either on the application or in the interview for classroom teachers.

/s/Peter Westerman
Lyle Wilkins
[67 other signatures attached
to the petition.]

EXERCISE 53 POLICE COMMITTEE REPORT

Write a story based on today's installment in the continuing conflict between the police chief and the Police Committee of the City Council.

Background and suggestions. Let's assume that this is the gist of a fifty-page report that contains an appendix full of documents, letters, interview transcripts and news clips, all documenting the alleged misdeeds of the Police Department during the five years that it has been directed by Ernest Hudson. The task here is to bring it down to its essence, quoting some of the specifics, but still not getting too bogged down in detail.

For purposes of this story, assume that the report has been released early this morning and that you are writing for today's afternoon paper. Assume that the first public notice of the conflict was the story in Chapter 1, which we'll say appeared six months ago. The report is on the agenda for the regular meeting of the City Council next Monday at 8 p.m. in the council chambers. Assume that you called Hudson, Wheelock and Dmytryshyn but none would comment until they've studied the report. Hudson says he will call a news conference tomorrow at 9 a.m. to respond.

Be sure to include background. Use any material from previous exercises that you deem important.

CITY OF FAIRFIELD
Police Committee

MEMORANDUM TO: Honorable Mayor and City Council, City of Fairfield
FROM: Police Committee, Eleanor J. Beatty, Douglas Hixon, Kenneth Wheelock
RE: Special Report
This is a special report of the Police Committee in lieu of an annual report. Special circumstances have prompted us to abandon our annual report because we have been involved in a number of discussions with the management of the Police Department.

The responsibilities of the Police Committee are to monitor the activities of the department, to suggest ways in which the department can better serve the citizens, and to keep the council and the electorate apprised of the needs and problems of the department.

We believe our community is witnessing increased crime and violence at a time when the Police Department is experiencing a crisis in management. In the years since the appointment of the incumbent Chief of Police, it is clear that our Police Department has become increasingly hostile to and alienated from the community. This has been reflected in the relations between the Chief of Police and the Police Committee. These relations, starting amicably five years ago, have deteriorated to the point where the Chief of Police seldom attends our meetings. We are not being consulted in matters of grave importance to the welfare of the community. We are being openly defied. A few specific instances will serve to demonstrate:

1. Whereas we had instructed the Chief of Police that we wished to see the department concentrate to some degree on the handling of loitering and drug usage occurring in parts of the downtown core, the chief has seen fit to ignore our wishes. Arrests for drunkenness, loitering, disorderly conduct, and narcotics violations have shown marked reductions in the past five years, even though there is no evidence these activities have declined. As a result much of our downtown core is deteriorating with major loss in property values and continued exodus of businesses to shopping centers in the suburbs.

2. Whereas we had instructed the chief that we wished to provide some control over the rioting and demonstrations occurring in our community, our wishes were again ignored. The downtown and the campus area have been the scene of every kind of riot and demonstration imaginable, for whatever cause, good or bad, legal or illegal, and often against the best interests of the community. While the committee is in favor of free speech and all that, there must be obvious and well-defined limits to what is permissible and what is not. Since the Police Department has been delegated the task of issuing parade and demonstration permits, it is clear that the chief of police is issuing permits to anybody and everybody, without regard to what perfidious influences or what sinister points of view might be promulgated upon our children. As a result our town has been treated to such spectacles as Communistic and Marxist points of view, homosexuality extolled, abortion favored and opposed, and we have even seen obscene and pornographic materials distributed by groups exercising their rights of "free speech."

3. Whereas we had instructed the chief that we were satisfied with the then-existing organizational structure of the department, the chief almost from the start began rearranging the higher echelons of administration to suit himself. The result has been the destruction of the professional lives of several spendid career officers in favor of personnel imported from other locations. In many instances, positions once occupied by officers are now occupied by *civilian* personnel in sensitive financing, research, and policy-making positions. Conditions occasioned by such changes border on the chaotic. There is enormous turmoil and lowered morale.

4. Whereas we had instructed the Chief of Police to try to hold the line on budgets and to consult with us before making substantive changes, the city has witnessed increasingly strident demands for funds for programs that are unnecessary and often capricious. Police budget requests have traditionally been outrageously out of line, reaching requested increases of 67% over the previous year on one occasion. The return on this investment is often negligible—numerous times high-density crime patrols have spent entire evenings blanketing a section of the city only to emerge from an evening's work without a single arrest!

5. Contrary to our wishes, the chief has taken money and personnel from the already critically understaffed patrol and criminal investigation divisions to add equipment and personnel to the Community Service Patrol and the Crime Preven-

tion Unit, both of which are largely welfare or service units whose role is essentially public relations. The department does not need further public relations. It needs a few good arrests and narcotics busts that can come only from hard and dedicated police work by front-line anticrime units.

These are but a few areas that concern the committee. There are others. We shall state them briefly.

The chief has on several occasions called the narcotics laws "unenforceable." This is an appalling admission! It also is a self-fulfilling prophecy, for our Police Department has been singularly ineffective in controlling the rampant use of drugs in the city.

The chief has issued orders effectively gagging members of the department. One such order, issued shortly after he assumed office, forbade police officers from talking with members of the Police Committee or any other elected official, except with the permission of the chief.

He has made it equally clear that he will not tolerate approaches from elected officials on behalf of certain officers eligible for promotion or seeking transfers. So while exceedingly tolerant of street demonstrations in the name of free speech, he has effectively denied the same freedom to members of his own department.

Such problems have resulted in a dangerously low level of morale within the department. Interviews with and letters from officers who have dared to violate the chief's gag order in the interests of overall public welfare testify to this. We present some excerpts:

"We are working in a very negative environment. The detectives can go out and arrest 40 people and bust up a burglary ring, and there's not one word of encouragement said to them by the Chief of Police or by the higher command in the department. But put an unauthorized poster on the wall or violate some other standard operating procedure and you catch hell."

"There is a constant feeling with the rank and file that if you actually do *police* work—that is, if you really *lean* hard on some of the scum and hippies and riffraff—and some bleeding heart complains to headquarters, you'll find yourself on a limb with the Chief of Police wielding a chainsaw."

"The public has this view of cops as a horde of savage head busters who have to be kept in their cages or they'll beat the hell out of everybody in sight. As a result the high command has put shackles on us."

"There is a lot of heavy stuff going down in Fairfield—drugs and prostitution and even organized crime. You're not going to get at it by going out and making public relations contacts. You do it by following the movements of known criminals, cultivating informants, and leaning on people. But all they care about at headquarters is handling traffic, making computer studies, and avoiding complaints about police brutality."

A final problem the committee has encountered is the issue of police abuse and harassment of citizens. The committee has spoken out about this on previous occasions. Letters to the committee in the past six months certainly indicate that the problem has not abated. Nearly 150 communications have come to the committee in the last six months. If only a fraction of them are substantiated, it would point to an appalling number of instances of abuse of police power. This, admittedly, has been a longstanding problem that predates the present Chief of Police. But little has been done to improve it under the new command. Here are some excerpts of communications the committee has received:

The parents of two 15-year-old rape victims write: "When the girls were released after five hours of terror, they notified a friend who in turn notified the police. The police assured the friend that they would notify the parents that the girls were safe. We were not told of the release until almost 3 o'clock in the morning, three hours after the release. We suffered almost unendurable agony for eight hours, the final three hours of which were totally unnecessary and due only to the insensitivity of the police."

A 17-year-old boy had parked his car on a street. A car containing three adult men parallel-parked in front of the boy's car, hitting the bumper. The youth shouted an obscene remark, whereupon the second car backed into the bumper again, harder. The youth shouted additional remarks, and the three men got out and started beating up on the youth. When police arrived, they arrested the *youth* and let the men go. Later it was discovered that one of the men was a relative of the arresting officer. Naturally the case against the boy was dropped the moment it reached the district attorney's office.

A girl, 18, was driving a 1983 Camaro at admittedly excessive speed. She was stopped by an officer and greeted by several sexually suggestive remarks, such as, "I'll probably have to give you a ticket, but if you're cooperative, perhaps we can work something out. . . ."

A group of Carson College boys were stopped by an officer for running a red light. The officer called them a number of unpleasant names, such as "pervert" and "degenerate" when the students protested that the light actually had been yellow when they entered the intersection.

We do not mean to imply that the incumbent chief is totally to blame for every excess of power perpetuated by an officer. Nor do we mean to imply that Mr. Hudson is without merit as a police administrator. He is a forceful and persuasive man, a hard worker, a keen analyst, and a man possessed of great charm. At the time he was one of three finalists for police chief, members of this committee lent him their enthusiastic support.

It has now become clear, however, that the large-city methods brought to Fairfield by the present chief are not in the best interests of the community. We had hoped that this problem might be dealt with in a quiet manner without undue publicity that may threaten Mr. Hudson's future career. It appears that Mr. Hudson and the media have worked out their own stratagems for maximum publicity with resulting community turmoil. We regret this development.

In any event, and in view of the urgent matters outlined herein, the Police Committee recommends the passage by the council of the following resolution:

WHEREAS Ernest J. Hudson, Chief of Police for the City of Fairfield, has engaged in and acted upon policy decisions and changes against the wishes of the elected officials of the city, and,

WHEREAS said activities appear to have exceeded his authority as chief of police, and,

WHEREAS the result of such actions has been an atmosphere of turmoil and loss
   of morale within the Department, and,
WHEREAS the differences between the elected officials and the chief of police
   are irreconcilable,
BE IT THEREFORE RESOLVED that the following actions be taken by the council:

1. That the council respectfully request the immediate resignation of Ernest J.
Hudson as Chief of Police, or, in the event of a refusal to resign, that the council
terminate his services effective immediately.

2. That the council provide every assistance to Mr. Hudson in seeking other employment.

3. That the council appoint an acting Chief of Police and immediately, with the
help of the Police Committee, begin a nationwide search for a successor.

4. That a police-civilian review board be appointed from among members of the
council, the rank-and-file members of the Department, and the public at large to
review police policy and action, including investigation of reports of excesses of
police power.

5. That the council vest in the Police Committee full power for the employment and
dismissal of the Chief of Police and for the review of major policy changes within
the Police Department.

EXERCISE 54 POLICE REPORTS

Write news stories for each of the three police reports you'll find on the following pages.

Background and suggestions. Reporters who cover
the police beat routinely encounter the reports turned in
by police officers and use the reports as the basis of stories. They may seem a little difficult to understand at
first, filled as they are with police jargon and procedures,
but eventually one comes to comprehend them and use
the factual data from them. Police records are public
documents, though police procedures vary from one ju-
risdiction to another on the question of news media access to reports. Under most freedom of information
laws, police may withhold them from public view during
an investigation, which is to say while they are still
timely from a news standpoint.

Reporters should always verify names and addresses
in the *City Directory* and should not always depend on
police officers to spell names or even common words
correctly. Information from reports should always be attributed to the police (''police said'' or a similar refer-

ence). Reporters often supplement the police reports
with interviews with witnesses or participants; good feature stories often result from that practice. For these exercises, however, see what you can do with the material
at hand.

Note in the following instances that the reports come
in two-page units, one an ''Incident Report'' that presents the essentials, the second a ''Detail Page'' that presents the officer's account of the incident based on interviews with participants and witnesses. Some officers
type their reports; others, as here, write or print in long-
hand.

Assume in each case that you have encountered the
reports early in the morning. The reports will not indicate a specific date. Assume that the events occurred last
night or early this morning and insert the appropriate
dates.

INCIDENT REPORT: Armed Robbery, 895 E. 11th

ITY										

INCIDENT REPORT
LINCOLN COUNTY LAW ENFORCEMENT AGENCIES

☐ GOODPASTURE PD   ☑ FAIRFIELD PD   ☐ MAYBERRY PD
☐ HARRISONVILLE PD   ☐ WAGONTIRE PD   ☐ LINCOLN CO SHERIFF
☐ OAKVILLE PD

PAGE 1 OF 2
CASE NUMBER: 57-3131

	PAT	DET	ASGN OFCR	OSB	RCDRS
	PROP OFCR	CRME LAB	MED INV	RESD DPTY	JAIL
	JUV CT	CITY ATTY	DIST ATTY	MUN CT	DIST CT
	SPEC SRVC	FIRE DEPT	OLCC	CIVIL	INFO RLSE

CLA ___ PDS ___
SCO ___ PDDT ___
SVAL ___ LOG ___
HVAL ___ INI ___

Entry: AIRS LEDS NCIC LOCAL OTHER
Clear: AIRS LEDS NCIC LOCAL OTHER

1. INCIDENT: ARMED ROBBERY (ROBBERY I)
2. INCIDENT LOCATION: 895 E 11th
3. RPTD DATE: YESTERDAY   4. TIME: 11:50 P   5. OCC. DATE: ___   6. TIME: 11:30 P   7. NON CRME INCID.   OTHER

CUSTODY

8. LAST NAME	FIRST	MIDDLE	9. COMPUTER NO.	10. D.O.B.	11. AGE	12. RACE/SEX

13. ALIAS NAME/MONIKER | 14. HGT. | 15. WGT. | 16. HAIR | 17. EYES
18. RES. ADDRESS | 19. RES. PHONE | 20. SOC. SEC. NO.
21. EMPLOYER/SCHOOL & GRADE | 22. BIRTH STATE | 23. PHYSICAL IDENTIFIERS
24. PARENTS NOTIFIED BY | DATE/TIME | 25. DET TIME | 26. DET ADMIT PERSON | 27. AUTH. DETENTION

CHARGES

1. WARRANT/CIT. NO. | 28. COURT DATE TIME | 29. COURT | 30. BAIL
2. WARRANT/CIT. NO.
3. WARRANT/CIT. NO.

OTHER PERSONS

31. NAME (FIRM IF BUSINESS)	FIRST	MIDDLE	32. COMPUTER NO.	33. D.O.B.	34. RACE/SEX
(1) LINDLEY	CALVIN	RICHARD		9/11/43	W/M

35. ADDRESS: 895 E 11th | 36. RES. PHONE: 367-0084 | 37. BUS. PHONE: 226-1179 | 38. WORK HOURS: IRREGULAR

39. LAST NAME	FIRST	MIDDLE	40. COMPUTER NO.	41. D.O.B.	42. RACE/SEX
(1) ANDERSON	PRISCILLA	JANE			W/F

43. ADDRESS: 897 E 11th | 44. RES. PHONE: 368-4484 | 45. BUS. PHONE: — | 46. WORK HOURS: —

47. LAST NAME	FIRST	MIDDLE	48. COMPUTER NO.	49. D.O.B.	50. RACE/SEX
( )					

51. ADDRESS | 52. RES. PHONE | 53. BUS. PHONE | 54. WORK HOURS

SUSPECTS OR LOCATE PERSON

55. NAME, DOB, RACE/SEX, HGT., WGT., HAIR, EYES, ADDRESS, PHONE, PHYSICAL IDENTIFIERS, CLOTHING, ETC.

WFA. MED HGT., 125-135, BROWN HAIR, BROWN EYES, ABOUT 30, DARK COMPLEXION, WORE BLACK TURTLENECK SWEATER, DENIM TROUSERS, GRUFF VOICE "GIGGLED A lot."

VEHICLE INFO.

VEHICLE STATUS	E	AV	IV	LV	MV	RV	SV	TV	VV	56. VIN NO.	57. VALUE

VEHICLE INFO.	LIC. NUMBER	LIC. ST.	LIC. EXP. YEAR	LIC. TYPE	VEH. YEAR	MAKE	MODEL	STYLE	COLORS

PERMISSION USE: YES☐ NO☐ | DELIQ. PAYMENTS: YES☐ NO☐ | THEFT INS.: YES☐ NO☐ | BODY DAMAGE: YES☐ NO☐ | KEYS IN VEH.: YES☐ NO☐ | VALUABLES: YES☐ NO☐ | SPEC. EQUIP.: YES☐ NO☐ | DRIVEABLE: YES☐ NO☐

58. REG. OWNER | ADDRESS | PHONE
59. TOWED TO | TOWED BY | 60. REASON | 61. CIT. NUMBER
62. | DATE/TIME | NOTIFIED BY | I.D. NUMBER
VEHICLE RECOVERY COMPLAINANT NOTIFIED: YES☐ NO☐

DO NOT TOW

REPORTING OFFICER	I.D. NO.	REPORTING OFFICER	I.D. NO.	63. DATE AND TIME REPORT PREPARED
ROBERT W. GRAHAM	228			

	DIVISION	SHIFT	AREA	APPROVED BY

FILE COPY   5/75

DETAIL PAGE: Armed Robbery, 895 E. 11th

DETAIL PAGE
LINCOLN COUNTY LAW ENFORCEMENT AGENCIES

GOODPASTURE PD	☐	FAIRFIELD PD ☑	MAYBERRY PD ☐	PAGE 2 OF 2
HARRISONVILLE PD ☐		WAGONTIRE PD ☐	LINCOLN CO SHERIFF ☐	CASE NUMBER
OAKVILLE PD ☐				57-31131

ITY				
CLA		PDS		
SCO		PDDT		
SVAL		LOG		
RVAL		INI		

☐ FOLLOW-UP   ☑ PROPERTY   ☐ EVIDENCE

PAT	DET	ASGN OFCR	OSB	RCRDS
PROP OFCR	CRME LAB	MED INV	RESD OPTY	JAIL
JUV CT	CITY ATTY	DIST ATTY	MUN CT	DIST CT
SPEC SRVC	FIRE DEPT	OLCC	CIVIL	INFO RLSE

Entry	AIRS	LEDS	NCIC	LOCAL	OTHER
Clear	AIRS	LEDS	NCIC	LOCAL	OTHER

1. INCIDENT   ARMED ROBBERY (ROBBERY I)

2. INCIDENT LOCATION   895 E. 11th

3. RDTD DATE	4. TIME	5. OCC. DATE	6. TIME	7. NON CRME INCID.	OTHER

PROPERTY STATUS	E	AP	FP	IP	MP	RP	(SP)	VP

8. TAG/RECEIPT NO.	9. WHERE PROP. STORED	10. TOTAL STOLEN/RCVD. VALUE

11. PROPERTY RELEASE   DATE AND TIME   RELEASED TO: (SIGNATURE)

12.
FOLLOW THIS SEQUENCE FOR LISTING ALL ITEMS OF PROPERTY - USE PROPER STATUS CODES

ITEM NO.	(QUANTITY)	NAME	SER. NO.	BRAND/MAKE	SIZE/CALIBER	COLOR	ENGRAVING/INSCRIPT	OTH.DESC.INFO.	VALUE
A	1	WALLET W/CASH						$420 CASH	420
B	1	WRIST WATCH		TIMEX-ELECTRIC			"TO A REAL MAN"- IRMA		35
C	1	COLOR T.V.		GE/1200/23"		WALNUT			595
D	1	RIFLE		WINCHESTER 94/30-30				NEW	120
E	1	TROUSERS			38-30	BLUE			12
								T = $1182	

Lindley states he returned home about 11:30 p.m. after spending entire evening at Black Cat Tavern on Detroit Ave. Vict. entered premises thru front door w/house key & proceeded to bedroom where he encounteres susp. Female susp. apparently heard vict enter & was waiting for him w/gun he described as .45 Army type pistol (automatic). She forced vict. to stand w/hands against bedroom wall while she removed wallet containing $420 cash from a payroll check he cashed earlier that day. She also removed his watch. Then she forced vict. to disrobe & tied his hands behind back & forced him to walk thru front door to the street where she tied him to his own car bumper. Susp. last seen walking behind premises. Vict. waited several minutes then called neighbor's (Anderson) attention by loud yells. Upon arriving at the scene, this officer found vict. attired in bathrobe & seated in front room sofa. Writer observed entry gained by kicking in basement door. Vict is extremely anxious to prosecute.

REPORTING OFFICER	I.D. NO.	REPORTING OFFICER	I.D. NO.	13. DATE AND TIME REPORT PREPARED
ROBERT W. GRAHAM				

DIVISION	WATCH	AREA	APPROVED BY

4-78

FILE COPY

INCIDENT REPORT: Armed Robbery, Downtown Motel

ITY			
CLA		PDS	
SCO		PDDT	
SVAL		LOG	

INCIDENT REPORT
LINCOLN COUNTY LAW ENFORCEMENT AGENCIES

☐ GOODPASTURE PD	☑ FAIRFIELD PD
☐ HARRISONVILLE PD	☐ WAGONTIRE PD
☐ OAKVILLE PD	
☐ MAYBERRY PD	
☐ LINCOLN CO SHERIFF	

PAGE 1 OF 2
CASE NUMBER
57-32004

PAT	DET	ASGN OFCR	OSB	RCDRS
PROP OFCR	CRME LAB	MED INV	RESD DPTY	JAIL
JUV CT	CITY ATTY	DIST ATTY	MUN CT	DIST CT
SPEC SRVC	FIRE DEPT	OLCC	CIVIL	INFO RLSE
OTHER				

Clear Entry

AIRS	LEDS	NCIC	LOCAL	OTHER
AIRS	LEDS	NCIC	LOCAL	OTHER

1. INCIDENT **ROBBERY I**

2. INCIDENT LOCATION **Downtown Motel 133 E 7th St**

3. RPTD DATE	4. TIME **6:57PM**	5. OCC. DATE	6. TIME **6:50 PM**	7. NON CRME INCID

CUSTODY

8. LAST NAME **CASSELL**	FIRST **STEPHEN**	MIDDLE **JAMES**	9. COMPUTER NO.	10. D.O.B. **4/17/57**	11. AGE	12. RACE/SEX **W/M**

13. ALIAS NAME/MONIKER **"CASS"**	14. HGT. **5'10"**	15. WGT. **170**	16. HAIR **BRW**	17. EYES **BRN**

18. RES. ADDRESS **No Permanent Address**	19. RES. PHONE	20. SOC. SEC. NO.

21. EMPLOYER/SCHOOL & GRADE	22. BIRTH STATE	23. PHYSICAL IDENTIFIERS **Missing left index finger**

24. PARENTS NOTIFIED BY	DATE/TIME	25. DET TIME	26. DET ADMIT PERSON	27. AUTH. DETENTION

CHARGES

1. **Robbery I**	WARRANT/CIT. NO.	28. COURT DATE TIME	29. COURT **Circuit**	30. BAIL **$25,000**
2. **Eluding a police officer**	WARRANT/CIT. NO.		"	**$10,000**
3. **Resisting Arrest**	WARRANT/CIT. NO.		"	**$10,000**

OTHER PERSONS

31. NAME (FIRM IF BUSINESS) **(1) Downtown Motel**	FIRST	MIDDLE	32. COMPUTER NO.	33. D.O.B	34. RACE/SEX

35. ADDRESS **133 E. 7th St.**	36. RES. PHONE	37. BUS. PHONE **343-4874**	38. WORK HOURS

39. LAST NAME **(2) GRIMM**	FIRST **Elizabeth**	MIDDLE **Anne**	40. COMPUTER NO.	41. D.O.B. **1/2/39**	42. RACE/SEX **W/F**

43. ADDRESS **1601 Westway Ave**	44. RES. PHONE **268-1109**	45. BUS. PHONE **343-4874**	46. WORK HOURS **12-7PM**

47. LAST NAME **( )**	FIRST	MIDDLE	48. COMPUTER NO.	49. D.O.B.	50. RACE/SEX

51. ADDRESS	52. RES. PHONE	53. BUS. PHONE	54. WORK HOURS

SUSPECTS OR LOCATE PERSON

55. NAME, DOB, RACE/SEX, HGT., WGT., HAIR, EYES, ADDRESS, PHONE, PHYSICAL IDENTIFIERS, CLOTHING, ETC.

From witness/vict. Grim: white-male-adult, 25-30, 5'11" 175 lbs., long brown hr., Brw eyes, missing 1 finger left hand, Black leather jacket w/skull and crossbones on back, black boots, knife in sheath on belt, small earring left ear. 1-2 days beard stubble.

VEHICLE INFO.

VEHICLE STATUS	Ⓔ	AV	IV	LV	MV	RV	SV	TV	VV	56. VIN NO.	57. VALUE

VEHICLE INFO.	LIC. NUMBER **X/2321**	LIC. ST. **Any**	LIC. EXP. YEAR	LIC. TYPE **m/cycle**	VEH. YEAR **1923**	MAKE **Hartey**	MODEL **361**	STYLE	COLORS **Black**

PERMISSION USE	DELIQ. PAYMENTS	THEFT INS.	BODY DAMAGE	KEYS IN VEH.	VALUABLES	SPEC. EQUIP.	DRIVEABLE
YES ☐ NO ☐	YES ☐ NO ☐	YES ☐ NO ☐	YES ☐ NO ☐	YES ☐ NO ☐	YES ☐ NO ☐	YES ☐ NO ☐	YES ☐ NO ☒

DO NOT TOW

58. REG. OWNER **Stephen J. Cassel**	ADDRESS **See Above**	PHONE

59. TOWED TO **Impound**	TOWED BY	60. REASON **Evidence**	61. CIT. NUMBER

62. VEHICLE RECOVERY COMPLAINANT NOTIFIED.	YES ☐ NO ☐	DATE/TIME	NOTIFIED BY	I.D. NUMBER

REPORTING OFFICER **JON W. MARX**	I.D. NO. **061**	REPORTING OFFICER **Patrick L. Smith**	I.D. NO.	63. DATE AND TIME REPORT PREPARED

FILE COPY

5/75

DIVISION	SHIFT	AREA	APPROVED BY

DETAIL PAGE: Armed Robbery, Downtown Motel

DETAIL PAGE
LINCOLN COUNTY LAW ENFORCEMENT AGENCIES

GOODPASTURE PD	✓ FAIRFIELD PD		MAYBERRY PD
HARRISONVILLE PD	WAGONTIRE PD		LINCOLN CO SHERIFF
OAKVILLE PD			

PAGE 2 OF 2

CASE NUMBER: 57-32004

✓ FOLLOW-UP ✓ PROPERTY EVIDENCE

1. INCIDENT: ROBBERY I

8. TAG/RECEIPT NO. 472
9. WHERE PROP. STORED: FPD
10. TOTAL STOLEN/RCVD. VALUE: $266

RELEASED TO: (SIGNATURE) Elizabeth A Grimm(s)

12. FOLLOW THIS SEQUENCE FOR LISTING ALL ITEMS OF PROPERTY - USE PROPER STATUS CODES

This officer was dispatched to Downtown Motel, 133 East seventh st. at approx 7 p.m. in response to a reported armed robbery. Victim Grimm, the hotel clerk, states that a "Hells Angel" type man rode into the motel drive and entered the office where Grimm was working alone. Susp. pulled a knife from a sheath on his belt and said "Get the money," Grimm said. Grimm said she gave the man all the bills in the cash box, estimated to be excess of $200 cash. The man told her to lay down behind the counter and not get up or she would get hurt. Grimm heard the motorcycle ride off and she called the office. Suspect matching Cassell's description observed at 7:10 p.m. on west 11th st. by patrolman Smith. Suspect vehicle pursued west on West 11th st. for approx 2 miles where, at intersection with Bertleson Road, suspect hit loose gravel and overturned. His speed on West 11th was excessive causing him to loose control of vehicle. He was not injured and scuffled with patrolman Smith although he did not use a knife on a belt sheath. Patrolman Smith subdued susp. and read him his rights at appoximately 7:15 p.m. and transported to city jail. Approximately $260 found on susp.

REPORTING OFFICER: J. W. MARX
REPORTING OFFICER: Pat C. Smith
13. DATE AND TIME REPORT PREPARED

FILE COPY

EXERCISE 55 FATAL MOTOR VEHICLE ACCIDENT

Write a news story based on this final police report, one considerably more complicated than the others.

Suggestions. Here you will find a series of documents, including: the traffic accident report form; a police officer's sketch of the accident; a report by Officer Graham, who was the first on the scene; and another report by Detective DeHaviland, who was assigned to interview witnesses.

In writing about this event, be discreet about using eye witness reports. Not all police jurisdictions would share reports like these to news media when an investigation is continuing for fear of jeopardizing what could ul-

timately become a criminal case. Don't be careless in assuming that the event was in fact a late-night drag race down Fairway Avenue unless you find an authority to whom you can attribute that information. At least one of the participants in this accident has become prominent through earlier pages of this text, so you may want to include background information from previous exercises.

Avoid using police jargon from the reports. Attribute information to the police.

CASE NO. 58-61073

Fatal MVA—13th & Fairway
Supplemental Report

PERSONS INVOLVED:	DIAMOND, Terrence Lyle 1104 University Avenue Fairfield (Age 20)	McCORMACK, Linda Ann 1196 Onyx Avenue Fairfield (age: 17)
	DOFFERMAN, Billy Joe 555 Westway Avenue, Apt. 39 Fairfield (age: 18)	
WITNESSES:	CHALMERS, Danny Ray 2234 E. 32nd St. Fairfield (age: 17)	UVERS, Dianne Christine 1911 W. 14th St. Fairfield (Age 17)
	PERRIN, Stacy Ann 617 E. 14th St. Fairfield DOB 5-17-1919	

DETAILS: While on patrol in the area of W 16th and Fairway I was stopped by a passing motorist and advised that there was a serious MVA at the intersection of 13th and Fairway. After advising radio dispatch of this information, I arrived at scene at 0220.

Upon arrival at the scene I observed a Blue Volkswagen sitting on the sidewalk, crossways, and the Blue Camaro sitting crossways in the left lane of Fairway Avenue. The body of the deceased was observed laying on the sidewalk with the head pointing south down Fairway. The entire area was littered with parts of cars and broken glass.

I then observed McCORMACK who when contacted was laying on a blanket on her back on the sidewalk by Fairway Avenue. She was in severe pain with possi-

TRAFFIC ACCIDENT REPORT: Fatal Accident, Fairway Avenue and 13th Street

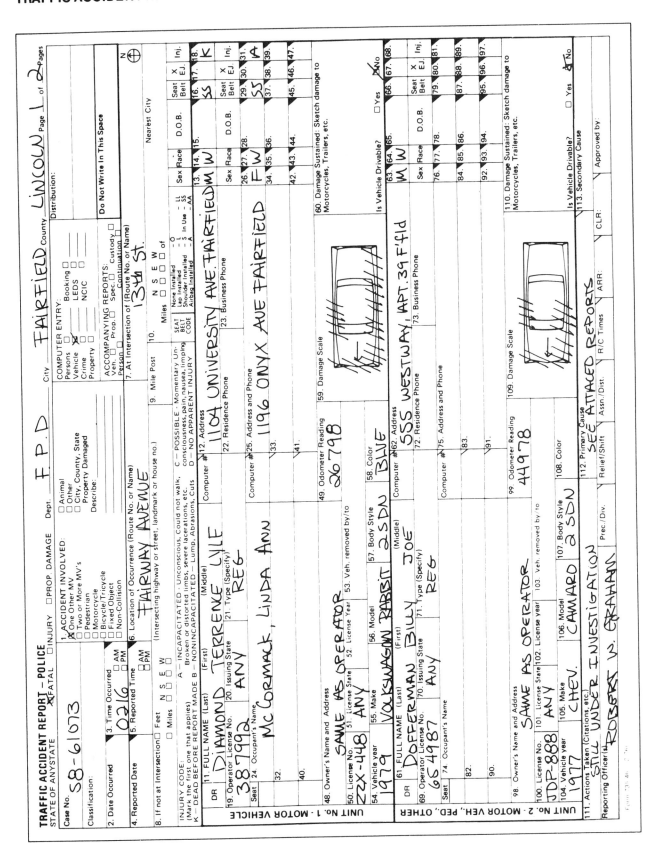

TRAFFIC ACCIDENT SKETCH: Fatal Accident, Fairway Avenue and 13th Street

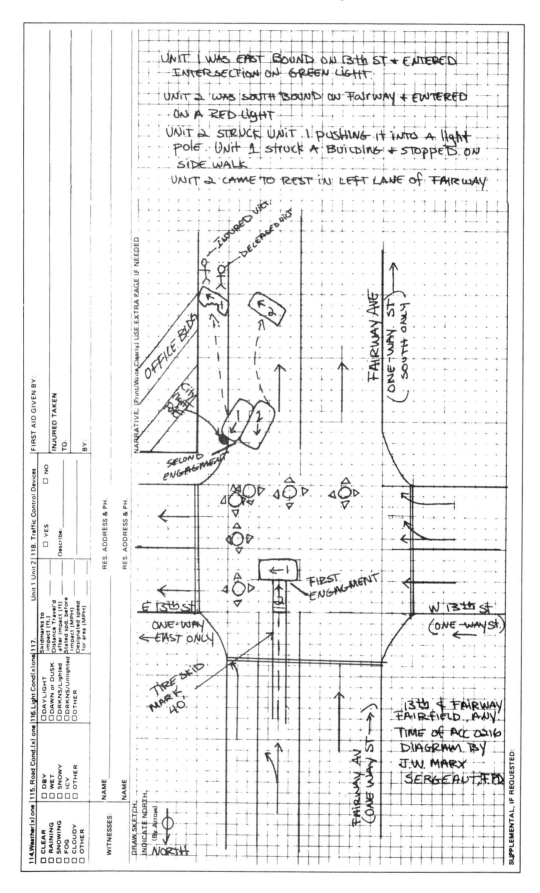

ble fracture of the left leg. She was conscious and complained of severe abdominal pain. I radioed for ambulance and administered first aid.

At the time I made contact, DOFFERMAN was in a dazed condition and was wandering around the scene of the accident. This subject was unable to relate what had happened and had a cut on his head on the right side. With the arrival of the assisting officer, I contacted the witnesses and arrangements were made to transport same to City Hall for statements.

In compliance with instructions from Lt. Kingsley, I advised subject DOFFERMAN of his rights at 0225.

It was determined through my observations at the scene that the Volkswagen, driven by DIAMOND and with McCORMACK as passenger had been east bound on 13th Street and had entered the intersection on a green light, and that DOFFERMAN, traveling alone in the Camaro had been south bound on Fairway, that he entered the intersection of 13th and Fairway on a red light and had struck the Volkswagen broadside, pushing it into a light pole and then into the building where it came to rest.

See statements obtained by Det. DeHaviland, this case No.

After traffic had been controlled and at the direction of Lt. Kingsley, I transported DOFFERMAN to Providence Emergency where he was examined by the duty doctor and a blood alcohol test was taken at the request of the subject. Subject was then transported to City Hall where he was released.

Robert W. Graham
Patrolman, FPD

CASE NO. 58-61073
Fatal MVA—ADDITIONAL

Time 0640 [date]

CONTACTED: CHALMERS, DANNY RAY
             UVERS, DIANNE CHRISTINE
             PERRIN, STACEY ANN
             MCCORMACK, LINDA ANN

NOT CONTACTED: WFJ, name unknown, 5-2, slender, dark blonde hair

EVIDENCE: Two (2) tape recorded statements

DETAILS: At approximately 0220 this date, writer was advised of a fatal traffic accident at 13th and Fairway. At request of Lt. Kingsley, writer contacted witnesses and took statements as follows:

At approximately 0230 writer contacted DANNY CHALMERS. Chalmers stated that he was proceeding south on Fairway in the right traffic lane. Beside him in the left lane was the Camaro and they proceeded side-by-side for a distance of approximately four blocks. Danny Chalmers stated that both vehicles were stopped for a red light at Fairway and 11th. When the light turned green he accelerated his vehicle rapidly for a short distance, going to an estimated speed of 30-40 mph after which he slowed down both by engine compression and brakes. At a point about one-fourth block north of 13th he stated that he observed a red light in the right hand lane. He stated further that the Camaro which was behind him accelerated very rapidly and did not appear to slow down for the red light. Chalmers stated that the light had been red for some time and that he could not understand why the driver of the Camaro was going to drive through a red light. On questioning, Chalmers stated that he had had nothing to drink during the evening, and when asked several times regarding racing or conducting a speed contest, he denied that they were involved in this activity. At approx 0250 writer began a tape recorded statement with Danny Chalmers which ended at 0305. It should be noted that Chalmers vehicle was a 1982 Mercury Cougar.

Writer briefly contacted DOFFERMAN. This subject was asked if he wished to discuss the incident, and his rights were outlined by Lt. Kingsley. DOFFERMAN indicated he did not want to discuss the incident without an attorney being present.

At approx 0337 this date, writer contacted UVERS. She states that she was a passenger in the Cougar driven by Chalmers. She states as follows, that they had been driving home from a motion picture and that they were proceeding at a normal rate of speed south along Fairway in the right lane. They stopped for a traffic light at 13th and Fairway. Miss Uvers states that she did not see the approaching Volkswagen as it entered the intersection. She states that she did not hear nor see the Camaro as it was continuing south until just before the moment of impact. At approx 0355 writer began a tape recorded statement with Miss Uvers in the presence of Sgt. Marx who had been with writer through the conversation. Taped statement ended at approx 0413.

Writer then contacted PERRIN, however, after hearing her version of what had occurred it was obvious that she was incorrect and unsure of what happened. No tape recorded statement was taken from Mrs. Perrin. As a point of information it should be known that Mrs. Perrin stated that the two cars traveling south on Fairway were going side-by-side at an extremely fast rate of speed.

At approx 0504 this date, writer contacted LINDA ANN MCCORMACK at Providence Hospital along with Lt. Kingsley. As this witness had just undergone emergency treatment for a broken left leg, possible concussion, and numerous facial cuts and abrasions, she was under sedation for pain. She had just come out of emergency where a cast had been prepared for her leg. Under the circumstances and at the request of the doctor, the interview was kept brief.

Miss McCormack states that she had been to a fraternity party with the deceased subject. Terrence Diamond. She states that they had spent some time driving around Fairfield after the party and were enroute to her home at the time of the accident. She stated that Diamond had had "two or three" beers at the fraternity party. Miss McCormack stated that they were driving eastward along 13th Street at approx 25-30 mph and that the light was green and traffic was light. Miss McCormack states that she observed a vehicle approaching from the left at an extremely high rate of speed. She estimated the speed at 60 mph. She stated that she warned Diamond of the approaching vehicle by shouting "Look Out." She states that she observed Diamond turn the steering wheel sharply to the right and that she heard tires screeching. She states that she could remember nothing else until she found herself lying on a blanket.

Walter L. DeHaviland
Detective, CID

EXERCISE 56 A CRIMINAL INDICTMENT

Write a story based on the following information. Assume that the accident occurred about two weeks ago.

Background. An accident such as the one depicted in Exercise 55 often has legal implications, which means it may be taken to court to determine if one or more of the participants was guilty of a criminal act. In this case, the police investigation of the accident that led to Terrence Diamond's death has convinced authorities (the district attorney, in this case, who is the official charged with prosecuting criminal cases in the county) that the accident involved some criminal activity. So the case of Billy Joe Dofferman has been presented to the Grand Jury, a group of citizens drawn together to consider whether a crime has been committed. If the jury agrees

that it has, an indictment is issued that charges the defendant with a crime and sends police out to arrest the defendant and place him in the county jail.

Police arrested Dofferman this morning at 9:45 and lodged him in the county jail. He will appear in Circuit Court tomorrow at 9 a.m. to enter a plea (guilty or not guilty) to the charge. Bail has been set at $3,000. Witnesses examined by the Grand Jury in reaching its decision were Robert W. Graham, Walter DeHaviland, Jonathon W. Marx, Linda Ann McCormack, Danny Ray Chalmers, Dianne Christine Uvers and Stacy Ann Perrin.

In the Circuit Court of the State of Anystate for Lincoln County

THE STATE OF ANYSTATE
              Plaintiff

vs.   INDICTMENT

BILLY JOE DOFFERMAN
              Defendant

The above named BILLY JOE DOFFERMAN is accused by the Lincoln County Grand Jury by this Indictment of the crime of

NEGLIGENT HOMICIDE

Committed as follows:

The said BILLY JOE DOFFERMAN on or about the [insert date], in the county aforesaid, then and there being the driver of a motor vehicle southbound on Fairway Avenue, a public highway in the City of Fairfield, did then and there willfully and unlawfully drive said motor vehicle carelessly and heedlessly in reckless disregard of the rights and safety of others in a grossly negligent manner to wit:

1. By failing to keep a proper lookout for other traffic upon or crossing said public highway;
2. By failing to stop, turn or otherwise exercise the care and caution required to keep his vehicle under control and to avoid collision with the vehicle driven by Terrence Lyle Diamond, deceased, as alleged herein;
3. By failing to stop and obey the traffic control signal located at the intersection of 13th Street and Fairway Avenue;
4. By driving his motor vehicle at a speed greater than reasonable and prudent under the conditions then and there existing;
5. By attempting to engage and engaging in a race with a motor vehicle operated by Danny Ray Chalmers while said motor vehicle was then and there southbound on Fairway Avenue within the City of Fairfield, Anystate;

and the said defendant while driving said motor vehicle in the manner and under the conditions aforesaid, did thereby then and there collide with a vehicle operated by Terrence Lyle Diamond, which motor vehicle was then approaching from the defendant's right and travelling east on 13th Street, a public highway in the City of Fairfield, thereby inflicting and causing to be inflicted bodily injuries to the said Terrence Lyle Diamond, who, as a proximate result of said injuries did die on the [insert date] contrary to statute and against the peace and dignity of the State of Anystate.

Dated this [insert date] at Fairfield, Lincoln County, Anystate.

/s/VICTOR A. SMITH, District Attorney

EXERCISE 57 PERSONAL INJURY LAWSUIT

Write a news story about this second legal fallout from Billy Joe's accident: a "civil" lawsuit.

Background. By "civil" lawyers differentiate from the "criminal" procedures depicted in the previous exercise. Dofferman could go to prison if convicted of negligent homicide, a criminal offense. In this civil action brought by Linda McCormack's attorney, damages are sought to compensate Linda for her injuries, some of which are permanent and disfiguring. Both the criminal and civil cases could go before a Circuit Court jury, which could send him to jail for the criminal indictment or order him (or his insurance company) to pay compensation to Linda. Write a story about this lawsuit. For background, assume that the accident occurred three months ago, also that Dofferman pleaded guilty to negligent homicide and served 120 days in the state penitentiary. Assume that Linda is still 17 years old. Use whatever background about her from previous exercises that you deem useful.

IN THE CIRCUIT COURT OF THE STATE OF ANYSTATE
FOR LINCOLN COUNTY

LINDA ANN MC CORMACK, by Edward W. McCormack, her Guardian ad Litum	
Plaintiff	Case No.
vs.	COMPLAINT
BILLY JOE DOFFERMAN	(Action at Law
Defendant	Bodily Injuries)

Plaintiff for her cause of action, Alleges:

I

Plaintiff is a minor and brings this action through her father who has been appointed her Guardian ad Litum.

II

At all times material herein Fairway Avenue was a paved, two-lane, one-way street upon which traffic moves in a southerly direction, and 13th Street was a paved, two-lane, one-way street in which traffic moves in an easterly direction. A traffic signal device controls traffic at the intersection of Fairway Avenue and 13th Street.

III

On or about [insert date] Plaintiff Linda Ann McCormack was riding as a passenger in a Volkswagen Rabbit then operated by Terrence L. Diamond and traveling east on 13th Street. Defendant was then operating a Chevrolet Camaro traveling south on Fairway Avenue. Defendant drove the Chevrolet Camaro into the side of the Volkswagen in which Plaintiff was a passenger, violently knocking it across the intersection and into the side of a building at the corner.

IV

At the time and place aforementioned, Defendant was negligent in one or more of the following particulars.

1. In failing to stop in compliance with the red stop light located at the intersection which at that time was stopping traffic on Fairway Avenue.
2. In failing to yield the right-of-way to the Volkswagen, in which Plaintiff was a passenger, and which had entered the intersection on a green light.
3. In driving at a speed greater than was reasonable and prudent under the circumstances and conditions then existing.
4. In participating in a speed race with another motor vehicle traveling south on Fairway Avenue at the time and place mentioned.
5. In failing to keep and maintain an adéquate lookout for other traffic upon and crossing Fairway Avenue.
6. In failing to keep the Chevrolet Camaro automobile under adequate control.

V

By reason of the negligence of the Defendant in one or more of the particulars alleged herein, the collision occurred and Plaintiff was caused to suffer serious and extensive bodily injuries, including an injury to the head with concussion of the brain and injury to the central nervous system, lacerations of the face and head, injury to the left leg with multiple fractures to bones of said leg, and multiple bruises and abrasions about the head, body, and limbs, and was caused to suffer physical and emotional shock. Said injuries were permanent in nature, and by reason of the injuries, Plaintiff has and will continue to suffer pain, discomfort, inconvenience, disfigurement, disability, and mental anguish, all to her general damage in the sum of $350,000.

VI

By reason of the injuries, Plaintiff has been required to have an ambulance, to be hospitalized, and to have the services of physicians, nurses, technicians, and the use of special medical and physical therapeutic equipment, medicines, and supplies, all at the reasonable expense of $3,088.97, to her special damage in that sum. Plaintiff will by reason of her injuries continue to require medical care for an indefinite period of time in the future, and the total of her medical expenses is unknown. The Complaint will be amended when the full amount of her special damages is known.

VII

By reason of the injuries, Plaintiff has been unable to participate in interscholastic athletics, and as a result has had to decline a proffered college athletic grant-in-aid in the amount of $500 a year for four years, to her special damage in the sum of $2,000.

VIII

By reason of the injuries, Plaintiff has been unable to maintain part-time and summer employment with resultant loss of wages in the amount of $1,500, to her special damage in that sum.

WHEREFORE, Plaintiff prays for judgment against the Defendant for general damages in the sum of $350,000 and special damages in the sum of $6,588.97, for costs and disbursements herein incurred, and for such other and further relief as to the court may seem proper.

Susan C. Graham
Attorney for Plaintiff

Chapter Seventeen

THE NEWS CONFERENCE

News conferences are called by public officials and celebrities largely as a means of handling the frequent requests for information. When such people are involved in newsworthy situations, the inquiries from reporters are frequently so constant that they could literally spend all their time talking individually to media representatives even in a small city like Fairfield. Clearly the solution is to call them all in and speak to them at once.

The typical conference is a little like the presidential news conferences you see on television, though it usually has fewer media participants. The speaker and the reporters are "performing" a little as a rule, especially if the conference is being telecast. Reporters find it hard to get a good line of questioning going because each reporter has his or her own ideas of what questions should be asked. The results tend to be disjointed, broad and superficial. Some reporters have reputations for asking convoluted questions, and some tend to phrase their questions in a provocative manner, hoping for provocative answers. Other reporters participate little in news conferences. Through it all, key questions often are not asked, and the answers given sometimes have little connection with the questions that have been asked.

EXERCISE 58 NEWS CONFERENCE

The conference depicted here with Chief Ernest Hudson is typical. He calls the conference to respond to the Police Committee Report, released yesterday and depicted in Exercise 53. He provides a handout showing the results of a recent public opinion survey conducted by an opinion research class at Carson College under the direction of Julia Nathan, professor of sociology. Write a news story for today's paper based on this material.

A. [Hudson]: Let me explain the document that I handed you. Dr. Julia Nathan came to me a few weeks ago and asked if I'd be interested in having an opinion survey done on public attitudes toward the Police Department. I said yes. She had fifteen graduate students from one of her classes run the

---

SURVEY RESULTS

1. Do you think that the police in Fairfield do an excellent, good, fair, or poor job of enforcing the law?

Excellent	17%
Good	40%
Fair	26%
Poor	8%
No opinion	9%

2. How good a job do the police do in protecting the people in your neighborhood?

Very good	39%
Pretty good	33%
Not so good	14%
No opinion	14%

3. How good a job do the police do in being respectful to people like yourself?

Very good	59%
Pretty good	22%
Not so good	9%
No opinion	10%

---

survey using personal interviews by telephone with a random sample of 350 residents. She tells me the margin of error is about five percent. You have the results which I believe show good citizen support of the department. Okay, now I'll try to answer your questions.

Q. *[Bill Williams, Channel 3 News]: Chief Hudson, how do you feel about the Police Committee's Report?*

A. Generally speaking, I'm opposed to it except in one extremely important respect—

Q. *[Mel Jackson, Channel 9 News]: Chief, you're quoted in the report as saying narcotics laws are unenforceable. What's the reason for that? Is it because of difficulty of smoking out—if you'll pardon the expression—the users of dope? I'm just curious why you would make such a blatant statement, and my second question is, don't you think the police abuses are kind of getting out of hand, I mean, it's pretty rough on the parents of kidnap victims when the cops don't bother to inform them that their daughters are safe, and I also think that—*

A. Let me assure you, Mr. Jackson, that we are trying to enforce the laws to the best of our ability. My

comment about the unenforceability of narcotics laws was taken out of context. My point is that to arrest someone for narcotics in Fairfield is a little like snipping one leaf off a vigorously growing weed. Fairfield is merely at the end of a highly complex and well-organized drug distribution system. Hacking away at the outer branches of a well-oiled pipeline network is not going to accomplish much.

Q. *[Jackson]: Chief, this report suggests that you've really strong-armed some of your pet measures through and that you listen to nobody. How do you feel about that? Does this represent the actuality of your relationship with the committee? And my second question is—*

A. Mr. Jackson, the Police Committee and I obviously disagree on some things. My philosophy is that a police department should be closely integrated with the citizens of the community. It should try to rid itself of the macho, tough-guy image. We have spent time doing that.

Q. *[Jackson]: Like what? Isn't it true, Chief, that you've strong-armed your way through the last five years?*

A. We have established community service patrols and we have sent officers out to speak to school groups in an effort to prevent future crime. The officers have talked about drugs, burglary, fast cars, alcohol, shoplifting and a whole set of police problems. Though we can't prove it, we think the result of this has been the prevention of criminal activities, particularly among the young. We've put crime statistics into the computer so that we can determine crime patterns and then devise ways of coping with them. We have improved our training programs. We want trained men and women out on the street, acting and looking sharp and crisp and courteous—

Q. [Jackson]: It just doesn't cut it with me, Chief, don't you think—

A. Please hear me out. We have rewritten documents and procedures calculated to give the maximum service with the minimum physical risk to the officer. And with these improvements we have cut our response time—the time it takes a patrol car to reach the scene of an emergency—in half. Now, the Police Committee doesn't agree with all of this. They see the officer as being more aggressive, more forceful, more controlling of people's behavior. They are particularly distressed by what they see as a lessening of law and order, as shown by the increasing number of street demonstrations and parades over such things as apartheid in South Africa or pro- or anti-abortion advocates. Well, my position is that you really don't want your police department making decisions as to who shall be allowed to demonstrate or hold a parade and who shall not. You can't be in a position of allowing the anti-abortion people to demonstrate because you agree with their views and not the pro-abortion because you disagree with theirs. The department does not take a position on apartheid or abortion or legalization of marijuana or firing the football coach or anything else people might demonstrate about. We enforce the laws, and we allow all demonstrations so long as they conform to the rules that we have established and which have been approved by the City Council.

Q. [Sandy Macklin, Rocket, alternative paper]: Sir, isn't there a constitutional question here?

A. On the right to demonstrate, you mean? Of course. Also a common sense question. Our procedures manual, which I wrote myself, is very clear on this point. It says that peaceful and lawful demonstrations should be looked upon by police agencies not as a threat but as a safety valve. All we ask is that they comply with the law.

Q. [Macklin]: Have they done so?

A. I have no complaints. They even picketed the Police Department one cold day in December a year or two ago. Not only did they secure the required permit, but we all had a good time. I could see that they were getting tired and discouraged, so I sent out for coffee and doughnuts and invited them in. We had a nice chat.

Q. [Barbara Miller, Telegram]: What were they picketing about?

A. I think we were holding a young man on a burglary charge, and they wanted to show their support, even spring him loose if possible.

Q. [Miller]: Does Julia Nathan's survey suggest to you that the public sides with you and against the Police Committee in this ongoing conflict?

A. I'd prefer to let the figures speak for themselves. The curious thing about the survey is that the Police Committee had a copy of it, provided to them by Dr. Nathan. They chose to ignore it.

Q. [Miller]: Can you suggest why they ignored it?

A. Ask them.

Q. [Jackson]: Chief, you seem to be insinuating that the committee deliberately stacked the cards against you.

A. As I say, they chose to ignore it. I can't say why.

Q. [Macklin]: Sir, what about women? I mean, is the increased use of women police officers to be considered as one of your accomplishments?

A. We currently have eleven female officers on our staff of one hundred sworn officers, and of the eleven, five cover regular beats in the patrol cars just like men. The others are in juvenile and detectives divisions. We have not a shred of evidence that they are any less effective doing patrol work, and we have some evidence that they do especially well in other areas, particularly detectives and juvenile. I have been quoted as saying the council should consider a woman as our next police chief.

Q. [Williams]: That brings up the main question— Chief, do you plan to resign?

A. No.

Q. [Williams]: Will you fight to keep your job?

A. You bet! Not only to keep the job but to protect the integrity of one of the best small-city police departments in the country.

Q. [Jackson]: Chief, surely you're not serious about being replaced by a woman?

A. Mr. Jackson, police chiefs try to operate on brains, experience and courage—and maybe a tad of political and administrative savvy. There's no reason a woman who has those qualities can't do splendidly as a chief of police. If anything is in the way of this, it would be only that women generally have not been in this work long enough to have gained the experience and administrative seasoning required of the job. This is the twentieth century, darned near the twenty-first, and times change. So let's not burn that bridge before we cross it.

Q. *[Miller]: You've mentioned personal vendettas a time or two in the past. Do you think Mr. Wheelock is carrying out some kind of personal or political vendetta against you?*

A. Police chiefs and their departments tend to be fair political game, Ms. Miller, especially in this day and age. I tend to feel that our philosophical disagreements have fanned their feelings—those of the committee—beyond the stage of rational discussion of our differences. The committee in recent weeks has tended to be contentious and confrontative, and I have little doubt that they'd feel more comfortable with another person administering the department. In some ways it reflects the stresses of changing attitudes among our citizens and in society generally.

Q. *[Miller]: Changing from what to what?*

A. From the macho, law-and-order image to a more tolerant society.

Chapter Eighteen

LIBRARY RESEARCH

Every newswriter should be at home in a library, particularly the section that contains the general reference books. Most newspaper libraries also contain a selection of reference books in addition to the indexed clippings of stories previously published in the paper. Some papers have their files on electronic databases. News agencies can also subscribe to national databases, such as Dialog or Nexus, which allows them to scan indexes in mere seconds.

Use of the library ranges from acquisition of facts, such as how many people immigrated to the U.S. between 1901 and 1910 (consult the *Statistical Abstract of the United States*), to biographical rundowns on celebrities such as businessman and philanthropist Gordon P. Getty (*Current Biography*) or novelist Jean Auel (*Contemporary Authors*). By consulting such reference works as *Reader's Guide to Periodical Literature* or *Business Periodicals Index*, you will find articles that have appeared in magazines and business papers that will be useful as background. If actress Farrah Fawcett were to visit your community and you were assigned to interview her, your interview will proceed much better if you know a lot about her—information available from such sources as *Current Biography* or magazine articles culled from the *Reader's Guide* index.

All of the questions in this chapter can be answered by consulting one or more of the following references:

Almanacs (*Information Please Almanac*, and several others)
Biography Index
Book Review Digest
Books in Print
Books of quotations (such as Bartlett's, Oxford and others)
Business Periodicals Index
Congressional Directory
Congressional Quarterly Almanac
Contemporary Authors
Current Biography
Encyclopedias (such as *Encyclopedia Britannica* and others)
Encyclopedia of Associations
Facts on File
Famous First Facts
Guinness Book of World Records
IMS Directory of Publications
Medical Encyclopedias

Moody's Complete Corporate Index
New York Times Index
Public Affairs Information Service
Reader's Guide to Periodical Literature

Statistical Abstract of the United States
Who's Who
Who's Who in America
Yearbooks (*Collier's, World Book,* and others.)

EXERCISE 59 STATISTICS

Answer these questions by consulting the Statistical Abstract of the United States.

1. How many persons have immigrated to the U.S. since 1820?
2. What was the ten-year period of highest immigration to the U.S.? How many persons immigrated during that period?
3. How many immigrants came to the U.S. in the most recent year for which figures are available?
4. What are currently (latest figures) the three leading countries of birth for immigrants to the United States?
5. What is the life expectancy for a white female, age 50? A nonwhite male, age 50?
6. What was the life expectancy of a U.S. citizen in (1) 1920, (2) 1930, (3) 1940 and (4) latest available?
7. What was the difference in the life expectancy rates between white females and nonwhite females in 1920? How about now (latest available)?
8. What percentage of the land is owned by the federal

government in the states of Alaska, California, Hawaii and Rhode Island?
9. Who has the most aircraft carriers among the world powers: U.S., the Soviet Union, or France? How about submarines?
10. How does the U.S. compare to the Soviet Union in per capita military expenditures? How about military expenditures as a percent of gross national product?
11. What countries of the world rank the highest in military expenditures as a percent of gross national product?
12. How many people attended college football games in the most recent year for which figures are available?
13. What percentage of U.S. children are orphans?
14. Has the number of farms in the U.S. increased or decreased in recent years? Cite the relevant figures.
15. What percentage of U.S. farmland (area) is in large farms of 2,000 acres or more?

EXERCISE 60 QUOTATIONS

Newspaper librarians say that books of quotations are heavily used by writers seeking quotes appropriate to a topic they are addressing in an article. Or they may be seeking to identify the author or the exact wording of a quotation they vaguely remember. Each quotation here comes in rather a mangled form—just as you might expect to retrieve it from memory. Cite the author and the exact wording of each one.

1. "Journalism is not readable whereas literature is not read."
2. "I disagree with what you say, but you have a right to say it."
3. "It's always darkest before the dawn."
4. "Go West, young man."
5. "Real learning is always accompanied by pain."

6. "I'd rather be right than president."
7. "Damn the torpedoes—full speed ahead!"
8. "Cowards die a thousand deaths, the brave but once."
9. "There is no rest for the wicked."
10. "The road to hell is paved with good intentions."

EXERCISE 61 SEARCH FOR FACTS

For each question, write the answer and cite the name of the reference book you consulted as a source.

1. List the names of any books currently in print authored by novelist Ursula LeGuin.

2. Cite excerpts from two critical reviews of Jean M. Auel's 1980 novel, *The Clan of the Cave Bear.*

3. Name at least one Japanese language publication in the U.S.

4. Cite the names, circulation and location of offices of publication of at least two publications directed specifically at brides.

5. The police chief says your chances of being killed in a highway accident are greater than on an airliner. Cite supporting statistics.

6. How does one qualify for membership in the Daughters of the American Revolution? How many members does it have?

7. How many members are in the Air Line Pilots Association? What's its purpose?

8. Farmer Hank Tubbs has grown a gigantic radish in his greenhouse: 8 pounds 4 ounces. Is it close to a world record?

9. A news story about a mountain rescue says a victim suffered from "hypothermia." What is it?

10. Cite the date and place of birth, education and noteworthy accomplishments of Donald Kent Slayton.

11. Who is Lady Antonia Fraser? What has she accomplished?

12. Who was the first female college president in the U.S.?

13. Who was the first U.S. President to resign from office? When?

14. Who piloted which aircraft that was the first to fly faster than the speed of sound? When?

15. What is the length and source of the Nile River?

EXERCISE 62 BIOGRAPHICAL SKETCHES

Let's assume that each of the following persons is speaking or performing in Fairfield, or in your community. For each one, write a succinct biographical summary (or write a complete news story, inserting your own details of when and where the public appearance will be). Be sure to include sources of information.

1. Charles Monroe Schulz, born 1922.
2. Jane Ellen Brody, born 1941.
3. Peter Victor Ueberroth, born 1937.

4. Dr. Robert K. Jarvik, born 1946.
5. Diane Sawyer, born 1945.

EXERCISE 63 NEWS FACTS

The following questions are drawn directly from newsroom experiences. Please provide the information requested, and cite your source(s).

1. What is the origin of the "Miranda Warning" used by police?

2. What was the first Negro college to open in the U.S.?

3. What is the birthdate of James Earl Carter, Jr., his wife's maiden name and the dates he served as governor of Georgia?

4. A news story refers to John Llewellyn Lewis. Who is or was he?

5. Which has the longest ocean (and gulf) shoreline: California, Florida, Alaska or Hawaii?

7. What was the date of Patricia Hearst's capture by the FBI? How long was she held by the Symbionese Liberation Army?

8. What was Patricia's grandfather, William Randolph Hearst, famous for?

9. List the names of all U.S. authors who have won the Nobel Prize for literature since 1901.

10. How many airplanes does Delta Air Lines operate? How about United?

11. What was Procter and Gamble's net sales figure for the latest year available?

12. What spot on earth has the highest average annual rainfall?

13. List the members of the Senate Foreign Relations Committee.

14. State the major economic support of the state of Kansas.

15. How much water is in Lake Michigan?

EXERCISE 64 TOPIC RESEARCH

By consulting various indexes, locate published articles and other research materials that would help you develop a national perspective on the following topics. Cite the names and dates of likely sources, and also cite the names of the indexes through which you located them.

1. Police abuse or brutality. Is it a problem only in Fairfield? What is happening in other parts of the country? Are other police officials in political hot water in their communities?

2. Let's say the high incidence of rape in Fairfield is to be the topic of a comprehensive article. What national material can you find to provide perspective?

3. An article is being prepared on a Carson College physics professor who is conducting experiments on solar energy. Find sources for background material that you can use in preparing for an interview with him.

4. A major article is being researched on the high cost of hospital care in Fairfield (or in your community). Locate sources of material that will bring a national perspective to your story.

5. One T. Boone Pickens Jr., born in 1928, will make an unannounced visit to Fairfield to inspect the Acme Manufacturing Company plant, according to reliable sources. Who is he, and why might citizens of Fairfield be concerned about such a visit?

EXERCISE 65 A VISITING CELEBRITY

It happens (we'll assume) that a Fairfield resident, Janis Jones, is a personal friend of film actress Farrah Fawcett. Janis's husband, Dan, teaches drama classes and directs plays at Carson College. Janis invited Farrah to visit her in Fairfield, and, to her surprise, Farrah accepted. She's scheduled to arrive tomorrow night, and Farrah will spend the following day in Fairfield visiting drama classes at Carson College. Write a story about this, but first go to the library to find background information about Farrah Fawcett. Here is some additional material from an interview with Janis Jones.

Q. Where did you know Farrah Fawcett?

A. At the University of Texas. We were in classes together.

Q. What was she like then?

A. I hate to admit this, but we girls used to tease her all the time. We made fun of her.

Q. Really? Why?

A. Oh, she was so damned cheerful and optimistic then when it was fashionable among college students to be dreadful cynics. She had that patently fresh-scrubbed look, like a dream vision out of the 1950s. That was a time when the unkempt look was very much in. And her clothes! There was hardly a time when she didn't parade around like a fashion model. This, mind you, was a time when the fashion was patched jeans and tattered sweatshirts—what we used to call "grubbies" or "scuzzies." So naturally we used to give her a lot of flak over that.

Q. How did she respond to all that flak?

A. Cheerfully! And with a big smile! Doesn't that beat all?

Chapter Nineteen

LEGAL RESTRAINTS

The exercises in this chapter will give you practice in dealing with potential legal dangers. The laws relating to mass communications are complex and rapidly changing. Libel is the area of most concern to reporters. The exercises in this chapter are based on the five chapters on media law in the back of the *AP Stylebook and Libel Manual*. Those chapters are the least a student should consult when considering matters of media law.

Libel is defined as defamation in writing: an untrue or unprivileged statement that tends to hold a person up to public contempt, ridicule, or hatred; or to injure a person's reputation; or to cause a person to be shunned or avoided; or to injure a person in business or professional pursuits.

Although it is not possible to present a complete discussion of the laws of libel in this chapter, there *are* some warning signs that should alert you to danger. The *AP Stylebook* says that most libel suits result not from big investigative reports, but from run-of-the-mill stories from police, the courts, public meetings and business activities. Perhaps 95 percent of those come from charges of crime, immorality, incompetence and inefficiency. Be cautious when you encounter the following:

1. Any accusation of criminal activity unless documented by police, court or other public records or said in or by a governmental agency protected by "privilege." (The proceedings of government agencies are protected by *absolute privilege*, which means libel suits cannot be brought against elected officials speaking in Congress, state legislatures, city councils, courts of law, executive pronouncements and so on. The media that report such matters are protected by *qualified privilege*, which means they cannot be sued for a reasonably accurate, balanced account of the proceedings).

2. Any loaded word or words tending to ridicule a person or accuse him or her of moral or legal wrongdoing: whore, nazi, racist, swindler, child molester, plagiarist and so on.

3. Any quotation of another person who makes an untrue or unprivileged accusation of wrongdoing. Quoting the other person does not absolve you of responsibility.

4. Any offhand, gossipy remark made in casual conversation, even if made by a public official. Thus a comment made by a member of the city council is privileged if made in the official proceeding of that body, but not privileged when made informally outside the council chambers.

5. Libelous remarks made in meetings *other* than official government agencies. Meetings of the Rotary Club or the National Association of Manufacturers are not privileged. News conferences are not privileged.

Defenses against libel suits are:

1. **Truth.** The statement must be *provably* true in court, however. It is not enough to prove that you accurately quoted someone saying it; the statement itself must be accurate. To report that Jane Doe was arrested and lodged in jail on a charge of armed robbery is provably true if you can produce the jail records and court documents that substantiate it. You must be careful with proper identifications, particularly when reporting police activities. This is why occupations, ages and addresses are essential. To report without further identification that "John Smith" was arrested for a crime could libel several John Smiths in the community.

2. **Privilege.** As noted, statements made in official proceedings of government agencies are not actionable for libel, and media are protected in reporting accurately a balanced account of such activities. Most government documents are privileged.

3. **Fair comment.** Criticism of works of art—books, play performances, architecture of public buildings,

paintings, concerts, movies, actors, exhibitors—is not libelous so long as it consists of comment and opinion and does not misstate the facts. The comment must be done "fairly and with an honest purpose," according to one judicial opinion.

4. **First Amendment defense: The New York Times Rule.** A landmark case decided by the Supreme Court in 1964 drew a classic distinction between public officials and private citizens, resulting in a kind of double standard of liability for libel. In *New York Times vs. Sullivan,* the court said that for a public official to collect damages, actual malice must be proved—malice defined as knowing the statement was false or acting with reckless disregard as to whether it was false or not. Private citizens, on the other hand, must prove only "negligence" in most states, meaning that the journalist had been careless with the facts. The First Amendment defense, then, is to show that in the case of public officials or "public figures" that no actual malice was present in the libel.

EXERCISE 66 EDITING FOR LIBEL

Assume that you are editing material written by other reporters and columnists. Which of these statements might be legally dangerous, and why? For each statement, suggest what action should be taken, if any, to minimize the legal danger. If no, or minimal, danger exists, explain why. When appropriate, rewrite the statement to minimize the danger. For reference, consult the libel chapters in the AP Stylebook *and* Libel Manual.

1. Sue Graham, 30ish, address unknown, was arrested by police Thursday and lodged in the Lincoln County Jail for being a prostitute.
2. William L. Dilley, 77, former coal miner, died this morning from an operation performed by Dr. Chesley Worthington.
3. Testifying in Circuit Court today, Linda McCormack identified the defendant, rapist Orville Dixon, as the man who attacked her and stole her purse.
4. Billy Joe Dofferman, 18, 555 Westway Ave., pleaded guilty today to negligent homicide in the death of Terrence L. Diamond. Circuit Judge Raphael Gutierrez sentenced him to four months in the state penitentiary.
5. "You're a menace on the streets and highways," Judge Gutierrez told Dofferman from the bench. "A stretch in the pen will give you time to learn that a high-performance automobile is not a toy."
6. In the City Council last night, Councilman Ken Wheelock accused Police Chief Hudson of "incompetence that borders on corruption."
7. Ernest Hudson raped a young girl one time years ago,

Kenneth Wheelock confided to a reporter Friday at lunch. "I know it happened," he said, "I just can't prove it."
8. The book "Liar" by George F. Hoyt is so hopelessly dull that this reviewer cannot in good conscience suggest that you buy it.
9. And it's small wonder Hoyt has written such a dull book, given his boozy affliction for the bottle!
10. County Commissioner Del Hudson says his opponent in the forthcoming election is unfit for office because "he's nothing but a petty thief." [Assume that you've checked the records and found three convictions on the opponent's record: one for shoplifting, two for petty larceny.]
11. There are some lousy teachers at Carson College, Rotarians were told today by the college's student body president, Ellie Chase.
12. The absolute worst teacher at Carson College, Ms. Chase continued, is Julia Nathan, who is "dull, slovenly and totally without knowledge about the subjects she teaches."
13. The Department of Community Health today closed

the Black Cat Tavern, 400 Detroit Ave., because of alleged unsanitary conditions.

14. The Fairfield chapter president of the Woman's Christian Temperance Union was arrested last night by Fairfield police on a charge of driving while under the influence of intoxicating liquor.

15. Charges against the WCTU president (item #14) were dismissed today. Police said her actions, which led officers to suspect influence of intoxicating liquor, were actually an adverse reaction to a prescription drug.

EXERCISE 67 RAPIST IN CUSTODY

Write a story for today's paper based on this information. Note that the paper's policy precludes publishing the names of victims of sex crimes.

From a police report: Orville Yancy Dixon arrested today at 10 a.m. at his place of employment, the Lincoln County Rock Quarry on McKinley Road. Suspect offered no resistance. Age 34. Address 4311 Enterprise Road, Fairfield. Held in Lincoln County Jail in lieu of $50,000 bail.

Charges from Grand Jury Indictment:

1. Rape. Victim: Allison Deanne McKenzie, age 16, 4030 Truman Ave.; Parents: Alice D. and Gordon M. McKenzie, same address.

2. Sodomy. Victim: Allison Deannne McKenzie, age 16.

3. Rape. Victim: Marjorie Ann Young, age 27, 600 Oak Avenue.

4. Sodomy. Victim: Marjorie Ann Young.

5. Assault with deadly weapon (knife). Victim: Marjorie Ann Young.

6. Aggravated assault. Victim: Linda Ann McCormack, age 17. Parents: Edward and Dorothy McCormack, 1196 Onyx Ave.

7. Attempted Robbery. Victim: Linda Ann McCormack.

Excerpt from interview with county jail guard, Alex Bierbaum:

Q. What can you tell me about this guy Dixon?

A. Well, they finally got that rat. And about time! He's the famous "Redbeard," the rapist. They're not through with him yet—I'll lay you odds that there's gonna be another fifteen or twenty charges against him yet. He's been terrorizing women around Pioneer Park for a year now, and he's just about the lowest kind of scum there is. I personally would be happy to bash his skull in. The women he raped all said he had this red beard, and nobody could figure out who he was because it didn't seem like there could be that many red-bearded cats around. Well, it turns out that it was a false beard, as one of the victims discovered when she yanked on it and it came off. I understand he's confessed everything. A lot of people are gonna sleep easier tonight with Orville Dixon in jail. Truly the scum of the earth!

EXERCISE 68 COURTROOM TESTIMONY

The newspaper is covering a murder trial in Circuit Court. Below is the essence of today's segment in which the defendant is being cross-examined by the district attorney. Write a story based on this material. Be sure to include background. In choosing what to include, apply your knowledge of the "privilege" concept.

Background. Tania W. Blanck is on trial, accused of first-degree murder in the death of a man alleged to be her lover. Today she is on the witness stand. This is the fifth day of the trial in Circuit Court with Judge Carl E. Wimberly on the bench. Blanck is 33. She is accused in the death of one Stanley J. Klutzmann, 27. His body was found at the bottom of an elevator shaft in Ms. Blanck's apartment house. Earlier testimony indicated that the state crime lab had found traces of blood matching Klutzmann's type in Blanck's apartment, had found drinking glasses with his fingerprints, had even found a gun in a ventilator shaft of her apartment that a crime lab expert said was the one that killed Klutzmann. A jury of seven women and five men is hearing the case. The district attorney is Victor Smith; defense attorney is Charles Stoneroad.

Q. *Miss Blanck, during direct examination this morning, you stated that you were home all evening last June 17, the night of the murder.*

A. Yes.

Q. *And that you had no callers.*

A. Yes.

Q. *Can you explain the traces of blood found in your apartment by the crime lab?*

A. No, sir, I sure can't.

Q. *How about the neighbors who testified that they heard a loud argument in your apartment that night?*

A. I think it must have been the TV.

Q. *And the two shots they said they heard?*

A. The TV again. Or maybe backfires from cars on the street.

Q. *The gun in the ventilator shaft?*

A. It wasn't mine. I sure don't know anything about it.

Q. *Miss Blanck, did you greet Mr. Stanley Klutzmann at the door of your apartment the evening of June 17 with a gun in your hand?*

A. No, sir.

Q. *And you did take that gun and shoot Mr. Klutzmann twice in the chest?*

A. No, sir. But I'll tell you this—if someone did shoot him, it was justified. He was an animal.

Q. *An animal?*

A. Yeah.

Q. *Ah, what kind of an animal.*

A. A rat, I'd say.

Q. *A rat?*

A. Yeah, the worst kind of rat. A married rat. He had a wife. He lied to me. He deserved to die.

Q. *And so you took a gun and—*

A. No, sir. I was merely expressing an opinion.

Q. *Miss Blanck, one final question. Is it true—and remember you're under oath—is it true that you worked as a call girl in Las Vegas?*

A. What a dirty, rotten thing to ask—

Q. *[Stoneroad, defense attorney]: Objection! The question is not relevant.*

A. [Court]: Mr. Stoneroad, I'm going to allow the question because the character of the defendant was made a point by the defense in direct examination earlier.

Q. *So what is your answer, Miss Blanck?*

A. It's not true—well, it's sorta true, I mean, I was an actress in Las Vegas, and, yeah, it's sorta true.

In the courtroom during recess, you chance to talk informally with Ms. Blanck for a moment. The following dialogue takes place:

Q. *Ms. Blanck, can you tell me how you feel the trial is progressing so far for you? Are you winning or losing?*

A. I'm not talking to nobody—and if you put that Las Vegas stuff into the paper you'll get your neck in a ringer so fast it'll make your head swim. I'll sue! Besides, the district attorney is a rat asking those kinds of questions—he's a wife beater—a child molester—why, he was even one of my regular johns in Las Vegas! Just ask him!

EXERCISE 69 HIGH SCHOOL DEMONSTRATION

Ellery Quick, 17, is student body president and yearbook editor at South High School. This morning there is a demonstration in front of the school involving about twenty students, many of them carrying placards such as these:

BRIAN JAMES IS A CROOK!
B.J. STEALS FROM STUDENTS
EMBEZZLER!
HEY, B.J., YOU OWE US $100!
THIEF! THIEF! THIEF!
BRIAN JAMES STEALS CANDY FROM BABIES!

On the scene you encounter Ellery Quick and conduct a sidewalk interview.

Q. What's going on?

A. We're showing Brian James our lack of support.

Q. Who's Brian James? And how come you're not supporting him?

A. Brian James is the principal. A week ago we had a food fight in the cafeteria—no big deal, just some of the guys pulling the exuberance number. So anyway Big Daddy Brian wants to know who started it, and nobody will tell him. So he says he's gonna take $100 out of the student body fund to pay for the damage! That crook! I think he must steal from church collection plates! So he goes, "You guys had better come clean and confess if you want your $100 back." So we're not gonna quit picketing until Big Daddy Brian coughs up the hundred!

Next you discuss the matter with Brian James:

Q. Mr. James, what are the facts in the situation?

A. This much is true—I did in fact remove $100 from the student body funds. These are funds collected from student body cards sold at the beginning of the school year. This is a penalty levied against the student body for infraction of rules clearly stated in the student handbook given to each student in the fall. The rules clearly state that students who cause damage to school property shall be responsible for making monetary restitution for the damage caused thereby. And because the student body officers, who know full well who are the perpetrators of this damage, refuse to identify the culprits, I am left with no choice but to levy the damage against the general student body fund. The money was used to pay for overtime janitorial services and for breakage of equipment. The bill came to $104.89, but I was willing to settle for an even hundred. This is a legal right vested in the principal, and I do feel the signs outside are a tad extreme in their rhetoric. Above all I am determined that no taxpayer funds be used to pay for wanton damage caused by students, and tax funds would have been the only other source of reimbursement for damages.

EXERCISE 70 FLYERS

Write a news story about an incident that occurred just prior to Saturday's big football game at Carson College.

Background. One of the paper's sports writers says a group of scraggly looking young men who identified themselves as members of the Revolutionary Student Brigade was standing on the sidewalk in front of the stadium handling out leaflets. The occasion was the game with archrival Ponderosa College, a small liberal arts school at nearby River City. One of the fans, upon reading a leaflet, turned and swung at one of the young men with her umbrella. He ducked and she missed. Otherwise the scene was peaceful, except for occasional shouts by fans at the young men. A police officer, Bob Graham, was on the scene, but took no action. Carson College won the game, 14–7. Holloway has been coach at Carson for three years, during which time his teams have won 13 games (including Saturday's game), lost 14 and tied 1. As fans left the stadium the young men were nowhere in sight. (See copy of flyer on page 126.)

By phone you interview participants for a story in the Sunday paper (assume the game was played on Saturday). Below is the essence of their answers.

A. [Coach Holloway]: No comment! I wouldn't dignify that bunch of dirty, smelly, rotten hippie types with any kind of reply. No way!

A. [Sue Thompson, chairwoman of Carson's Board of Trustees]: This is an outrage! I wouldn't dream of firing Chuck Holloway, but Clark Mansfield is going to have a lot of explaining to do. Those students should have been jailed immediately! Why weren't the police called? I can tell you I was shocked and dismayed by the absence of a firm stand on the part of the police and the college administration, and

I'll be calling a special meeting of the board within the week. It's just scandalous what's going on at the college anymore.

A. [Clark Mansfield, president]: It is a libelous and despicable flyer, no doubt about it. And there is not a word of truth in any of the accusations against Coach Holloway. Our coach is as fine a citizen as ever we could wish for. I am advised by legal counsel, however, that the students involved—if indeed they *were* students—were acting within the law so far as any criminal prosecution is concerned. We

FIRE CHUCK HOLLOWAY!!!

NICE GAME, COACH..

"THE THRILL OF VICTORY..."

Charles Holloway has been coach of football at Carson for three years. Without doubt the worst coach in the history of this institution!!! It isn't just that he's a LOUSY COACH who can't coach his way out of a paper bag!!! It is that he is dishonest with players, he fixes games, and he makes deals with his players to keep the point spread within certain limits in order to benefit through his gambling activities. EVERYBODY KNOWS THAT HE'S A GAMBLER!!! Even now he's at least $30,000 in debt in his consortium with ORGANIZED CRIME!!! (Why do you think his wife is working???) These are just a few of the reasons why we, members of the Revolutionary Student Brigade, urge all football fans to rid Fairfield and Carson College of scum like coach Holloway. It wouldn't be so bad having a dishonest coach around if he won games, but his record is lousy!!! Besides, most people don't know the REAL coach Holloway. He's a closet GAY!!!! Bet you didn't know that, eh? Do you want young boys left in the charge of a man who is a dishonest homosexual? Think about it!!! We urge the trustees to act now. FIRE COACH HOLLOWAY!! Let's replace this sickie with a real man.

/s/ Revolutionary Student Brigade

are advised that the sidewalk in front of the stadium is public property and that their activity on public property is entirely legal. Had they entered the stadium itself we could have removed them on the basis of trespass. We'll be consulting with our attorneys Monday to see if any civil action is feasible on the basis of the libelous flyers. Carson College, I must say, has always been in the forefront of liberal arts colleges in our encouragement of free and robust debate on the issues of the day, but these filthy little innuendoes go far beyond the confines of free and robust debate. Even so, if I may borrow a little

from Thomas Jefferson, I feel that the Carson student body takes no credence in these libelous comments, and reason may yet prevail to combat error.

A. [Officer Graham]: The students were within the law. City Ordinance 178–3, subsection A, allows such demonstrations without city permit so long as they occur on public property and contain fewer than ten persons. I observed the scene throughout the time they were present and there was no violation of the law.

EXERCISE 71 OFF-THE-RECORD COMMENTARY

Write a story based on the following interviews.

Background. "Off the record" is not a legal concept. It is a device used by public officials to relate information to reporters that might help the reporter with the

story but which is not to be published. Another term often used by officials is "not for attribution," which means the material can be used but should not be attributed to the source by name. Another term with similar meaning is "on background." Such requests are negotiable, however; a reporter is not bound by them legally, though one who violates a confidence may lose a source. Write a story based on this exercise, honoring the various requests for anonymity or "off the record." Let's assume that you have explained to various sources that you are trying to pull together a story that explains the political dimensions of the police controversy. In the first, Jon Marx has agreed to talk with you but has put some restrictions on how his comments may be used.

A. [Marx] What I tell you has to be in the strictest of confidence, purely off the record. I hope it will help in directing your future inquiries. I'd be in a lot of hot water if my name got used. So are you agreeable to going off the record?

Q. *Yes.*

A. My theory is—and it's only a theory—that Hudson's problems can be traced to conditions existing before he got here. I was ready to quit the force when Hudson came in five years ago. He started making changes for the better. I was astonished. When I first came here, every officer above lieutenant had what we used to call a "hook." Have you ever heard that term?

Q. *No. Tell me.*

A. It means he got his promotion largely through politics. You're an ambitious cop, so you do some favors for a politician. He puts in a good word for you with the chief. Promote my boy to captain, says the hook, and I'll help you get the police budget through city hall. It's as simple as that. There was nothing formal about it, and the chief didn't *have* to promote that man, and if he didn't, well, maybe he'd get away without political repercussions, maybe he wouldn't. If he had a good reason for not promoting, maybe he could negotiate. But turn down the politician too many times and you're going to get in hot water sooner or later.

Q. *Sounds cozy.*

A. Until Hudson came. He transferred some of the political appointments to unimportant jobs. He demoted others. He eased some out through early retirement. He put a lot of civilians in jobs formerly held by officers. That was a splendid idea because civilians tend to operate independent from the police hierarchy, and so they perform more effectively.

Q. *So how does Wheelock figure in?*

A. Ken Wheelock couldn't quite cope. Wheelock was a powerful political figure until Hudson came. He was never a hook so far as I could tell—he was above all that. But he had certain cronies in the department that he stood behind, and when Hudson started pushing some of them around, demoting them and all, Wheelock began to fight back. Now this is just a theory, mind you, not for publication. I can't prove a thing.

Eleanor McPherson, member of the Fairfield City Council:

A. What you're seeing is power politics played in a grand and classic manner. It truly puts one in awe. It's a fascinating study, really. As chair of the Police Committee for eleven years, Ken Wheelock wields great power in police matters. At least he used to, before Hudson arrived. Along comes Ernie Hudson, riding tall like Marshal Dillon, only he has a master's in criminology and big-city experience and all kinds of new ideas about how a police department should be run. Such a grand confrontation we're now seeing, something worthy of a great playwright, maybe even a contemporary Shakespeare! Ernie has slowly undermined Ken's political dynasty, and what we are now seeing is the final denouement in this grand conflict.

Eleanor Beatty, member of the City Council, member of the Police Committee:

A. Ken Wheelock and I have opposed the fascist tendencies of the present chief of police. You just cannot talk to that man. There is no communication. We are locked in a test to see whether we are going to have civilian control of the department or police fascism.

Mayor Dmytryshyn:

A. Until Ernie came, our police chief was Ken Wheelock. Hudson's predecessor [the late Elmer Gann, who died in office six years ago at age 67 after twenty-seven years as chief of police] was totally ineffectual his last ten years. Don't quote this, but Gann's funeral was the best I ever attended. It meant that certain roadblocks had been removed in the way of a more efficient police force. We specifically hired Ernie Hudson to do some house cleaning, and that's what he's done. But the process upsets so many people and encroaches on so many political enclaves that it's only natural that Ernie would run out of goodwill after five years.

He's stepped on too many toes. He's accomplished a lot, but I don't know if we can keep him here. It's a problem by no means confined to Fairfield.

Q.   What about political hooks where politicians would back cops for promotion?

A.   I think it's accurate to say that, before Hudson, politics did intrude on the police department. After Hudson, no. Good Lord, no! Hudson was so straight-arrow from the start that he actually became pretty heavy handed. He would tolerate no deviance from departmental honesty.

Q.   What about police corruption? Were there cops on the take?

A.   Not to my personal knowledge.

Q.   Were cops fixing tickets?

A.   I confess that when I used to get parking tickets, I just sent them to Elmer Gann, and that was the last I heard of them. I'd never do that with Hudson. I don't want to go to jail. Ken Wheelock did that once, so I hear, and got burned.

Q.   How so?

A.   Ernie shot back a letter saying Ken had obviously misdirected the citation, which should be handled in Municipal Court.

Q.   You actually saw such a letter?

A.   Several of them. And not just to Ken. I remember Ken's more vividly because he was so incensed. He fumed for a week. People used to come to me to complain, but I always backed Hudson.

Ernest Hudson:

A.   Let me take you off the record to explain why I can't comment just now. I have a little political debate going that will take some finesse. I don't ob-

ject to your writing about the situation, but it should be clear that you're doing so on your own initiative and not at my instigation and not with my overt cooperation. Some time in the future, perhaps when I decide to retire from office, we can talk.

Q.   Could I ask one clarifying question—on the record?

A.   You can try.

Q.   Did people send you tickets to be fixed when you became chief?

A.   There were a few instances where traffic citations appeared to have been misdirected to my office. I don't know whether this was intentional or not. Sometimes people get confused about which office does what in a bureaucracy as big as city hall.

Q.   What did you do with them?

A.   We devised a form letter, a polite little missive that suggested that this citation somehow got misdirected to the wrong office, and would they kindly take care of it in Municipal Court, Room 459 in City Hall.

Kenneth Wheelock:

A.   Seems to me this business has been sensationalized and blown all out of proportion. I would have nothing further to say.

Q.   May I ask if you ever sent a traffic or parking ticket to former Chief Elmer Gann to be taken care of?

A.   No, of course not!

Q.   Did you ever send one to Hudson to be taken care of?

A.   I'll not be answering those kinds of questions. This interview is terminated. [Hangs up.]

Chapter Twenty

ENDINGS

Reporters find that newsmakers often weave in and out of their professional lives. Some hang around for weeks, months, even years, while others enter fleetingly and are never heard from again. Some have jobs—public officials, for example—that keep them in the public eye. Others merely enjoy the notoriety and seem to insert themselves into the media's field of vision when they can. A few seem to emerge in the news for no apparent reason other than fate thrusting them into public notice whether they wanted it or not.

So it is with some of the characters in this book. Some of those keeping us company through the preceding chapters—Ken Wheelock, Ernest Hudson, Linda McCormack, to name a few—have served us well in simulating real-life situations. Though any exercise book must by necessity be reduced to essentials, the characters nonetheless serve to suggest that news is often an ongoing series of events, with a history and quite possibly a future that bears watching.

To suggest that these stories have an ending, much as a novel has an ending, may seem artificial at first glance. Professionals know, however, that an alert reportorial vision and sensitivity will often produce occasions when an old story logically ends. A popular feature in many newspapers and magazines is the "whatever happened to _____ ?" approach, which contains high reader inter-

est. Interviews conducted weeks, months, even years later can provide splendid endings to stories that, in the haste of daily reporting, never quite get resolved.

A fiction writer dealing with such characters as Hudson and McCormack would seek a touch of irony, perhaps, in the final scene, along with a resolution of conflict and perhaps a new beginning in some new direction, the "Tomorrow Is Another Day" approach. Real life endings sometimes match those elements. Or they can be more variable, ironic, surprising, suspenseful, lustful, or violent than most fiction writers could imagine—the truth-is-stranger-than-fiction syndrome. They can also be duller, more routine, more corny, more predictable than any imagined by a fiction writer.

The most important point to be made here, however, is that reporters should look for an end of the story whenever possible.

That means finding a point where a sequence of events logically reaches a conclusion, a resolution of conflict or a departure in some new direction. Sometimes it means reviewing the entire series of events to see what can be learned from it. Often an ultimate lesson emerges from such events as the conflict over the police chief. Perhaps the reporter sees it, or at least sees the need for asking the questions that will yield the deeper meanings possible through such journalistic reviews.

Sometimes reporters get so involved with the day-to-day fragments of a story that they lose track of their overall context and therefore their deeper significance. To cite an example, an astonishing number of triumphs and tragedies have focused on one character, the high school swimming star, Linda McCormack. If she is human (and her character is based on real people), she cannot help but react to and learn from the events that have occurred. So even in her youthful perception, lessons may be learned that are useful to other people. A reporter treating the whole story of Linda—through all the high and low points—may be able to impart an educational or inspirational message to the readers that goes beyond the mere recounting of events.

The ability to do so, however, attaches to the most sensitive, perceptive and curious of reporters. It takes a certain kind of perception—or ''vision'' as fiction writers often call it—to see the significance of events. It comes with experience and maturity. It is never easy, but it is worth considering, even at this early stage of your journalistic career. It comes to those who are lifelong students of the human condition. It comes to those who learn and grow from each experience. To some, of course, it may never come at all.

It comes most easily to the curious, learning, growing kind of reporter. This could be one of those crossroads decisions referred to in Chapter 15, the personality feature. If you want to be that growing kind of reporter, this is a place to start.

This book has given lists of tips for accomplishing certain ends. Perhaps only one tip is required here: Strive, whenever possible, to present events in narrative form, bringing in as much background as necessary, so that you are presenting essentially a case history that has a significant point to make. In some cases the point should be noted early in the story. Sometimes it comes at the end. Sometimes it's so dramatically obvious that it need not be specified at all.

EXERCISE 72 VANDENBOSCH

See if, in the story here, you can focus, in part, on the character of the late Mr. VanDenBosch. Assume that his death occurred one year ago.

In accord with several provisions of the will of the late Mayor Ivan R. VanDenBosch, three boys and three girls were assembled to discuss the future of Huck Finn Island.

Debbie Tippets, 9, 213 W. 6th (Parents: John and Beth Tippets).

Edie O'Connor, 9, 990 Eisenhower (Edith O'Connor).

Katie Christensen, 10, 1676 Lincoln (Anne and Stan Christensen).

Johnny Petruzzelli, 11, 2417 Agate (Dom and Helen Petruzzelli).

Kenny DeHaviland, 11, 1809 W. 34th (Walt and Maggie DeHaviland).

Daryle Dion, 11, 1889 Onyx (Jack and Irene Dion).

After two hours of discussion, the kids concluded that the following should be added to the island.

1. A pile of driftwood hauled in from Pacific Ocean beaches.
2. An old truck body or boat hull.
3. A pile of old lumber and blocks of wood.
4. A large pile of sand.
5. Lots of newly planted trees.

Here is a fragment of an interview with Scott Steubing, director of parks and recreation.

Q. So is that it? Is that what you're going to do?

A. Yes, indeed. That's what we intend to put out there. I think old man VanDenBosch would be delighted. It's just what he had in mind when he wrote that oddball provision in his will.

Q. Were there any other suggestions that didn't make the final list?

A. Some of the kids didn't want to put anything there at all. They liked it fine just the way it is. It almost came to a point where we were going to have to accept that notion, because our lawyers kept saying we couldn't do it—we couldn't take all that driftwood and stuff out there. There was too severe a liability problem. They were afraid kids would drown trying to get to the island. So finally we decided to build a footbridge to the island—and that's when the lawyers stopped dragging their feet on Van's project.

Q. *You're going to haul driftwood all the way from the west coast?*

A. Right. I know a beach on the Oregon coast just full of contorted bits of driftwood.

Q. *How soon will the island be ready with all the new developments?*

A. In about six weeks.

EXERCISE 73 WHEELOCK

Under the laws of Anystate, public bodies may meet in "executive session" (closed to the public and news media) when discussing personnel matters, such as the hiring and firing of appointed officials. The Fairfield City Council discussed the performance of Police Chief Hudson for two hours last night in executive session. They emerged to report that the council had unanimously endorsed the performance of Hudson as chief of police. Councilman Kenneth Wheelock then read a statement to the council and the public. Write a story that sums up the long-standing police controversy.

This is a statement on behalf of myself and Mrs. Beatty. It does not necessarily represent the views of the third member of the Police Committee, Mr. Hixon. It appears that this Police Committee is in a distinct minority with regard to Mr. Hudson. We do not believe that the community will benefit from further discord between the committee and the Police Department. Accordingly, we wish to make two announcements: (1) We withdraw our request for the resignation of Mr. Hudson, and we wish him continued success, and (2) we, councilpersons Wheelock and Beatty, herewith offer our resignations from the Police Committee, effective immediately.

It is apparent to us now that we ourselves are partly responsible for the disharmony with the Police Department. Although we have not substantially changed our minds, we now concede that the management problems in the department are far more complex than we had imagined. We apologize to Chief Hudson for any anxiety our actions may have caused him or his family. We thought we were acting in the best interests of the community. We now concede that we acted unwisely.

Kenneth J. Wheelock
Eleanor J. Beatty

Additional Information. Mayor Dmytryshyn appoints councilpersons McPherson and Johnson to the Police Committee and appoints Hixon its chairman. The council also approves that portion of the Police Committee's Resolution that called for appointment of a civilian review board. The vote was 7–0 in favor. Details to be worked out by the Police Committee. Council discussion includes this comment from Hudson:

Hudson. I want to thank all those who supported me through these past months, and I particularly want to thank Ms. Beatty and Mr. Wheelock for their courage in making their public announcement. I know that was not an easy moment for them. Your apologies are accepted. I bear no one ill will.

EXERCISE 74 GRAY

Localize this wire story, drawing in background as needed.

BY SALLY CHESTER

VALLEY CITY (AP)—Miss Valley City was chosen as the new Miss Anystate Saturday night by the judges at the Miss Anystate Pageant.

She is 21-year-old Barbara Kretsinger of Valley City. The 5-foot-7, 118-pound, blonde, blue-eyed beauty won the evening gown competition Friday night and placed in two other events—third in talent and second in swimsuits. Kretsinger is a broadcasting student at Valley City Community College and also works part time for a local television station.

First through fourth runners-up in order, are Jeanne Gray, 22, Miss Fairfield; Rachel Lantyern, 19, Miss Middleton; Deborah Lynn, 20, Miss River City; and Betsy Ann Yamata, 23, Miss Sussix County.

Elected Miss Congeniality by the contestants was Jeanne Gray, Miss Fairfield.

Winners of the four events were: evening gown, Barbara Kretsinger; talent, Rachel Lantyern; interview, Deborah Lynn; and swimsuit, Jeanne Gray.

Part of a telephone interview with Jeanne Gray following the pageant:

Q. *Hi, this is Fred Scott from the* Telegram. *I hear you won the swimsuit event. Congratulations!*

A. Isn't that a kick? All this time I thought I was too skinny. They tell me that skinny is *in* this year. In-stead of giving you points for how much you got, they give you points for how little.

Q. *How do you feel about coming in second?*

A. Great! I mean it! I expected to be 18th out of 18.

Q. *And how about being elected Miss Congeniality? I thought you said women hated you!*

A. Not this bunch! They're a great bunch of girls! I think it's because we're *all* universally hated that we got along so well.

Q. *Did you blow it on the interview? You said earlier you might.*

A. I was my usual smart-alecky self and I think the judges thought I was being obnoxious. They were right.

Q. *So what was your overall impression of the experience?*

A. I *loved* every minute! But I wouldn't do it again. What I *really* loved was meeting Barb Kretsinger. She's into television and imagines herself as an anchorwoman some day. She and the rest of the pageant experience may have changed my life. I get a $4,000 scholarship as the first runner-up. I'm thinking of going back to school for a master's in telecommunications. Don't laugh! *Somebody's* got to replace Barbara Walters!

EXERCISE 75 MCCORMACK

Let's assume that it has been nine months since the accident that caused death to Terrence Diamond and disfiguring injuries to Linda McCormack, the high school athlete. Susan C. Graham, Linda's attorney, has accepted a "generous" out-of-court settlement (amount undisclosed) from the insurance company in the personal injury claim against Billy Joe Dofferman. Here are the major points of Barbara Miller's interview with her. Write a story based on this information plus any background you may care to include. The information lends itself to a narrative kind of treatment, like a case history with touches of homespun philosophy.

Q. *You'll be finishing high school at the end of this school year—what do you plan to do now?*

A. College—I definitely will go to college, but I don't know where yet. I lost all my athletic scholarship possibilities.

Q. *What do you plan to study?*

A. Medicine, maybe. I could do that. My dad says I'd be good at that. Maybe I could get into emergency medicine—I could be a doctor or an emergency technician. My dad says I should try that—you should listen to your father, even if you don't agree. It's crazy, you know? Dad and I have had a thousand discussions in the last few months.

Q. *About what?*

A. Everything. About swimming. About putting your life back together after it's been shredded to pieces by things you can't do anything about. About working your way out of dark rooms or dungeons or—

Q. *Dark rooms?*

A. It's all kind of silly. . .

Q. *It actually sounds interesting—about the dark rooms, I mean, and how one works her way out.*

A. Okay, it's like every person lives in a dark room. You're born there, I guess. Your whole life—everybody's life— is a search for light. Doors swing open for you, depending on your skills and intelligence and how hard you work. You know? Like me, I can swim pretty good—or I could once—and so there's a door that's open with light streaming in and so your life goes in that direction. Is this making sense?

Q. *Yes.*

A. But then the door slams shut. You can't swim anymore. It's inky black and you're doomed and you spend your time feeling sorry for yourself. You have plenty of help—people holding doors for you or wanting to help you down the stairs. So, all right, there's a stairway in this dark room and it's possible to fall down. Also a few trapdoors and landmines. But if you just open your eyes! Other doors are there, slightly open, a crack of light coming through. You don't see them at first but only because you're so wrapped up in your own misery. If you ever get out of your misery—that's the secret—I mean, get out of your self-concern for a moment and peek through some of those other doors and—Wow!—you might be surprised by what you see. Whole new horizons open up! I'm sure this makes no sense at all—it's just how I feel.

Q. *I think it makes great sense.*

A. It's just that for the first time in my life I've had to rely on my head instead of my body. I'm finding powers and resources I didn't know I had. I have a tiny scar on my face from the accident. So, okay, I won't try to be a fashion model. The doctors say I'll always have a slight limp. So, okay, I won't try to play basketball. But I can still swim—maybe not in competition but I can do all right.

Q. *You sound like you've given all this some serious thought.*

A. I know, I know. It sounds awful. I've been thinking a lot of things I've never really put into words before. I do a lot of thinking now—and a lot of reading over the past few months. Maybe I grew up a little. I even read *Moby-Dick*. You know who I sound like?

Q. *Who?*

A. Terry. Terry Diamond. God, how I miss him! What people don't know about Terry is that he was crippled as a child, and people said he'd never be like a normal child—that he'd always be kind of sickly. Well, it made him mad. Really mad. So he fought his way out of that hole, that dark room, and he became a football player.

Q. *You seem almost to be saying the accident has changed your life—maybe even for the better. Maybe not. What do you think?*

A. For the better! Can you believe that? Everything has to change, has to grow. People have to change, have to grow up. That's the way it has to be unless you're just gonna stagnate. But if nothing happens to you, there's no reason to change, to grow. You know? And the thing that brings about the change always seems at first like the worst possible disaster. Does that make any sense? It's like dark clouds have silver linings. What a lousy cliche! I'm sorry—I'm really sorry you couldn't have gotten a better interview. Maybe some other time I'll have something to say. . . By the way, tomorrow's my eighteenth birthday!

EXERCISE 76 HUDSON

Perhaps there are two stories in this exercise, one a spot news story, the other a more analytical feature.

CITY OF FAIRFIELD

Police Department
Chief of Police

To: Honorable Mayor and City Council

Please accept my resignation as your Chief of Police, effective June 30. I have accepted a position with San Francisco State University as associate professor of criminology. I look forward to establishing a new career in the academic world. It has been a pleasure to be of service to the City of Fairfield.

Sincerely yours,

Ernest J. Hudson, Chief of Police

Q. Wow, chief, this was kind of unexpected!

A. No chief of police should stay on the job forever. People should change jobs or spouses every five or seven years. And since I'm pretty fond of the woman I married seventeen years ago, it had to be the job. Around the country, police chiefs are falling like leaves in a whirlpool. In the past year or so I can name you a dozen chiefs who have been fired or quit under cloudy conditions. After five years a public servant begins to break his oar hacking away at the problems. It's like having a bank account of brownie points of goodwill. You make an unpopular decision or arrest the wrong person or oppose the wrong pressure group or enforce the law *equally*—and you start to draw down that account. Pretty soon there's nothing left but bleached bones.

Q. Why teaching?

A. It appeals to me. There's a lot of personal freedom on a college campus, assuming you can avoid serving on committees. You don't get caught up in petty political hassles, unless you happen to enjoy that kind of thing. And I think you can accomplish things beyond your immediate area. I used to be a police training officer. Training is the one area where you can make changes without a lot of money. You can tighten up operating procedures, you can rewrite the manuals, you can make sure nobody goes out on the street without proper preparation. I've written lots of manuals, and some of my ideas are now standard operating procedure in departments all over the country. Now I may write a book.

Q. What on?

A. Police training. It's a scandal in most departments. Do you know that in this state, a beauty operator has to get 1,000 hours of training before she can get a license? But a cop has to get only 250 hours. And that cop is making life-and-death decisions every day. He has to react with split-second precision. His life may depend on it. My first week as training officer I rewrote the manual on hot pursuit. Until then we'd had more officers hurt in car wrecks than in all the street fights and shootouts put together.

Q. What do you think you've accomplished here in Fairfield?

A. The improvement I'm most pleased with is response time. That means how long it takes an officer to respond to an emergency call. When I became chief it was seven minutes. Now it's down to three on the average. We made computer studies on where emergencies were most likely to occur, and when, and we had patrols in those areas ready to go into action quickly. Sometimes we can get to an emergency scene in less than ninety seconds.

Q. Do you feel you were forced out by the Police Committee?

A. Not at all. I had the offer from San Francisco over a year ago. I was about to accept until they started picking on the department. If Ken Wheelock and his crowd had kept their mouths shut, they'd have been rid of me a year earlier. I decided that for the sake of the department and the next chief, I had to stick around and see this one through. If Wheelock had won, the Police Department would have been set back to the Dark Ages. We'd have had to buy a torture chamber and build a dungeon. It was a fight we *had* to win.

Q. You put up a good fight.

A. If you have to fight, it's nice to do so aloof from it

all emotionally. My career wasn't really on the line. When you're not emotionally involved your mind is clear and you can be devastatingly effective. The outcome of the fight was never in doubt. I knew we'd win. That's because we had gained public support and acceptance. We eliminated problems, eliminated political interference. We retired a lot of tired, old cops and replaced them with fresh, crisp, courteous young men and women. We tried to deal fairly with everyone, even the media. I think we made some friends.

Q. How do you want to be remembered?

A. Probably as the cop with the corny metaphors. I didn't talk that way when I first came here. Then I met old VanDenBosch. Remember his famous line—we're gonna pave Easy Street and then we'll all lie in clover? I used to tease him about that. But then pretty soon I was talking that way myself. It got to be a habit. It just attached itself to my personality, like barnacles in a rainbarrel.

Appendix A

COPY EDITING
AND STYLE

Newspapers are in the process of rapid technological change so far as the handling of "copy" is concerned. (In newspaper parlance, *copy* means any material written for publication.) Where newspapers once produced copy typewritten on paper, most newspapers today use electronic copy-processing methods. For the reporter this means typing a story on a video display terminal, which is a computer-linked electric typewriter. Your words don't show up on paper; they appear as images on a television screen.

The purpose of these changes is to produce the paper faster and more efficiently. Instead of giving the typed copy to a typesetter, who would merely rekeyboard what the reporter has already written, today's copy-processing methods set photographic type via computer. And they do so using the original keystrokes of the reporter.

In view of this, is there still a need for journalism students to learn the traditional copy editing symbols for working with paper copy?

The answer is yes. In the first place, much material written for publication (books, magazine articles, brochures, advertising copy, catalogs, and many newspapers) is still being written on paper. Second, a need still exists in most journalism classes for student-teacher communication on paper.

Chart of Copyediting Symbols

Symbol	Purpose	Example
≡	Capitalize letter	He lives in phoenix, ariz.
/	Use lower case	What's His Address?
⊙	Add period	She lives in Boston

(continued on next page)

Symbol	Purpose	Example
⬭	Abbreviate or spell out	She moved from Logan, UT, to Phoenix, Arizona.
⬭	Use number or spell out	He owns twenty-six airplanes. She suffered 5 years of pain.
|	Separate words	He left for New Mexico
⌒	Close up extra space	It's a 12 per cent increase.
⌒ (with line)	Delete letter & close up	The citty has personnel problems.
∿	Transpose letters	The emmo was raedy yestreday
⌣ (with P)	Insert letter	The mayr resined today.
⌃	Insert comma	So he said this is the end
⌣ (with =)	Insert hyphen	A 5 year old child won the race.
/—/	Insert dash	He gave her a stone.
∨∨	Insert quote marks	Help, help! she screamed.
L	Start new paragraph	She got on the bus. He went home.
⌢	Delete words and close up	He is a very handsome man.
⌣	Insert word(s)	She is a superb runner.
⊐ ⊏	Center words	⊐ By Charlie Gibson ⊏
⊏	Flush left	⊏Work started today.
⊐	Flush right	History⊐
No ¶	No paragraph	It was cold today. It will be colder tomorrow.
⌐_⌐	Transpose words	The house that built Jack.
‥‥ Stet	Ignore correction; let the original stand	Police went on strike today. Stet
———	Set italic	Continued on p. 12
∿∿∿	Set in bold face	By Jane Clevinger
=	Set in (caps and) small caps	By Jim Brothers
o̅ m̅ n̅	Overscore the letters o, m, and n in handwritten copy to distinguish them from a, w, and u respectively	Conference
a̲ w̲ u̲	Underscore the letters a, w, and u to distinguish them from o, m, and n in handwritten copy.	Walkup

Symbol	Purpose	Example
	Set type flush left and ragged right	John Smith, on the far left in the above photo, named Fairfield City manager by the council last night. (Staff Photo.)
-30- or #	End of story	

EXERCISE 77 USING COPY-EDITING SYMBOLS

Using the proper copy-editing symbols, make the requested changes. Follow AP-UPI style.

1. Capitalize the appropriate letters: new york, chicago, denver.

2. Insert quotation marks where needed: The novelist said, My writing has been influenced profoundly by many of Truman Capote's works, particularly his nonfiction novel, In Cold Blood.

3. Delete the extra letters and close up: Paciffic, Atlaantic, South Chiana Seea, Pollar Cap, Floraida, Gullf Coast.

4. Transpose letters as needed: liesure, beleive, releive, pageant, vengaence, cieling.

5. Lowercase the Words That should Not be capitalized.

6. Add a comma: Medford Mass.

7. Add a period

8. Insert lettrs where they are neded.

9. Center this line:

    By Joseph Cone

10. Make this line all capital letters.

11. Italicize this line.

12. Make this line bold face.

13. Make this line bold face and italic.

14. Transpose words: To be not or to be. The banner star-spangled.

15. Insert hyphens where needed: transAmerica, 5 year old child, good looking boy.

16. Center this byline, caps and small caps:

    By Richard Smith

17. Insert commas: "Oh boy" he said "this is a tough game.

18. Separate the words: Those were hardtimes back inthe30s.

19. Transpose the letters: Sacramneto, Chciago, Bffualo.

20. Insert apostrophes: a ladys purse, a boys bike, the childrens toys.

21. Write the word "omniverous" and overscore and underscore the appropriate letters.

22. Make this set

    of lines flush

    right and ragged

    left.

23. Substitute dashes for commas: She ran fast, and how!, to win.

24. Spell out: Ala., Penn., and Wash.

25. Use numerals: twenty-six, thirty-four, and fifty-nine.

EXERCISE 78 COPY EDITING

Using the appropriate copy-editing symbols, correct teh misspellings and typographical errors in this story. Please follow the [interjected] instructions as they appear.

By Barbara Miller [caps and small caps, centered]

Staff Writer [italics, centered]

Fairfield [paragraph indent] should do away with diagonal parking on First [close up] St. [spell out] and impliment parallel parking instead.

That was the recomendation of the Police Committee to the Common Council of the City of Fairfield Thursday night. [Make it read: Fairfield City Council.]

Counselman Ken Wheelock cited two safety prloblems with diaganal parking— banged car doors and danger in backing out into the street—in his recomendation to the council. [Delete last three words.]

"I feel any times theres a safety factor involved people shouldn't drag their feet. said Wheelock. "Im sure the police can tell you there have been more accidents on First St. than anywhere.

The council Will discuss the issue in a work sesion August [abbreviate]9.

"In fairness, I think the merchant's on First Street should be notified of a work sesion," reccomended Counselwoman Kelly Estelle. "I move that we send a leter to eacch of the bussinesses involved to notify them of the work session.

Estelle's motion was passed by the council. [Insert *unanimously*.]

EXERCISE 79 MORE COPY EDITING

Using copy-editing symbols, correct the misspellings, punctuation errors, and typographical errors in this story. Follow any interjected instructions that appear. Watch carefully for subtle punctuation errors and typos.

By Barbara Miller [all caps, bold face, flush left]

Staff Writer [italics, flush left]

A thirty-thousand-dollar [use numerals] grant has been awarded to a womens literary and arts magazine published in Fairfield.

The editors of Women's Literary Review, a 1,200 circulation magazine by and about women were notified of the grant yest erday by the National Endowment for the Arts. [Start new paragraph.] Funds will be used to help make the magazine sefl-supporting, and to pay for manuscripts, Editor, Ellen Herndon, said.

Herndon a professor of English at Kit Carson College said the magazne was founed five years ago to, ''encourage and maintain the female tradition in the ifne arts.'' The magazine published quarterly features fiction poetry essays and visual arts by and about women.

the Magazine is [change to: has been] fin anced primarily by Carson College and by foundation grants and subscription sales. The magazines goal is to increase paid circulation 1,200 from to about 5,000 over the next two years, Ms. Herdon said.

EXERCISE 80 STYLE QUIZ

As intended here, style means uniformity of usage. If you were to cite a place-name as Sandy, Ore., then presumably all place-names would be handled in a consistent manner—with state names abbreviated: Shreveport, La.; Medford Mass.; Buffalo, N.Y.; and so forth. (States with short names—Ohio, Utah, for example—are exceptions.) If you say 5-year-old girl in one sentence, using the numeral, you would not say five-year-old girl, spelling out the number, in the next.

To maintain consistency, most newspapers operate by a stylebook. The most commonly used one is that of the wire services, Associated Press and United Press International. They are identical. The exercises on these pages are designed with the AP–UPI style in mind.

The phrases that follow require knowledge of style. From the choices given, select the one that conforms to the style used in your newswriting class.

GROUP 1: CAPITALIZATION

1. Hudson [River, river]
2. Democratic Party, Democratic party, democratic party
3. Democratic principle, democratic principle, Democratic Principle

4. Democratic and Republican [parties, Parties]
5. [Dist. Atty., dist. atty.] John Smith
6. Victor Smith (district attorney, District Attorney]
7. J. Chesley Worthington (M.D., m.d.]
8. 893 E. 11th [st., St., street, Street]
9. 44 [MPH, mph]
10. 8 [p.m., P.M.]
11. [the Rev., the rev.] Billy Graham
12. First and Apricot [streets, Streets]
13. Apricot [street, Street]
14. U.S. [Congress, congress]
15. a [Congressional, congressional] committee
16. Ph.d., PH.D., ph.d.
17. [Electrical Engineer, electrical engineer] R. L. Burnside
18. Ponderosa [College, college]
19. [Editor, editor] Ellen Herndon
20. [Ex-Mayor, ex-Mayor, ex-mayor] Ivan R. VanDenBosch

GROUP 2: ABBREVIATIONS

1. [Lieutenant Governor, Lt. Gov.] William Perry
2. He left today for [Ala., Alabama].
3. Springfield, [Ill., Illinois]
4. Moscow, [Ida., Idaho]
5. Acme Manufacturing [Co., Company]
6. [Prof., Professor] Gregory Jackson
7. [Sen., Senator] Charles Percy (R-Ill., R-Illinois]
8. Austin (Tex., Texas]
9. [Lt. Gen., Lieut. Gen., Lieutenant General] John Doe
10. [P.F.C., Pfc., PFC] Gerald Moore
11. [Sgt., Sergeant] Delbert Tokay
12. [Govs., Governors] Hugh Penfold and Victor Atiyeh.
13. [M. Sgt., M/Sgt., Mstr. Sgt., Master Sgt., Master Sergeant] George Wood
14. [Chief Petty Officer, CPO, Chf. Pty. Ofcr.] John Miller
15. He went from [Michigan, Mich] to [O., Ohio].
16. She flew from Redding, [Cal., Calif., California], to Provo, (Utah, Ut.], in two hours.
17. Hilo, [Hi., Hawaii]
18. former [Pres., President] James Carter
19. She entered the Army in [Aug., August].
20. She was born [March, Mar.] 5, 1947.

GROUP 3: NUMERALS

1. World War [II, 2, Two]
2. Thanks a [million, 1,000,000].
3. About [30, thirty] persons attended.
4. The council needs [three, 3] more members.
5. He read [10, ten] pages.
6. Freddy Gopher, [6, six], and Jimmy Jones, [11, eleven], were missing.
7. Police today searched for [7, seven]-year-old Wanda Johnson.
8. [300, Three hundred] freshmen started classes yesterday.
9. They drove to [9, nine] Ellerby Road.

10. 104 E. [7th, Seventh] St.
11. Jane Doe, [twenty-six, 26], has [two, 2] children, Ellen, [5, five], and Sally-jo, [6, six] months.
12. He was in his [40s, forties].
13. Present were Linda, [16, sixteen], Amy, [9, nine], and Myra, [7, seven].
14. He flew in a [DC-Nine, DC-9].
15. [First, 1st] Amendment to the Constitution
16. the [14th, Fourteenth] Amendment
17. His lectures covered the [9th, ninth] century and the [14th, fourteenth] century.
18. He's on TV Channels [3 and 14, Three and Fourteen, Three and 14].
19. He represents the [4th, Fourth] Congressional District.
20. The Supreme Court, in a [5-4, five-four] decision,
21. He'll arrive June [1, one, first, 1st].
22. She is [5, five] feet [10, ten] inches tall.
23. He drove [9, nine] miles.
24. the U.S. [Sixth, 6th] Fleet
25. Interstate Highway [I-5, I-Five]
26. He asked for [$1,000, $1 thousand].
27. It was a [$4.3 million, $4,300,000] purchase.
28. She paid [$9, nine dollars] and sold it for [$14, fourteen dollars].
29. The mine cost [$1 million, $1,000,000, one million dollars].
30. The temperature dropped to [5, five] degrees last night.
31. It was [nine, 9] below zero.
32. Alabama [6, six], Stanford [0, zero].
33. Alabama beat Stanford [6-0, six-zero].
34. The golfer finished [18, eighteen] holes [2, two] under par.
35. He scored [6, six] points on a sweep from the [2, two]-yard line.
36. The wind blew about [five, 5] miles an hour.
37. The sailboat was going at least [4, four] knots.
38. The ratio of victory was [2-to-1, two-to-one].
39. About [two-thirds, ⅔] of the members left early.
40. Beethoven's [5th, Fifth] Symphony

EXERCISE 81 STYLE AND COPY EDITING

Using the appropriate copy-editing symbols, correct the style, punctuation, and spelling errors in the following sentences. Some are correct as they stand.

Example: She Drove East on Route I-80 and finally settled in the south.

1. She drove from Los Angeles, Calif., to Springfield, Mass. and back.
2. It was a .9 per cent increase.
3. $1,000s have been spent this year repaving roads in Lincoln County.
4. The meeting is at six PM Sunday.
5. Walter Valentine, Vice-President of the Acme Manufacturing company, will speak tomorrow.
6. The companys taxes rose from $1.9 million to $2,300,000, a 21% increase.

7. The route took them West into the midwest, then northwest and finally into Calif.

8. The team returns home today after losing 9 of 14 games on the road.

9. Sen. Mark O. Hatfield, R-Ore. is in town.

10. He has sailed the Atlantic and Pacific Oceans.

11. 33 persons escaped injury in a bus accident yesterday.

12. He lives on Baker St.

13. She lives at 224 W. Baker Street.

14. The president will speak at noon (9 a.m. PST.)

15. Robert W. Hutchinson, Deputy Superintendent of Public Instruction, died last night.

16. Two negroes and five White men were in the party.

17. Prof. Ellen Herndon teaches History 103 in room 4, Gilbert hall.

18. The victim was Jane Roe, a go go dancer at the Red Light club.

19. The police chief served 3 years in the navy before joining the Honolulu police department.

20. Relations between the state and the Federal Government are deteriorating, the governor said today.

21. as a Graduate student in history, she was awarded two Federal grants.

22. Reverend Hiram Weaver was a Sergeant in the Army and an F.B.I. agent before attending Seminary school.

23. Stationed at Ft. Lewis, Wash., Sergeant Bill Brady decided to climb Mt. Rainier and Mt. Hood.

24. The price of a hamburger at Duffy's has increased from $0.85 to $1.05.

25. The Chronicle of Higher Education is considered the Bible of college administrators.

EXERCISE 82 A FINAL COPY-EDITING EXERCISE

Copy edit the following story, paying close attention to misspelled words and names, addresses, punctuation, typographical errors, and style.

It doesn't work the black magic it once did. But this Friday the 13th you might still see a few people muttering incantations to ward off evil spirits.

That is in places other than Fairfield you might.

Folks here just don't seem to hold to those old fashioned beleifs. In fact most are downright skeptical.

''No, I'm not really into the supersticion scene,'' said Linda M. Deauville, 23, of 876 Buchanan Ln., Fairfield. ''I'm just not afraid of anything.

Deauville, one of several Fairfield residents asked about their feelings on Friday the 13th couldn't recall any phobias.

''I won't step under a ladder if I can avoid it but golly that's just common sense,'' Deauville said. What if there's a workman on the ladder and he spills paint or drops a hammer on you?''

Another residnt, Christine Rannow said she was 10 years old when she encountered a rhyme and she's never forgotten it.

''See a button, let it lay, pas it by, have bad luck all day.''

''To this day I canot pass by a button without picking it up.'' she says. ''It's silly I guess but I wouldn't term mysefl supersticious.''

Another woman who did not want to be identified, admits to being ''horribly supersticious.''

On one Friday the 13th her father was injured.

On another Friday the 13th her father went to the hospital for a blood clot.

And on a third Friday the 13th she and her husband were divorced.

''Black cats,'' said the woman, ''really freak me out.

Janice Westerman, 44, of 11 Reagan Avenue, said her 20 years of full time working have taught her nevr to worry about any Friday the 13th.

''It's always Monday the 15th that I dread,'' She said.

Dr. Katsuki Sakamoto, psychology department chairman at Kit Carson college, said supersticions are largely a thing of the past.

''Bad luck can occur most any day, but people take not of it more particularly should it occur on Friday the 13th or shortly after a black cat has crossed your path,'' he said.*

*Adapted from a story in the *Eastern Oregon Review*, La Grande, Oregon.

SPELLING

The following lists come largely from experience—that of teachers and newspaper copy editors who keep track of such things as misspelled words. The most often misspelled word may well be accommodate *(remember: two* c's *and two* m's*). The words are arranged in groups of 24 each. Please study them a group at a time and be prepared to take a quiz on any or all words (including those on the self-test in Chapter 2).*

GROUP 1

accessible	coolly	primitive
admissible	employee	propeller
awkward	escape	sizable
bulletin	forecast	seize
busing	gauge	successor
commitment	independent	tangible
competent	lien	tobacco
condescend	prejudice	weird

GROUP 2

adviser	dissipate	parallel
allegiance	embarrass	peninsula
amok	expendable	permissible
assessment	fiendish	recommend
bestial	hitchhiker	reprehensible
bookkeeper	impostor	reversible
changeable	lightning	rhythm
confluence	miscellaneous	serviceable

GROUP 3

aesthetic	descendant	maneuver
affidavit	dilemma	naive
amortize	discernible	nauseous
barbiturate	enforceable	newsstand
bureaucracy	esophagus	panicky
cigarette	focused	paralysis
compatible	innocuous	tariff
corollary	liquefy	veterinarian

GROUP 4

amnesia	hymnal	professor
baccalaureate	incalculable	remembrance
calendar	incidentally	soliloquy
colonel	millionaire	suffrage
demagogue	parliamentary	superintendent
dissipation	pasteurization	symmetrical
ecstasy	perseverance	traveling
equilibrium	possession	villain

GROUP 5

bicycle	indictment	restaurant
canoeing	license	sacrosanct
counterfeit	maintenance	scissors
disastrous	medicine	sergeant
edible	monstrous	souvenir
eligible	peaceable	synopsis
emigrate	remembrance	tepee
heinous	repellent	wondrous

GROUP 6

accidentally	foreign	roommate
acquittal	laboratory	shield
allotment	misshapen	sufficient
consensus	mustache	temperature
deferment	neighbor	transferred
dilapidated	optimistic	vein
discipline	quizzes	weight
drunkenness	receipt	withhold

GROUP 7

asinine	inaugurate	poignant
brusque	incalculable	repetitious
confectionery	inflammation	resuscitate
courtesy	khaki	subtleties
criteria	knowledgeable	supersede
exacerbate	memento	vacillate
exhilaration	pavilion	vacuum
hypocrisy	perspiration	verbatim

GROUP 8

acetylene
ambidextrous
corroborate
diarrhea
dilettante
entrepreneur
espresso
fusillade

guerrilla
hors d'oeuvres
idiosyncrasy
iridescent
kaleidoscope
meringue
miscegenation
mischievous

paraphernalia
proselytize
renaissance
restaurateur
sacrilegious
sauerbraten
sauerkraut
surveillance

Homonyms

A homonym is a word that sounds like another word but is spelled differently and has a different meaning. *Capital* (stock or monetary assets) sounds like *capitol* (the government building). *Affect* sounds like *effect*, *berth* like *birth*, *counsel* like *council*, and so forth. The following list contains some of the most commonly confused (and thus misspelled) homonyms. Please review the list to make sure you understand the differences in both meaning and spelling. Look them up in the dictionary if necessary. Be prepared to take an exam in which your instructor will pronounce the word and give its meaning but will expect you to know how to spell it. Example: *Principal*, a school administrator.

affect/effect
allusion/illusion
altar/alter
bizarre/bazaar
canvas/canvass
carat/caret/carrot/karat
censor/censure

compliment/complement
counsel/council/consul
desert/dessert
discreet/discrete
faze/phase
ingenious/ingenuous
mantel/mantle

ordinance/ordnance
populous/populace
premiere/premier
principle/principal
stationary/stationery
tenant/tenet

GRAMMAR EXERCISES

This segment contains a series of grammar exercises. It begins with a review quiz that you can score yourself. These exercises have been prepared with two standard references at hand: the *AP Stylebook and Libel Manual* (1985) and the *Prentice-Hall Handbook for Writers*. Authorities don't always agree; in case of differences the *AP Stylebook* will prevail. All newswriters should have a dictionary and a language skills reference book available; see Appendix B, page 167, for suggestions.

EXERCISE 83 A GRAMMAR QUIZ

This quiz covers some of the most common grammatical problems that newswriting students encounter in their work. To take the quiz, make the required choices or corrections and then turn to Appendix B for an answer key.

Pronoun-Antecedent Agreement

1. The football team lost [its, their] nerve.

2. Each of the seven women checked [her, their] purses before entering.

3. The couple split up after deciding to live [its, their] lives separately.

4. The United Mine Workers held [its, their] meeting in Denver.

5. The jury, composed of seven women and five men, delivered [its, their] verdict.

Subject-Verb Agreement

6. Present at the meeting [was, were] Tom Savage and Fred Scott.

7. The firm's president, along with his secretary, [is, are] under indictment.

8. Neither John nor his sisters [stand, stands] to gain from petty quarrels.

9. There [was, were] a series of riots in the city in 1970.

10. Selling the marijuana cigarettes to the undercover agents [was, were] a mistake.

11. Some of the tomatoes [is, are] in the box.

12. Most of the sand [comes, come] from the ocean.

Case of Pronouns

13. Sergeant Savage gave Private Bowman and [I, me] a stern lecture.

14. The sergeant criticized [us, our] being late.

15. Savage is a man [who, whom] we have always admired.

16. He is also a man [who, whom] they say deserves a medal.

17. The sergeant has been in the Army longer than [we, us].

18. He will replace us with [whomever, whoever] can do the job properly.

19. He gave the rifles to [her and I, she and I, her and me, she and me].

20. [Us, We] soldiers have a lot to learn.

Verb Tenses

21. The doctor told her patient to [lay, lie] down.

22. The gun [lay, laid, lied] on the street all day.

23. She [lay, lied, laid] the magazine aside and greeted her visitors.

24. She [set, sat] the vase on the table.

25. When they returned home, they found that a burglar [stole, had stolen] their silverware.

26. Police said the prisoner had [drank, drunk] two bottles of wine.

27. The valley [lay, lied, laid] in front of them as the pioneers crested the summit.

28. If she [were, was] governor, she'd pardon the prisoner.

Miscellaneous Troublemaking Words

29. She felt [bad, badly] about spilling the acid.

30. She was hurt [bad, badly] by her husband's criticism.

31. She felt [fine, finely] after a good night's sleep, however.

32. Tom is the [most, more] aggressive of the two boys.

EXERCISE 84 NUMBER AGREEMENT

Select the correct verbs or pronouns in the following sentences to ensure that they agree in number with subjects or antecedents.

1. The captains and three battalions of officers [was, were] on the range.

2. Her best friend and confidante [is, are] in town today. [Same person.]

3. Every woman on the softball team [was, were] jubilant about the victory.

4. Half of the money [were, was] stolen from the cookie jar.

5. Half of the people present [was, were] in favor of the amendment.

6. Forty dollars [is, are] too much to pay for the hat.

7. Riding in the car [was, were] Jerri, Diane and Carol.

8. There [is, are] no redeeming social values in this book.

9. Rusting in the rain [is, are] the remnants of a once-proud Army tank corps.

10. A series of robberies [make, makes] the police chief nervous.

11. Every one of the men [was, were] proud of [his, their] service.

12. The news media [seem, seems] to sensationalize acts of terrorism.

13. Neither the coach nor the players discussed salary when [he, they] [was, were] at the news conference.

14. The couple [is, are] seeking a reconciliation.

15. Managerial personnel seldom [agree, agrees] on company policy.

16. The book with its many chapters of intense violence and sadism [was, were] upsetting to read.

17. The many chapters of lust and greed [was, were] fun to read, however.

18. In the box [was, were] an apple and three turkey sandwiches.

19. Mathematics [is, are] a difficult subject for journalism students.

20. Sgt. Tom Savage is the only one of the soldiers who [hold, holds] the Medal of Honor.

EXERCISE 85 PROBLEM VERBS

Select the correct choice of verbs in the following sentences.

1. When the pioneers crossed the mountains, they saw a wide valley [laying, lying] before them.

2. When police arrived, three bodies [lay, laid] on the street.

3. She wishes she [was, were] a princess.

4. She missed the dance because she had [tore, torn] her dress.

5. Police told her to [lay, lie] the gun on the table.

6. He [lay, laid] in the hospital bed for an hour before help arrived.

7. The officers told the suspect to [lay, lie] flat on the ground.

8. The child [sat, set] the doll on the table.

9. After she [lay, lied, laid] there an hour, she awoke refreshed.

10. She would have liked to [see, have seen] the play when it was in town.

11. The plane looked as if it [was, were] in trouble.

12. The governor insisted that his aides [are, be] on time.

13. By the time she was 20, she [won, had won] 15 scholarships.

14. If she [was, were] governor, she'd eliminate the sales tax.

15. The baby [sits, sets] in its highchair.

EXERCISE 86 CASE OF PRONOUNS

1. You can't judge a book by [its, it's] cover.

2. It was a long voyage for Sharmayne and [I, me, myself].

3. The captain criticized [him, his] using an unmarked squad car.

4. She hates [him, his] driving fast.

5. The [fireman, fireman's] entering the burning building was a brave act.

6. Fire Chief Bowers is a man [who, whom] the mayor says deserves a medal.

7. [Who, Whom] do you prefer for president?

8. I prefer [whoever, whomever] can do the job best.

9. It was Smith and [her, she] [who, whom] you saw.

10. My brother [who, whom] is smarter than [I, me] graduated with honors.

11. It was [her, she] [who, whom] the police wanted for questioning.

12. [She, Her] and [he, him] will drive to Sandusky tomorrow night.

13. She has worked longer than [I, me].

14. The children brought [there, their, they're] books.

15. The body of the victim, [who, whom] police say was wanted on a felony warrant from Florida, was transported to the morgue.

16. Police said the purse was [hers, her's].

17. It was a private conversation, just between [he and she, him and her].

18. The mayor gave the prize to [us, we] boys.

19. [We, Us] girls will give a concert Thursday.

20. The judge could not understand [him, his] pleading guilty when so little evidence was brought against [he, him].

EXERCISE 87 MISPLACED SENTENCE SEGMENTS

Sometimes a meaning you did not intend results from awkward construction of a sentence. Consider this example:

The woman went to a doctor with a sore throat.

Does the phrase with a sore throat *refer to the doctor or the woman? Chances are the writer meant it to apply to the woman, but its location just behind the doctor suggests that the doctor has the sore throat, a possible but unlikely meaning. The sentence must be recast with the elements in their proper place. Here are two ways to do so:*

The woman with a sore throat went to the doctor.
The woman went to the doctor about her sore throat.

The following sentences have similar misplaced segments that cause an unintended meaning. Rewrite each sentence to clarify its meaning. If you are unsure which is the intended meaning, choose the one you prefer.

1. Forty different kinds of rhododendrons grow in the Indonesian Islands, many of which have been transplanted to Pioneer Park.

2. For $20 you only get two tickets.

3. Lieutenant Kingsley almost jogs 10 miles a day.

4. The bearded fugitive fired the revolver at the policeman with vengeance in his eye.

5. Disguised as repairmen, police said it was easy for the burglars to gain access to the building.

6. Sitting on the beach, the woman in the purple beach robe slowly walked toward him.

7. Violent and uncaged, the zookeeper searched for the missing tiger.

8. Thoroughly stewed, Jan decided the let to pot simmer for another ten minutes.

9. While hiking in the mountains, the trails were covered with snow.

10. While lowering the landing gear, the plane's engine sputtered and quit.

11. Driving along the highway, the billboard distracted us.

12. Filled with gas, Mary said the car worked fine.

13. The ship's captain told his crew constantly to be on the alert for storm clouds.

14. The governor wore a plastic construction worker's helmet.

15. Be sure to make your corrections with a blue editor's pencil.

EXERCISE 88 USING THE RIGHT WORD

This exercise contains sentences with words that are frequently misused. Many of them are homonyms—words that sound alike but have different spellings and different meanings. Others are commonly misused terms such as like *when you really meant* as though *or* as if. *Select the appropriate choice for each sentence. Consult a dictionary or the* AP Stylebook *for any you're unsure of.*

1. The accused murderer received good [counsel, council] from her attorney.

2. From her cell, she wrote the warden on pink [stationary, stationery].

3. The rain, she told him, should not [effect, affect] the harvest.

4. She's an [ingenious, ingenuous] lady—trusting, gentle, naive.

5. She looks [like, as if] a goddess but talks [like, as if] she were a cold-blooded killer.

6. The council passed an [ordinance, ordnance] to make jaywalking illegal.

7. The boxer [fainted, feinted] to the left and delivered a right cross.

8. The dog broke [it's, its] foot.

9. It takes [capital, capitol] to rebuild the state [capital, capitol] building.

10. The scholars [pored, poured] over the ancient manuscript.

11. Mayor Dmytryshyn told an interesting [antidote, anecdote] about city hall.

12. The school [principle, principal] is guided by the highest [principles, principals] of educational philosophy.

13. Captain Cook's vessel left the dock with a full [compliment, complement] of men.

14. It is the most [populace, populous] part of the city.

15. The troops moved [further, farther] inland yesterday.

16. When the children were [all together, altogether], they made [all together, altogether] too much noise.

17. The governor's speech [inferred, implied] an increase in taxes.

18. From such a speech, one could [imply, infer] an attitude of indifference in the governor's office.

19. Washington and Eisenhower Avenues are the two streets [that, which] citizens want repaved next spring.

20. It was Linda McCormack [who, whom, that] received the lifesaving award.

21. Sergeant Savage is a strong-willed man, [that, which] makes him a little cantankerous.

EXERCISE 89 PARALLEL STRUCTURE

Parallel structure means using the same sentence construction to accommodate several variations. Note the first example is unnecessarily complicated. The second, using parallel structure, makes it simpler.

> **Not parallel:** On their vacation, the Jones family dodged tornadoes in Kansas, with windstorms in Texas, and then had to endure heavy rain in Louisiana.
> **Parallel:** On their vacation, the Jones family dodged tornadoes in Kansas, fought windstorms in Texas and endured heavy rain in Louisiana.

Note how each variation is introduced by a verb: dodge, fought, endured. *Simplify the following sentences by using parallel structure. (Additional exercises are in Chapter 12, Exercise 37.)*

1. Jeanne Gray finds French easy to read but she can't converse it very well.

2. The captain was both a good policeman, and he inspired his officers.

3. Skydiving and flying aerobatic maneuvers will be the highlight of tomorrow's air show.

4. He is guided in principle by his wife's love, the respect of his daughter, and his father showed much paternal concern, which also formed some of his principles.

5. Walter likes driving, to cook, and going out with women is another pleasure of his.

6. The storm brought ten inches of snow, and the temperature dropped to minus-8 degrees, and slippery highways resulted from this.

EXERCISE 90 COPY EDITING

Here are two news stories that contain grammatical, spelling, style and word-use errors. Please make corrections, using the appropriate copy-editing symbols.

A. The Fairfield City Counsel Monday night recommended the Black Cat Tavern be granted a beer and wine lisence, despite a petition and verbal protests to the counsel urging them not to allow reopening the tavern.

Some 40 odd residents of the Eastside neighborhood objected to reopening the tavern at 400 Detroit avenue because of loud music, indecent behavior and the fact that nearby property often gets damaged by inebriated patrons.

The Anystate Liquor Control Commission closed down the tavern by yanking it's license last month after the counsel declared it a ''public nuisance.''

The counsel agreed Monday to reccommend reissuence of the lisense which would reopen the tavern on a 3-1 vote, with 2 abstaining.

The new owners, Tony and Henrietta Cooperman, agreed to counsel demands that music not be played after 9 o'clock. Cooperman said they planned to improve the tavern's rough-and-tumble immage by adding a restaurant.

B. The class of [insert year] of North High School held their 10-year class reunion last weekend.

The class dinner-dance was held at the Sandy River Inn Saturday, and the class picnic was held at Pioneer Park on Sunday, which was catered by Sourdough Jim's Restaurant.

Prizes were given for those coming the furtherest, Sue Butler from Guam; the most kids, Sue Ann (Liberty) Davidson, Juanita (Pendergast) Schneiter and Fred and Linda Sue (Tate) Ormsby, who all have four children; the persons who had changed the least were David Valentine and Jacqueline O'Farrell; the persons changing the most, Kenneth Wellington who got skinnier, and Ellie Hyman got more beautiful; the person with the most hair was Ken Dutton; and the judges selected the two people who looked the youngest as Betty Jane Paterson and John Tippets.

PUNCTUATION EXERCISES

Before doing the exercises here, you may wish to review the rules of punctuation in a standard reference guide such as the *AP Stylebook* or a good dictionary. Although the references agree substantially on the principles of punctuation, some differences do exist. Among the most notable of them is the use of commas in a series. Should it be one, two, and three? Or one, two and three? In short, do you put a comma before the and? Most advocates of formal writing say yes, but most newspaper editors say no as do the AP and UPI stylebooks. To encourage you to learn the usage you're most likely to encounter in professional news work, the exercises below will follow the AP-UPI style.

EXERCISE 91 COMMAS

Correct the following sentences for placement of commas. Do not change the wording, only the punctuation. Some sentences are okay as they stand.

1. The speaker was lively talented and personable.

2. "Where" she asked "do we park the car?"

3. A trip by Amtrak if you really want to go by train is an enjoyable experience.

4. She's a tall slim self-assured woman.

5. The important gains the speakers all seemed to say came in the field of employee morale.

6. Some fire runs turned out to be, false alarms the fire chief said.

7. Although the meeting was controversial most of the issues were resolved.

8. Diane Smith and her roommate Melody Montana enjoy living in New York.

9. Mayor Dmytryshyn after months of indecision finally fired his secretary.

10. Police Chief, Ernest J. Hudson, left today on vacation.

11. She gave a copy of the memo to the mayor, and another to the council president according to reliable sources.

12. In reaching its unpopular decision the City Council exhibited, great courage, Mayor Dmytryshyn said.

13. The witness said ''I saw the defendant pull a gun and shoot the victim.''

14. The judge called the witness a, ''brave lady.''

15. Dr. Frederick Remington chief medical pathologist for Lincoln County pronounced the woman a member of a socially prominent family dead of asphyxiation.

16. The flight stopped at Boise Idaho and Salt Lake City Utah before making the emergency landing at Flagstaff Ariz.

17. The captain said that a sudden emergency had occurred and he took over the controls to make the emergency landing at Flagstaff.

18. ''As a family'' she explained ''we expanded our vision of the world became intimately exposed to different cultures and countries and developed a profound awareness of what it means to be an American.''

19. It was Carol not Marsha who answered the phone.

20. ''Where do we go from here,'' she asked.

Note: Just to be sure you're on the right track with commas, which are the most important and often the most difficult of punctuation marks, check your corrections with the key in Appendix B.

EXERCISE 92 QUIZ ON COMMAS

Correct any errors in comma usage that you find in the following sentences. Some are correct as they stand.

1. District Attorney, Victor Smith, rested his case at noon today.

2. The defendant said ''No sir I did not fire the revolver.''

3. The woman 44 has a 9-year-old daughter Amy Lou.

4. Her mind was made up and there was no turning back.

5. The queen had eggs toast and coffee for breakfast.

6. "Oh I always get terrible grades on the first exams" she said.

7. Because of the blizzard all flights have been canceled.

8. The police car cruised down a dark dirty dangerous street.

9. The President left for Washington and later for Paris.

10. Mary Tyler of Boring Md. and Lonnie Pritchard of Boring Ore. met in Paris France.

11. Speaking of Oregon did you know it rains almost constantly, there?

12. In court that afternoon, the witness testified that accused killer, John Doe, was, "staggering like a drunk" but the judge told the jury to ignore that remark.

13. The witness said, "He came at me with the knife and shouted, 'Your money or your life!' so I gave him the money."

14. Whenever John gets behind the wheel of a car he feels a strong sense of power.

15. Any woman, who is honest sincere and hard-working, will succeed.

16. Sandy Montgomery who is honest sincere and hard-working will succeed.

17. In winter storms frequently lash the Pacific Northwest coast.

18. Girls, who want to be athletes, should run a mile every day.

19. Police detectives however failed to identify the suspect.

20. Our newspaper covers such minor sports as cross-country running tennis swimming and sailing.

EXERCISE 93 COMMAS, COLONS, SEMICOLONS

Each of the following sentences contains a problem that can be solved with a comma, a colon or a semicolon. Please make the appropriate corrections. Do not use periods and do not change the wording. Follow AP style.

1. Present at the meeting were the following city officials Rodney Dmytryshyn mayor Richard L. Bowers fire chief and Ernest J. Hudson police chief.

2. He said they would "live together" she said it was "marriage or nothing." [Do not try to solve this one with a period; do not change the wording!]

3. To Governor Penfold, all the major crises revolve around one problem lack of funds.

4. Her lips said no her eyes said yes.

5. He sailed westward with no destination in mind adventure was his goal.

6. The posse searched the mountains and found the child playing in a meadow.

7. Governor Penfold said of his opponent, ''He's honest courageous worthy isn't it too bad he's such a loser?''

8. Betty Lou Elwell who lives on Monroe Avenue witnessed the shooting.

9. Betty Lou Elwell 3876 Monroe Ave. witnessed the shooting.

10. Betty Lou did not however talk to the officers about it.

11. The pilot made a smooth landing but the plane skidded on the runway ice.

12. Throughout the ordeal she could think of only one thing getting out alive.

13. He assembled a fortune in oil royalties moreover he inherited millions from a wealthy uncle.

14. Her application was ten days past the deadline therefore she was eliminated from active consideration.

15. She had three virtues optimism loyalty and sincerity.

EXERCISE 94 APOSTROPHES

Check the following sentences. Most have errors in the use of possessives or apostrophes. Be sure to note the difference between **its** *(possessive) and* **it's** *(contraction of it is). Add an* **s** *wherever appropriate in your corrections. Follow AP style.*

1. A masked gunman broke into the girls [plural] locker room.

2. It was the governor's first press conference in three months.

3. The dog and its owners were gone when police arrived.

4. His grades included three Bs and two As.

5. All DC-10s were flying the Los Angeles-Hawaii route.

6. The childrens bikes were stolen.

7. The story of Jesus life is inspiring.

8. The waitresses [plural] uniforms were splotched with ketchup.

9. ''Its a girl!'' the doctors assistant exclaimed.

10. The witness [singular] testimony was brief.

11. The witness [plural] sarcasm was predictable.

12. Karl Marx theories are considered valid today, she said.

13. The hostess patience was wearing thin.

14. He read Strunk and White book, ''The Elements of Style.'' [Joint authorship.]

15. Hemingway and Steinbeck literary efforts are remarkable. [Separate authorship.]

EXERCISE 95 HYPHENS

Insert hyphens as needed in the following sentences. Authorities don't always agree on the proper use of hyphens; therefore the AP Stylebook *should be consulted for guidance. Some sentences are correct.*

1. The 3 year old girl was lost for seven hours.

2. He had a good time on his easily remembered vacation.

3. They say he is a well read teacher.

4. It's a nine hour flight with a four hour layover in Hawaii.

5. Let us not prejudge this preeminent person for his premarital escapades.

6. It was a predawn raid.

7. The soldiers reformed their battle line.

8. For the jury he was able to recreate the events of the day in which he engaged in many recreational activities.

9. The judge handed him a 10 to 15 year sentence.

10. He lived in a preChristian era.

11. The museum displayed 16th and 17th century paintings.

12. The witness exhibited a know it all attitude.

13. He was a big business man. [He stood 5 feet tall but owned a gigantic, multi-national company.]

14. She is a well known author.

15. She is a widely known actress.

EXERCISE 96 QUOTATION MARKS

Correct any errors you find in the use of quotation marks. Be sure to watch for errors in capitalization and punctuation as they may relate to the use of quotation marks.

1. John said ''What's the governor's next move?

2. ''The mayor will probably resign'' said Fred.

3. ''The mayor'' said Mark ''does not discourage easily.''

4. The witness testified that she ''didn't know the gun was loaded.''

5. He said it was a ''splendid anthology'' where will it be published? [Please try to solve this problem without using a period.]

6. Her testimony continued: "I said to the defendant, "Please don't point that thing at me," and he said, "Face it, Baby, your time has come," and then the gun went "Bang!" actually it was more of a "Pop!" than a "Bang!"

7. Were your parents the kind who always asked, "Where are you going"

8. "Did you actually see the defendant fire the gun" he asked.

9. "Where," she asked, "can I expect to find 'War and Peace

10. Is this what you call "modern fiction"?

11. Mike said, "I once wrote a book entitled The Complete Works and Other Stories of Mike O'Brien, but I couldn't find a publisher.

12. She accused him of being a "shiftless hippie" however, she married him anyway, explaining that he was really a "sweet man."

13. His speech, titled What's Right with America, was discussed on the Today show.

14. She stood up and remarked, "Do you remember when your grandpa used to say, "You don't get the soap lessn' you boil the hawg

15. He said his opponents want to, "abolish" city government.

EXERCISE 97 GENERAL PUNCTUATION AND SPELLING

Correct the following sentences as needed. Some are okay as they stand.

1. As the search party slowly worked its way south the fugitive climbed the hills to the north.

2. The sheriff moved east his deputy moved west.

3. Second baseman, Royce Calhoun, hit three home runs.

4. He nominated three names for the award Henry Deerfield Kathleen Peterson and Cindy Dawson.

5. It was Oscar Wilde who said in his book The Portrait of Dorian Gray "There is only one thing worse than being talked about and that is not being talked about."

6. Four long hard desperate months lay ahead for the beleaguered garrison.

7. After we had finished eating the horse ran away.

8. The team that has the best win-loss record deserves the trophy.

9. She told the children she'd tolerate no "fooling around" the children immediately rebelled and told her to "get lost" [Try to solve this one without using a period.]

10. Betty Johnston who was the first doctor to reach the scene of the tragedy said there were no survivors.

11. "Its time" Maggie Davis said "that my horse found its way home."

12. Jane Ziff's final words of advice to me were terse. "Billie" she said "just remember to cross your ts and dot all your is and youll get along just fine."

13. Because she is a first rate novelist Barbara Justice's widely known books command a highly enthusiastic following.

14. Sheriff Bud Kuykendall who won last falls election by a landslide has decided to resign.

15. "I was driving home," the witness testified, "when a tall dark stranger came up from behind and stuck a gun in my ribs. He says "Give me all your money.""

Appendix B

EXERCISE KEYS

Language Skills Bibliography

This bibliography includes general reference books useful to consult whenever technical questions arise on grammar, punctuation, and word usage. The answers and explanations on the language skills quiz (Chapter 2, Exercise 1) are based on three primary sources: The *Associated Press Stylebook and Libel Manual,* the *Prentice-Hall Handbook for Writers* and *When Words Collide.* Where authorities disagree, the *AP Stylebook* prevails.

French, Christopher W., Eileen Alt Powell, and Howard Angione. *The Associated Press Stylebook and Libel Manual.* New York: The Associated Press, 1984.

Hodges, John C., and Marry E. Whitten. *Harbrace College Handbook.* 9th ed. New York: Harcourt Brace Jovanovich, 1982.

Kessler, Lauren, and Duncan McDonald. *When Words Collide.* Belmont, Calif.: Wadsworth, 1984.

Lakritz, Joyce. *Verbal Workbook for the ACT.* New York: Arco, 1983 [ACT: American College Testing program.]

Leggett, Glenn, C. David Mead, and William Charvat. *Prentice-Hall Handbook for Writers.* 8th ed. Englewood Cliffs, N.J.: Prentice-Hall, 1982.

Lewis, Norman. *Correct Spelling Made Easy.* New York: Dell, 1963.

————— . *Word Power Made Easy.* New York: Pocket Books, 1978.

Towers, Veronica F. *Spelling and Vocabulary Simplified and Self-taught.* New York: Arco, 1984.

Exercise Keys

Exercise 1 Self-test

1. accommodate
2. acoustics
3. all right
4. appalling
5. awful
6. believe

7. benefited
8. cemetery
9. consistent
10. correspondent
11. defendant
12. definite
13. diesel
14. development
15. exaggerate
16. fiery
17. fluorescent
18. harassment
19. hemorrhage
20. hygiene
21. inoculate
22. liaison
23. occasionally
24. occupant
25. occurred
26. picnicking
27. privilege
28. responsible
29. sacrament
30. satellite
31. separate
32. sheriff
33. subpoena
34. temperament
35. terrific
36. A five-year-old girl was injured yesterday. [Insert hyphen.]
37. Dr. John Messerle, father of the bride, failed to show up. [Set off phrase by commas.]
38. Police said that the suspect returned Monday night. [Remove unnecessary comma.]
39. Captain Johnson asked, "Where's the guilty party?" [Use comma to introduce quote.]
40. How did you like "Tale of Two Cities"? [Question mark outside quotes; it is part of overall sentence, not the book's name.]
41. "She was gone for only a moment," the child's mother said. [Insert apostrophe.]
42. He said the city is in "dire need of a financial boost." [No comma used to introduce *fragmented* quotation.]
43. Inflation was up three percent; employment was down four percent. [Semicolon separates two complete sentences.]
44. Police arrested two men and a woman for trespassing. [Remove commas.]
45. Their work finished at last, the firefighters left the scene. [Use comma to set off introductory clause.]
46. Correct.
47. The driver, his face streaming with tears, said he did not see the child crossing the street. [Commas set off clause.]
48. "It's a girl!" the nurse said. [Apostrophe needed for contraction of "it is."]
49. Jones did not heed the mayor's advice; however, he later sold the property and gained a favorable response from city hall. [. . .advice, however; he later. . . . also okay; it depends

on meaning. Semicolon separates two complete sentences.]
50. The trees, which workers planted last spring, are dying. ["Which" introduces a clause that provides incidental intelligence.]
51. The trees that workers planted last spring are dying. [The word "that" defines the particular trees under discussion.]
52. "The team has been resting on its laurels too long," Coach Holloway said. [The word "its," when used as possessive, does not require an apostrophe.]
53. It was a dark and stormy night. [Commas not needed.]
54. "I don't trust the mayor; moreover, I think he's a crook," Smith said. [Semicolon separates two complete sentences within the quote.]
55. "Will you be at work tomorrow?" he asked. [Comma not needed.]
56. In tears Jane Doe told the judge, "He walked up the ramp and said, 'See you later, Sweetie,' and that was the last time I saw him alive." [Single quotes used for quote within quote.]
57. The slim, long-haired defendant left by the side entrance. [Use comma to separate two adjectives of equal importance.]
58. Correct.
59. He said he'd be in the Hilton Hotel in Atlanta, Georgia. [Comma separates city and state.]
60. Whose raincoat is that? ["Whose" is possessive; "who's" is a contraction of "who is."]
61. The defendant said the raincoat was hers. [Remove apostrophe.]
62. The children's beds were unmade. [Apostrophe for possessive.]
63. The girls' names were Carol and Marsha. [Apostrophe at end of plural possessive.]
64. Correct.
65. Snow, she said, is what she loves most. [Commas needed for clarity.]
66. Police reported seeing Charles' car in Circle City last week. [Apostrophe needed for possessive; Charles's also correct.]
67. A set of well-defined rules gives us a sense of order. [Hyphen needed for compound adjective.]
68. The victims were Jane Smith, 38, Boston; Joe Friday, 44, New York City; and Stephanie Cyphers, 19, Yonkers. [Semicolons needed for clarity.]
69. Police returned the gun to John and *her*. ["Her" is object of preposition "to."]
70. The tire chains she got for Christmas *make*. . . . [Plural subject requires plural verb.]
71. The team of eleven boys *was*. . . . [Singular subject "team" takes singular verb.]
72. The woman *who* police believe was murdered. . . . [subjective case "who" required because it is subject of clause "who was murdered." Removing the superfluous "police believe" and similar phrases makes the structure of such sentences more clear.]
73. The county commissioners made little progress in *their*. . . . [Plural subject.]
74. The city council, composed of nine members, set *its* meeting for Thursday. [Council is singular subject.]
75. Annoyed *are* the readers when backward run the sen-

tences. [In this backward sentence, the subject is the plural "readers."]

76. Sitting in the car *were* three police officers. [Another backward sentence with "officers" the plural subject.]

77. He said the reward should go to *whoever* found the treasure. [Subjective case necessary here; "whoever" is subject of the clause "whoever found the treasure." It is *not* the object of the preposition "to."]

78. "Just between you and *me*. . . . ["me" is object of preposition "between."]

79. The forecaster said it looked *as if*. . . . ["like" is a preposition, "as if" a conjunction that joins the two clauses in this example.]

80. The witness said he felt *bad*. . . . ["bad" is a predicate adjective following the *linking verb* "felt." To feel "badly" would suggest an impaired sense of touch. It's comparable to the comment, "I feel fine" (not "finely"). Common linking verbs include *be* (and its variations, is, are, was, were, and so on) *lie, sit, look, prove, seem, grow, turn* and those dealing with personal senses: *sound, feel, look, smell, taste*.]

81. Jane, asked about her health, said she feels *fine*. (See #80 above.)

82. The doctor told the patient to *lie* down. [Present tense. "Lay" would be past tense.]

83. When he *lay* down, he fell asleep. [Past tense. In present tense, the sentence would read, "When he lies down, he falls asleep."]

84. She *laid* the gun on the table. . . . [As used here, "lay" means to set down or put in place; "laid" is past tense of lay.]

85. Neither Jones nor Smith *has* the answer. [Singular subject.]

86. Neither Jones nor his daughters *have* the answer. [When singular and plural antecedents are joined by "or" or "nor," the verb should agree with the closest antecedent—"daughters" in this case.]

87. Governor Penfold, *whom* the Republicans supported. . . . ["Whom" is the object of the verb, supported.]

88. It was *he*, Robert Redford, whom you saw in the hotel. ["He" is a predicate pronoun following a linking verb, "was."]

89. The council approved the *mayor's* taking a stand. . . . [Use possessive form here; the approval is of the mayor's stand, not the mayor.]

90. She testified that she could not imagine *his* shooting an innocent bystander. [As in #89, possessive pronoun needed here.]

91. The United Mine Workers *is*. . . . [The UMW is a singular unit and requires a singular verb.]

92. She *set* the bomb. . . . ["Set" here means to put into place; the words are often confused.]

93. If she were a princess. . . . [Use subjunctive mood for contrary to fact situations; see *AP Stylebook* for more on "subjunctive mood."]

94. She looks good *as* a princess should. ["As" joins the sentence with the succeeding clause; like is a preposition and should be followed only by a simple object: *She looks like a princess* or *the governor thinks like a politician*.]

95. All of the sand *was* dumped from the truck. [When using indefinite pronouns—all, some, none, most, more, any—the verb number depends on the noun to which it refers, the singular "sand" in this case.]

96. All of the dancers *were* aboard the ship. [See comment #95.]

97. The news media *are* on the job. [The word "media" is plural; "medium" is the singular form.]

98. She gave the basket to John and *her*. ["Her" is object of preposition "to" and thus requires objective case.]

99. *She and I* will leave for Denver tomorrow. [Both "she and I" are subjects of the sentence and require subjective case.]

100. Jane is taller than *I*. ["I" is subject of clause "I am tall," which is understood by the reader though not literally part of the sentence.]

Scoring: Allow one point for each correct answer.

95 or better: Excellent, a real professional.

85-94: Good, but some brushing up would help. Use a dictionary.

75-84: Consult frequently with spelling and grammar books.

Below 75: Inferior; concerted remedial effort needed.

Exercise 3 Rating the News

The set of local events described in Exercise 3 was turned over to a panel of professional newspaper journalists for discussion and rating. They rated them as follows:

1. President's unexpected visit to Fairfield, by far the top story, because of prominence, rarity, timeliness, proximity, action, with perhaps even a touch of mystery involved (why did the President come?).

2. Acme layoffs, rated ahead of mayor's announcement of possible new plant because it is definite (concrete), has economic impact (consequence, magnitude) and because Acme is well-known in the community (prominence).

3. Accidental deaths. A look at the *City Directory* will reveal that Yamashita, a circuit judge, and Zbytovsky, a bank manager, are the more *prominent* citizens, though violent death is always news in a local community like Fairfield.

4. Mayor's announcement of possible new industry. Very tentative possibility, indeed, and perhaps self-serving to mayor's political ends, but it contains an optimistic note (consequence), particularly if the community is economically beleaguered in light of Acme layoffs. One editor would merge the two stories into one.

5. The panel disagreed on ranking the remaining four items. The former governor's accident might rate a paragraph because of prominence, but timeliness is lacking and the incident is inconsequential. The former mayor's heart attack is worthy of minor note, they said, as is Linda McCormack's refusal to accept the medal (the rarity and potential conflict elements of the refusal make it a bigger story than a routine acceptance.) That leaves the marathon run. No doubt this annual event would be covered routinely by the sports department. Does the fact that a

former beauty queen set a new record for women make it more than routine? Much controversy ensued over that question, with answers ranging from "beauty queens are a dime a dozen nowadays" to "this one is different—a beauty queen whose talent is distance running!" The fact that she had resigned the queenship in favor of a principle gives her a certain minor infamy, thus enhancing *prominence*. In the end the consensus seemed to be that, if nothing more, the *controversy* element would boost it to more-than-routine status (but only slightly so). "If we're sitting around arguing about it, chances are the public will, too." Journalists know that controversy as a news element attracts public attention. Those with knowledge of sports also argue that the marathon time, 2:55:33, is not bad for an amateur runner—four and a half minutes faster would have qualified her for the Olympics.

Exercise 4 A Burglary Report

Two $300 stereo tape recorders and $18 cash were stolen last night from the Westside Middle School, 1700 River Ave.

Police said the school's janitor, Herman C. Melville, discovered the burglary this morning. Someone had smashed a window to the principal's office to gain entry. Police have no suspects.

Exercise 5 Resignation

John A. Elwell, Fairfield city librarian for the past three years, resigned last night because of "personal considerations."

The city Library Board will meet at 7 tonight to consider the resignation. Board chairman Frank Parker said today that he hoped the board could persuade Elwell to reconsider.

Elwell, 47, declined to elaborate on the reasons for the resignation, which is effective June 30. His letter to the Library Board said he wished to "reconsider my goals in life."

His departure, he added, comes at a "high point in the library's history, not a low point."

During his tenure, he said, the library has increased its circulation by 77 percent and has installed a computerized card catalog capable of providing telephone access by home computers. Other innovations include writer's workshops and a children's story hour.

If the board cannot convince Elwell to reconsider, it will appoint an acting librarian and begin a search for a replacement, Parker said.

"Mr. Elwell has brought a singular spirit of service to the Library in the past three years," Parker said. "It would be a shame to see him go."

Elwell served for five years as assistant librarian before taking his current position.

Exercise 6 Water Accident

A 3-year-old Fairfield girl drowned yesterday at Zumwalt County Park near Wagontire, the Sheriff's Office reported.

Terri Flemming, daughter of Donald and Dorothy Flemming, 880 Polk Ave., was pronounced dead on arrival at Providence Hospital.

A sheriff's report said the child disappeared from the swimming area at Zumwalt Park about 4 p.m. Searchers found her unconscious 10 to 15 minutes later about 100 yards downstream.

Attempts at artificial respiration failed.

Terri was the youngest of the Flemming's three children. Donald Flemming, a truck driver, was at work at the time of the accident.

[**Note:** The name is spelled Flemming, not Fleming. Always consult the *City Directory* for names; don't depend on police reports for accuracy—or on anyone else, for that matter.]

Exercise 9A Practice Leads

A squirrel short-circuited a power transformer about 2 p.m. yesterday, interrupting power to about 100 homes around West 40th Street for 17 minutes.

Exercise 12 Trash Collection

Seven jail inmates spent yesterday cleaning two truckloads of roadside litter from a 15-mile stretch of McKinley Road near the county waste disposal site.

Sheriff Charles B. Kuykendall called it an "interesting experiment" in the use of prison manpower and pronounced it a success.

The seven men, all volunteers from the minimum security section of the Lincoln County Jail, filled 100 plastic bags with trash, most of which had fallen off vehicles headed for the county dump. Citizen complaints prompted the sheriff to try using volunteer labor from the jail.

"We've had a zillion complaints from citizens about the looks of the roadways around the dump," he said.

But he lacks the personnel to enforce a county law that requires drivers to keep trash secured. So he called for volunteers from the jail and picked 7 of the 15 volunteers.

Within eight hours they had filled the two trucks. Among the litter was a wallet with two credit cards and $3 cash. It was returned to its owner.

Kuykendall said he planned to discuss the project with county officials to see if the experiment should be continued. The men worked under the supervision of a security guard.

The sheriff added a warning to drivers headed for the dump. You can be fined up to $500 and sent to jail for allowing trash to spill off your vehicle onto the roadways.

Exercise 20 Plane Crash

A 19-year-old Fairfield man died this morning when the small plane he was piloting apparently struck a power line and cartwheeled into a farm field four miles south of Fairfield.

Dead is Delbert W. Thissel, 555 Westway Ave. Sheriff Charles B. Kuykendall said Thissel was alone in the plane, which crashed and burned about 6 a.m. near

Highway 13. The craft had left Fairfield Airport about 15 minutes earlier.

Witnesses' accounts varied but generally agreed that the plane was flying low. Some said it struck a nearby 7,200-volt transmission line.

Virginia Tubbs, 18, who lives on the farm where the plane crashed, said the engine was going on and off.

"It was laying one wing over like it's about to turn upside down, and then it just hit the ground," she said.

A passing motorist, Audrey Brooks, 1345 University Ave., Fairfield, said she saw the plane skim low over the top of her car.

"One wing was kind of dipping low," she said. "I think it must have hit the power line, and it kind of toppled over onto the ground, kind of like a cartwheel."

It caught fire and moments later exploded into a "ball of flame," said Brooks.

A Fairfield Power & Light spokesman confirmed that the plane hit the line, causing a momentary fluctuation in electrical service.

The dead pilot was the son of Alan R. and Alice Thissel, 1607 West 17th St., Fairfield.

[Note the misspelled name—Thissel, not Thistle.]

Exercise 22 Ingram Death

Mattie L. Ingram, retired South High School English instructor who won a "Teacher of the Year" award in 1950, died yesterday. She was _____.

Miss Ingram retired in 1966 after teaching 40 years, 25 of them at Fairfield's South High School. She lived at 100 Eisenhower Ave.

Her career included extensive summer travel to 54 foreign countries and 49 states—all but Alaska. She conducted high school study tours in Europe in 1936, 1938 and 1953.

Born in Paynesville, Minn., in 1901, she earned bachelor's and master's degrees from the University of North Dakota and began teaching in Bismarck, N.D., in 1923. She also taught in Texas and California before moving to Fairfield in 1941.

She did postgraduate work at Stanford, UCLA, University of Chicago and University of London.

She is survived by a sister, Joy Brunner, Burbank, Calif.

Services are pending at Resthaven Funeral Home, Fairfield.

Exercise 26 Speech on Sexual Violence

The domestic war of the century is the war against rape and sexual violence, a police sergeant told the Fairfield Business and Professional Women in a luncheon speech yesterday at the Fairway Hotel.

"We don't really expect to eliminate sexual violence or child abuse entirely," Sgt. Kathy Anderson said, "but we plan to put up one hell of a fight."

Anderson works for the juvenile division of the Fairfield Police Department and chairs an organization called Women Against Rape. It was formed in 1984, a year after Fairfield had an all-time high crime rate for forcible rape—88.5 per 100,000 population. The statistical chance of being raped in Fairfield, she said, was then 70 percent greater than in New York City, twice as great as in Philadelphia, and a third greater than in Washington or Chicago.

A police interagency rape team was formed in 1986 to investigate incidents of rape and sexual violence. Fairfield's rape rate subsequently declined—to 44.6 last year, about the same as Philadelphia's.

Those statistics, Anderson said, do not reveal the problems as police officers see them—"the broken bodies and the often-grotesque psychological traumas" that are the aftermath of rape.

"Rape is not the only thing that concerns us," she said, "Only 22 percent of the cases we see are rapes of sexually mature females."

The other 78 percent include instances of child abuse and domestic violence, she said, such as "abused wives with black eyes, broken limbs and broken spirits."

"They are children," she continued. "Last year we processed the case of a 7-year-old girl raped with such abject brutality that she had to be hospitalized for a week—raped by her own father."

Anderson said funds are being sought to build a shelter home in Fairfield to house victims of rape, child abuse and family violence.

In a question and answer session, Anderson said police files were loaded with cases of women who had prevented a rape with creative solutions.

"One stuck her finger down her throat, which made her vomit, and the man left her alone," she said. "Another said she had herpes, a venereal disease, and the would-be attacker couldn't leave fast enough. Another told her attacker, 'Honey, let's go to my apartment.' She directed him to a busy intersection and, when he stopped for the light, she opened the door and walked away."

Anderson also said screaming was a good idea—"nothing is more attention-getting than a woman's screams. They're ten times more effective than a whistle."

She also advised women to yell "Fire!" in case of attack.

"If you yell 'Rape!' or 'Help!' people think it's a domestic squabble," she explained. "'Fire!' always brings them on the run—everybody loves a good fire."

Exercise 30 Planning Commission Meeting

A proposed home for unwed mothers at 880 East 11th St. was approved last night by the Fairfield Planning Commission despite protests from area residents.

The commission voted unanimously to allow Hosanna Children's Center, an interdenominational church agency, to house pregnant girls under the care of a counseling staff. The girls, aged 13 to 16, will be referred to the center by the state Children's Services Division or by local schools.

Two residents opposed the conditional use permit being sought by Hosanna Center. Cal Lindley, 895 East 11th St., saw the proposed home as "the first step toward deterioration of the neighborhood."

Lindley argued that the area was among the most historically picturesque in the city.

"If you permit them to move in there," he said, "I think you can kiss the historic preservation factor goodbye."

He also warned of possible crises at the center.

"These are highly charged and emotional young girls, and anything can happen," he said.

Another resident, Priscilla Anderson, 897 East 11th St., suggested that "there is a real danger of trouble in what has up to now been a very quiet neighborhood."

Paul Zweig, manager of the Hosanna Center, said the agency had outgrown its present location at 120 Eisenhower Ave. and was seeking a larger house.

"The type of home we are looking at is always needed," he said, "but unfortunately it's always needed in someone else's neighborhood."

He said the agency seeks to give pregnant girls an alternative to abortion. The new facility would house six to ten girls and three live-in counselors, with other counselors and tutors on call as needed.

"These girls are fine people no matter what you may think," Zweig said. "They are not troublemakers. They do not appeal to boys on motorcycles. This type of girl is not going to be out on the street looking for trouble. She's got enough trouble as it is."

The commission wil review the permit after one year's operation.

Exercise 42 A Quiz on Numbers

1. 30.9% increase
2. .312 batting average
3. 51.3% voted yes
4. 27.8% of community voted
5. $118.82 per dog
6. average: 23.1 years; median: 20
7. 1.4 rate for murder
8. 6.1% decline
9. 2.2:1 boy-girl ratio
10. roughly equivalent: 14.8% A's in physics: 15.2% in college
11. 1. Jones (82.8% pro labor votes)
   2. Johnson (77.8%)
   3. Smith (54.5%)
   4. Brown (52.4%)
12. 1. Carleton $8.62 hourly rate
   2. Acme $7.43
   3. Dalton $6.40
   4. Bijou $6.04
13. Cheltenham is lowest: 1:24.6; Caxton 1:27.2; Kennerly 1:28.6
14. 21.4% of employees are minorities (3/14)

Exercise 43 Council Attendance

Fairfield Mayor Rodney Dmytryshyn has not missed a meeting of the City Council in the four years he has served as mayor.

The mayor's perfect attendance record—104 meetings—was the best of the eight members of the council, according to figures provided by Margaret Christianson, chair of Citizens for Good Government. Here's the record for the others:

Eleanor McPherson missed 7 of 187 meetings held in 7 years (96% attendance).

Kenneth Wheelock missed 23 of 444 meetings in 27 years (95%).

Douglas Hixon missed 1 of 17 meetings in 8 months (94%).

Kelly Estelle missed 1 of 14 meetings in 7 months (93%).

Charles Johnson missed 17 of 139 meetings in 5 years (88%).

Eleanor Beatty missed 44 of 330 meetings in 13 years (87%).

Benjamin Dorris missed 33 of 75 meetings in 3 years (66%).

Exercise 83 Grammar Quiz

1. The football team lost *its* nerve.
2. Each of the seven women checked *her* purse. . . .
3. The couple split up after deciding to live *their* lives separately.
4. The United Mine Workers held *its* meeting in Denver.
5. The jury, composed of seven women and five men, delivered *its* verdict.
6. Present at the meeting *were* Tom Savage and Fred Scott.
7. The firm's president, along with his secretary, *is* under indictment.
8. Neither John nor his sisters *stand* to gain from petty quarrels.
9. There *was* a series of riots in the city in 1970.
10. Selling the marijuana cigarettes to the undercover agents *was* a mistake.
11. Some of the tomatoes *are* in the box.
12. Most of the sand *comes* from the ocean.
13. Sergeant Savage gave Private Bowman and *me* a stern lecture.
14. The sergeant criticized *our* being late.
15. Savage is a man *whom* we have always admired.
16. He is also a man *who* they say deserves a medal.
17. The sergeant has been in the Army longer than *we*.
18. He will replace us with *whoever* can do the job properly.
19. He gave the rifles to *her and me*.
20. *We* soldiers have a lot to learn.
21. The doctor told her patient to *lie* down.
22. The gun *lay* on the street all day.
23. She *laid* the magazine aside and greeted her visitors.
24. She *set* the vase on the table.
25. When they returned home, they found that a burglar *had stolen* their silverware.
26. Police said the prisoner had *drunk* two bottles of wine.

27. The valley *lay* in front of them as the pioneers crested the summit.
28. If she *were* governor, she'd pardon the prisoner.
29. She felt *bad* about spilling the acid.
30. She was hurt *badly* by her husband's criticism.
31. She felt *fine* after a good night's sleep, however.
32. Tom is the *more* aggressive of the two boys.

Exercise 91 Commas

1. The speaker was lively, talented and personable.
2. "Where," she asked, "do we park the car? [Insert commas]
3. A trip by Amtrak, if you really want to go by train, is. . . .
4. She's tall, slim, self-assured woman.
5. The important gains, the speakers all seemed to say, came. . . .
6. Some fire runs turned out to be false alarms, the fire chief said.
7. Although the meeting was controversial, most of the issues. . . .
8. Diane Smith and her roommate, Melody Montana, enjoy living. . . .

9. Mayor Dmytryshyn, after months of indecision, finally fired. . . .
10. Police Chief Ernest Hudson left today on vacation.
11. She gave a copy of the memo to the mayor and another to the council president, according to reliable sources.
12. In reaching its unpopular decision the City Council exhibited great courage, Mayor Dmytryshyn said.
13. The witness said, "I saw the defendant pull a gun and shoot the victim."
14. The judge called the witness a "brave lady."
15. Dr. Frederick Remington, chief medial pathologist for Lincoln County, pronounced the woman, a member of a socially prominent family, dead of asphyxiation.
16. The flight stopped at Boise, Idaho, and Salt Lake City, Utah, before making the emergency landing at Flagstaff, Ariz.
17. The captain said that a sudden emergency occurred, and he. . . .
18. As a family," she explained," we expanded our vision of the world, became intimately exposed to different cultures and countries, and developed a profound awareness of what it means to be an American."
19. It was Carol, not Marsha, who answered the phone.
20. "Where do we go from here?" she asked.

Appendix C

CITY DIRECTORY

Fairfield City Officials

CITY COUNCIL

Mayor	Rodney A. Dmytryshyn
Ward I	Eleanor H. McPherson
Ward II	Benjamin F. Dorris
Ward III	Kelly Estelle
Ward IV	Eleanor J. Beatty
Ward V	Charles V. Johnson
Ward VI	Kenneth J. Wheelock
At Large	Douglas K. Hixon

CITY PLANNING COMMISSION

Chair	Kelly Estelle
Member	James Bodoni
Member	Kaye Zolotow
Member	Roger Dombrowsky
Member	Ellen M. Herndon

ADMINISTRATION

City Manager	Victor M. Allen
Finance Director	Patricia Evans Hurst

Police Chief	Ernest J. Hudson
Dir Pub Works	J. Arnold Tippets
Dir Pks & Rec	Scott A. Steubing
Fire Chief	Richard L. Bowers
Municipal Judge	Sandra A. Manning
City Engineer	Craig V. Osterud
Librarian	John Elwell
City Attorney	George F. Burr
Dir Com Relatns	Kathleen L. McCarthy

Lincoln County Officials

BOARD OF COMMISSIONERS

West County	Lynn C. Buckley
East County	Janice Taylor
North County	Alfred T. Zinsser
South County	Margaret J. Wilkins
At Large	Delbert J. Hudson

ADMINISTRATION

County Manager	Glenn T. Cushing
Assessor	Jayne R. D'Arcy
Sheriff	Charles B. (''Bud'') Kuykendall
County Clerk	Olivia M. Mannix
Dept of Social Ser	David L. Yamata director
Dept of Com Relatns	Emily A. Webb director
Dept of Environ Mgt	Teresa B. Browne director
Dept of Vital Stats	Orville J. Holmquist director
Dept of Com Health	Dr. Harold J. Hemingway director
Medical Examiner	Dr. Frederick J. Remington
Juvenile Dept	A. Whitney Duvall director
District Atty	Victor A. Smith
District Court	Manfred A. Youngman presiding judge
	Judge Alfred B. Hawk
	Judge Sarah B. Weinberger
Circuit Court	Arthur G. Graham presiding judge
	Judge Raphael G. Gutierrez
	Judge Carl E. Wimberly
	Judge Helen A. Yamashita

Fairfield School District 4-J Officials

Board of Directors	Rebecca G. Tillinghast, chair
	Oscar Brooks
	Aaron W. Browne

	Robert S. Dailey
	William P. Odegard
	James B. Stumbo
	Samuel R. Sundram
Supt of Schools	Donald J. Axford
Deputy Supt	Tara A. Felgate
Dir Com Relations	Suzanne J. Corning
South High School	Brian James, principal
North High School	Eleanor M. Williams, principal
Eastside Middle School	Molly R. Moore, principal
Westside Middle School	John F. Lowry, principal
Baskerville Elem School	Lester W. Isaacs, principal
Caslon Elem School	James D. Gray, principal
Caxton Elem School	Daniel J. Houston, principal
Cheltenham Elem School	Frances D. Rodriguez, principal
Cochin Elem School	Tamara L. Stirling, principal
Cooper Elem School	Douglas K. Hixon, principal
Goudy Elem School	Kathleen M. Peterson, principal
Jenson Elem School	Scott R. Miller, principal
Kennerly Elem School	James A. Bodoni, principal

Kit Carson College Officials

Board of Trustees	Susan Thompson, chair
	Lester W. Burns
	C. Susan Graham
	Gordon M. McKenzie
	Catherine W. Marshall
	Walter Valentine
	Clark M. Quincy
	Carmen R. Wolfe
President	Clark R. Mansfield
VP for Academics	W. Montgomery Lee
VP for Administration	Robert L. Latch
VP for Development	Stephen J. Jaspers
Dir Information Bureau	Stephanie E. Odegard

Fairfield Power & Light Company Officials

Board of Directors	Samuel R. Sundram, chair
	Charles R. Blitz
	Carl W. Crawford
	Melissa H. James
	Daniel L. Jones
Manager	Jonathan W. Penrose
Chief Engineer	Ronald L. Burnside
Dir Community Relations	Emory W. Pokrzywinski

A

AASEN Kenneth J Dr (Evelyn) ownr Ridgeway Animal Hosp 11 Coburg Rd
ABEL Wallace L (Fern emp McKay's Mkt) mgr Overland Mtr Frt 330 Adams Av
ACKERMAN Andrew J (Arlene cnslr South HS) sales 1592 Nixon Av
ACME MANUFACTURING CO K L Walton pres 4000 River Av
ADAMS George S (Margaret wtrss) custdn Carson Col 334 E 19th St
AGAPE INN Tim Tremain mgr 754 E 10th St
ALDONOVICCI Dante A (Marie L) investigator Fire Dept 1715 E 14th St
ALLEN Pamela D ptnr Allen & Bernstein attys 990 Ford Av Suite 34
ALLEN Victor M (Pamela D atty) city mgr 2990 E 17th St
ALLEN & BERNSTEIN attys 990 Ford Av Suite 34
ANDERSON Josh L (Priscilla) emp Acme Mfg Co 897 E 11th St
ANDERSON William L (Kathleen S juv ofcr) sgt Hwy Ptrl 3349 W 29th
AVERY John L (Susan DMD) acct Acme Mfg Co 1140 Ford Av
AVERY Susan Dr dentist 990 Ford Av Suite 21
AXFORD Donald J (Wanda B hosp tech) Dist 4-J supt 1280 W 15th St

B

BANGOR Richard C (Anne M) sales mgr Frederick & Frank 3889 Royal Av
BARNETT Charles W (Addie nurse Prov Hosp) emp Acme Mfg Co 905 W 1st St
BASKERVILLE ELEM SCHOOL Lester W Isaacs prin 450 Lincoln Av
BEATTY Eleanor J asst mgr US Natl Bank 1395 Harris Av
BERNSTEIN Donna ptnr Allen & Bernstein attys 990 Ford Av Suite 34
BIERBAUM Alexander W (Dixie C) emp Sheriff Ofc 435 McKinley Rd
BLACK CAT TAVERN Anthony and Henrietta Cooperman ownrs 400 Detroit Av
BLANCK Tania W sales Frederick and Frank 400 E 38th St #405
BLANKENSHIP Robert W cmptrlr Acme Mfg Co 555 Westway Av #3
BLANKENSHIP Sarah W tchr Carson Col 400 E 38th St #238
BLITZ Charles R VP Acme Mfg Co 6580 Detroit Av
BODONI James A (Twila tchr) prin Kennerly Elem Schl 479 E 10th St
BOOTH Herbert S (Tara scty) ownr Resthaven Funeral Home 433 Ridge Dr
BOWERS Richard L (Eleanor) fire chf 2375 Truman Av
BRADFORD Barbara A artist 120 Edgewater Av #3
BROOKS Oscar (Audrey R scty) emp Overland Motor Frt 1345 University Av
BROWNE Aaron W (Teresa B) emp Calhoun Trucking Co 986 Oak Av
BROWNE Sharon A ptnr Quick Browne & Foxxe ad agcy 1644 Grant Av
BROWNE Teresa B dir Linc Co Dept of Environment Mgt 986 Oak Av
BROWN'S HOLE NIGHT CLUB Jarold Cohen mgr 222 Twickenham Ln
BURNS Lester W (Amanda) ownr Pioneer Valley Books 1900 Wellesley
BURNSIDE Ronald L (Jennifer L) engineer Fairfield Power & Light 1988 Kelly
BURR George F (Moira ownr Moira's Catering) atty 3866 Monroe Av

C

CABLE Fern F Mrs 111 Division Av

CALHOUN Arthur S (Helen acct) ownr Calhoun Trucking Co 19 Onyx St

CALHOUN TRUCKING CO Arthur S Calhoun ownr 1190 Monroe Av

CARSON COLLEGE see Kit Carson College

CASEY Janet Dr phys & surg ofc 22-A Twickenham Ln res 18 Polk

CASLON ELEM SCHOOL James D Gray prin 2405 Agate Av

CAXTON ELEM SCHOOL Daniel J Houston prin 300 University Av

CHALMERS Howard (Anne tchr Caxton Elem Schl) emp Acme Mfg Co 2234 E 32nd St

CHAMBER OF COMMERCE see Fairfield Chamber of Commerce

CHAPEL OF MEMORIES FUNERAL HOME Lawrence Pearson dir 565 University Av

CHASE Eleanor J stdnt Carson Col 1414 Kelly Blvd

CHELTENHAM ELEM SCHOOL Frances L Rodriguez prin 3559 Eisenhower

CHRISTENSEN Stanley C (Anne A artist) druggist 1676 Lincoln Av

CHRISTIANSON Theodore A Dr (Margaret) dentist 1631 Grant Av

CHRISTIANSON Theodore A Dr dentist (ofc) 220 W 5th St

CITY AMBULANCE SERVICE J R Wemple ownr 200 W 4th St

COCHIN ELEM SCHOOL Tamara L Stirling prin 2980 Ridge Dr

COHEN Jarold (Carmen Kennerly artist) mgr Brown's Hole Club 343 Oak Av

CONZEMIUS Andrea E drvr Calhoun Trucking Co 4578 Garfield Av

COOPERMAN Anthony and Henrietta ownrs Black Cat Tavern 1170 W 5th

CORNING John (Suzanne) sales Mattison-Kingsley Outdoor Store 3005 River Av

CORNING Suzanne J dir com relations Dist 4-J 3005 River Av

COUNTRY CLUB see Fairfield Country Club

CRAWFORD Carl W (Deborah P) ownr Crawford Chevrolet Cntr 111 Onyx Av

CRAWFORD CHEVROLET CNTR C W Crawford ownr 2000 Fairway Av

CUSHING Glenn T (Paula A rltr) Linc Co mgr 2277 Old Mill Rd

D

DAILEY Robert S (Melissa G rltr) surveyor 877 E 14th St

DALTON Roy K (Judy) emp Acme Mfg Co 567 W 14th St

D'ARCY Eric J (Jayne Linc Co assessor) prof Carson Col 2414 Onyx Av

DARNELL Jane C retd tchr 117 W 6th St

DAVIES Charles R (Maggie nurse) ancr KFLD 1179 Delta Rd

DAWSON Billie mgr Shell Service Cntr 34 Onyx St

DAWSON Clark E (Cindy photographer Telegram) sales 789 W 23rd St

DAY John H (Marsha mgr Zenith Bakery) ad mgr Telegram 788 Ford Av

DEAUVILLE Preston L (Linda M) sales 976 Buchanan Av

DEERFIELD Henry W (Shirley) owner River Av Mkt 711 River Av

DEHAVILAND Walter L (Margaret) city police det 1809 W 34th St

DIAMOND Terrence L stdnt Carson Col 1104 University Av

DIECKHOFF Robert A (Virginia tchr) ptnr R & R Texaco 777 E 29th St

DILLEY William L (Doreen G) retd 1734 Nixon Av

DION Jack L (Irene) emp International Business Machines 1889 Onyx Av

DIXON Orville Y rock crusher opr Linc Co 4311 Enterprise Rd

DMYTRYSHYN Rodney A (Lana H) CPA Dmytryshyn Allen & Ross 1151 Cherry Dr

DOFFERMAN Billy J emp Acme Mfg Co 555 Westway Av #39

DOMBROWSKY Roger L (Arlene beautician) acct 433 E 11th St

DORBLAND Susan A stdnt Carson Col 1515 Bogert Av

DORRIS Benjamin F (Roberta A) ownr Grocery King 2267 Nixon Av

DOWNTOWN MOTEL Fred Williams mgr 133 E 7th St

DuPRIEST Lillian (wid Thomas) tchr 444 W 26th St

DUVALL Alder Whitney (Priscilla J) dir Linc Co Juv Dept 1919 Ridge Dr

E

EASTERLING Jarold K (Ann Marie bkkpr) acct 2001 Old Mill Rd

EASTSIDE MIDDLE SCHOOL Molly Moore prin 2850 E 3rd St

ELWELL John A (Betty Lou tchr) city librarian 3876 Monroe Av

ESTELLE Kelly mgr Kelly Graphics 698 Curtis Av

F

FAIRFIELD CHAMBER OF COMMERCE Sandra Jones mgr Sandy River Inn

FAIRFIELD COUNTRY CLUB Richard Bernstein mgr 3345 Wellesley Dr

FAIRFIELD POWER & LIGHT CO J W Penrose mgr 400 McKinley Rd

FAIRFIELD PUBLIC LIBRARY John Elwell librarian 243 E 13th St

FAIRFIELD PUBLIC SCHOOLS Dist 4-J Donald J Axford supt 200 Monroe Av

FAIRFIELD TELEGRAM R J Poet ed & pub 975 E Broadway Blvd

FAIRVIEW MANOR apts Alan W Tichenor mgr 100 Eisenhower Av

FAIRWAY FURNITURE Clyde E Tanner mgr 500 Fairway Av

FAIRWAY HOTEL L W Scott mgr 9th & Fairway

FELGATE Tara A dep schl supt 4-J 1640 E 17th St

FIRST PRESBYTERIAN CHURCH W A Stout pstr 1182 W 13th St

FLEMMING Donald A (Dorothy) drvr TransAmerica Van Lines 880 Polk

FOREST LAWN CEMETERY 7500 Old Mill Rd

FOXXE Christina ptnr Quick Browne & Foxxe Ad Agcy 1280 Onyx Av

FRANKLIN Thomas (Elizabeth city police det) engineer 630 E 14 St

FREDERICK & FRANK DEPARTMENT STORE Harvey Underwood mgr 660 Fairway Av

FRIENDLY AV CHURCH OF GOD Hiram Weaver pstr 1106 Friendly Av

FRIENDS CHURCH Donald J Lamb pstr 670 W 5th St

G

GOUDY ELEM SCHOOL Kathleen M Peterson prin 2459 E 45th St
GRAHAM Arthur C (Ruth tchr South HS) circuit judge 680 Wellesley Dr
GRAHAM Carol S sales Pitchford Metal Wrks 555 Westway Av #88
GRAHAM C Susan tchr Caslon Elem Schl 1330 Adams Av
GRAHAM Robert W (Susan E acct) city police 1567 Parnell Av
GRAHAM Susan C atty 1515 Hilyard Av
GRAHAM Suzie actress 400 E 38th St #119
GRAVES Jonathan L (Muriel) retd librarian 777 Grant Av
GRAY James D prin Caslon Elem Schl 2060 Monroe Av
GRAY Jeanne tchr Goudy Elem Schl 555 Westway Av #14
GRAY Robert L (Rachel) emp Acme Mfg Co 333 W 11th St
GRAY Robert L Jr engineer C W Marshall Co 1104 Polk Av #4-E
GRIMM Harvey (Elizabeth hotel clerk) retail lumber 1601 Westway Av
GROCERY KING Ben Dorris mgr 11-A Twickenham Ln
GUTIERREZ Raphael G (Adrienne scty) circuit judge 977 E 14th St

H

HAMMITT Budd retd 100 Eisenhower Av
HAWK Alfred B (Carol J) district judge 1044 W 26th Av
HEATHERINGTON Anne E (wid Louis) 995 Alder Av
HEMINGWAY Harold L (Margo T) dir Linc Co Com Health 122 Polk Av
HERNDON Ellen M prof Carson Col 1899 E 7th St
HIXON Douglas K (Willa Jean scty) prin Cooper Elem Schl 153 Polk Av
HOLLOWAY Charles W coach Carson Col 786 W 17th St
HOLMQUIST Orville J dir Linc Co Dept of Vital Stats 1175 Delta Rd
HOSANNA CHILDREN'S CENTER Paul Zweig mgr 120 Eisenhower Av
HOUSTON Daniel J (Mary scty) prin Caxton Elem Schl 890 Polk Av
HOYT George F (widr Louise) writer & retd tchr 4880 Lincoln Av
HUDSON Delbert J (Marlene A) Linc Co commissioner 855 E 7th St
HUDSON Ernest J (Marilyn schl cnslr) city police chief 122 Polk Av
HUDSON Olivia R (wid Andrew) Rt 1 Box 246
HURST Patricia Evans city finance dir 4455 W 3rd St

I

INGLE Henry W & Darlene ownrs Oak Tavern 1105 Agate Av
INGRAM Mattie L retd 100 Eisenhower Av #35
ISAACS James M (Shirley cashier) mgr McKay's Mkt 1789 Villard Av
ISAACS Lester W (Karen M) prin Baskerville Elem Schl 193 Onyx Av

J

JACKSON Gregory L (Velda M acct) prof Carson Col 1300 Hayes Av
JACKSON Melvin G (Ellie machinist) ancr Ch 9 News 397 W 37th St
JAMES Brian (Louise atty) prin South HS 1714 Nixon Av
JAMES Louise atty (ofc) 77 Twickenham Ln
JAMES Melissa H loan ofcr State Bank 34 Onyx St
JAMES Robert A surveyor 3317 Edgewater Av
JASPERS Stephen M VP Development Carson Col 5680 Westway Av
JENSON ELEM SCHL Scott R Miller prin 7659 W 39th St
JOHNSON Charles H (Mary Ann electrician) printer 767 E 17th St
JOHNSON Charles J emp Shell Service Cntr 555 Westway Av #33
JOHNSON Charles N (Nettie) retd 1222 River Av
JOHNSON Charles V (Catherine) ownr Quik-Print 1672 Lincoln Av
JOHNSON C Wallace retd 767 Charnelton Av
JOHNSON Betty Lou stdnt Carson Col 555 Westway Av #55
JOHNSTON Betty Jane phys & surg ofc 111 Tower Bldg Suite D
JOHNSTON Betty Jane phys & surg res 11999 Old Mill Rd
JONES Betty A pharmacist 2344 Old Mill Rd
JONES Daniel L (Janis dance tchr) prof Carson Col 387 Onyx Av
JONES Eleanor A drvr Calhoun Trucking Co Star Rt Box 1160
JONES John P (widr Lila) retd 100 Eisenhower Av #45
JONES Joyce K stdnt Carson Col 888 E 11th St #3-A
JONES Richard L (Dianne artist) mgr Ffld Munic Airport 556 Monroe Av
JONES Sandra L mgr Fairfield Chamber of Commerce 622 W 17th St
JONES Xavier violin maker 123 Rarotonga Rd
JUSTICE Barbara writer Star Rt Box 884
JUSTICE Kelly M Ms mgr Lincoln Flight Service 5553 Old Mill Rd

K

KELLEY Hall J retd schoolmaster Kelley Point Estates Box 3466
KELLY GRAPHICS Kelly Estelle mgr 990 Ford Av Suite 11
KENNERLY ELEM SCHL James A Bodoni prin 7600 Fairway Av
KINGSLEY Edward R (Stephanie carpenter) police ofcr 880 E 19th St
KIRKWOOD Allen L (Patricia) emp Acme Mfg Co 501 Jefferson Av
KIT CARSON COLLEGE Clark R Mansfield pres 3500 Ponderosa Dr
KLINSKI Elizabeth L (wid Thomas) 1133 Market Ln
KRANSTON Ellery S mystery writer & tchr 11 Floral Hill Dr
KREWSON Billie-kay editor 1319 Freemont Av
KREWSON Peter R (Stephanie nurse) coach South HS 998 Hilyard Av
KUSCH James R (Molly nurse) ownr Sourdough Jim's 3015 College Av
KUYKENDALL Charles B "Bud" (Lila) Linc Co sheriff 2051 E 26th St

L

LAMB DONALD J (Marie candymaker) pstr Friends Church 677 W 5th St
LANGTRY Charles V (Darnella scty) pressman Acme Mfg Co 88 Onyx Av
LATCH Robert L (Kelly Jean) VP Adm Carson Col 5140 Fairway Av
LEE W Montgomery (Sandra) VP Academics Carson Col 543 Lincoln Av
LIBRARY Fairfield Public John Elwell librarian 243 E 13th St
LINCOLN COUNTY DAIRY PRODUCTS Mary Osborn mgr 37700 Old Mill Rd
LINCOLN FLIGHT SERVICE Ms Kelly M Justice mgr Fairfield Munic Airport
LINDLEY Calvin R drvr Calhoun Trucking Co 895 E 11th St
LOVE Adrian ownr Photo Creations with Love 555 Westway Av #45
LOVE Henry K sales Crawford Chevrolet Cntr 555 Westway Av #11
LOWRY John F (Henrietta tchr) prin Westside Mid Schl 1178 Taylor Av
LUNDQUIST Warren C (Heather prgrmr) prof Carson Col 900 Ridge Dr

M

MACKLIN Sandra L ed Rocket 5517 Old Mill Rd
MANNING Paul G engineer 2605 Bogert Ln
MANNING Sandra municipal judge 1233 Roosevelt Av
MANNIX Olivia M Linc Co clerk 1141 Hoover Av
MANSFIELD Clark R (Pauline writer) pres Carson Col 389 College Av
MARKVARDSEN John A (Sylvia bkkpr) dep shf Linc Co 1800 Sandy Rd
MARSHALL Catherine W ownr CW Marshall Engineering 1440 Delta Rd
MARSHALL C W ENGINEERING CW Marshall ownr 3777 Monroe Av
MARX Jonathon W (Stormy B) city police ofcr 2214 Lincoln Av
MATOBA Maggie mgr Red Baron Travel 400 E 38 St #200
McCARTHY Kathleen L dir Ffld com relations 991 W 9th St
McCORMACK Edward W (Dorothy art dir) financier 1196 Onyx Av
McGEE Duncan M (Olivia electronics technician) retd 880 W 14th St
McKAY'S MARKET James Isaacs mgr 13 St & Villard Av
McKENZIE Gordon M (Alice C) insurance sales 4030 Truman Av
McPHERSON Donald R Dr (Eleanor H) phys & surg 2990 W 26th St
McPHERSON Eleanor H persnnl mgr Frederick & Frank 2990 W 26th St
McLEAN Sheryl editor 88765 Old Mill Rd
McLOUGHLIN John chf factor Hudson's Bay Co 12 Vancouver Rd
MEEK Joe retd mountaineer Star Rt Box 1178
MELVILLE Herman C (Ruby) custdn Westside Mid Schl 1642 W 11th St
METRO CLUB Charlie Updegrave mgr 1000 Metro Bldg 10th & Fairway
MIDDLESWORTH Alfred J (Sally) tchr Caxton Elem Schl 480 Nixon Av
MILLER Barbara A reporter Telegram 77 W 57th St
MILLER Irving (Hillary bkkpr) mgr Retail Clerks Local 676 440 Truman Av
MILLER Scott R (Janet Casey MD) prin Jenson Elem Schl 18 Polk Av

MOIRA's CATERING Moira Burr ownr 101 Twickenham Ln
MOORE Murray J (Molly prin Eastside Mid Schl) sales IBM Co 980 W 26th

N

NATHAN Julia D prof Carson Col 590 E 27th St
NELSON William (Rebecca prof Carson Col) prof Carson Col 13 Polk
NICHOL Paul (Alana) mgr Providence Hosp 1555 Sandy Rd
NORTH HIGH SCHOOL Eleanor M Williams prin 3800 Ridge Dr

O

OAK TAVERN Henry & Darlene Ingle ownrs 300 Fairway Av
O'BRIEN Benjamin E (Lee Ann) trk drvr 1606 Eisenhower Av
O'CALLAGHAN Thomas J (Cynthia emp Dist 4-J) ofc mgr 2950 W 29th St
O'CONNOR Edith R clerk Acme Mfg Co 990 Eisenhower Av
ODEGARD Stephanie dir informtn Carson Col 4015 Monroe Av
O'ROURKE Alan M merchandising consultant 2244 Eisenhower Av
OESTREICH Paul J (May) farmer Rt 2 Box 667
OSBORN Mary A mgr Lincoln Co Dairy Products 36788 Old Mill Rd
OSTERUD Craig V (Belinda insur rep) Ffld cty engineer 119 W 7th St
OVERLAND MOTOR FREIGHT W L Abel mgr 4400 River Av

P

PARKER Frank D (Alicia bkkpr US Nat Bank) atty 450 Harding Av
PATERSON Betty Jane cnslr Linc Co Juv Dept 976 W 44th St
PEARSON Lawrence G (Melinda) dir Chapel of Memories 779 Nixon Av
PENROSE Jonathan W (Megan) mgr Ffld Power & Light 1333 Onyx Av
PERRIN HC CO acctng H C Perrin ownr 110 Fairway Av
PERRIN Howard C (Stacey) ownr HC Perrin Co acctng 615 E 14th St
PETERSON Kathleen M prin Goudy Elem Schl 2284 Division Av
PETRUZZELLI Dominic L (Helen J) clerk River Hotel 2417 Agate Av
PHOTO CREATIONS WITH LOVE Adrian Love ownr 11 Twickenham Ln
PIONEER VALLEY BOOKS Lester Burns mgr 100 Twickenham Ln
PLANTS Henry S (Samantha S wtrss) fry cook 1645 Bogert Ln
POET R J (Betty Johnston MD) ed & pub Telegram 876 Fairmont Blvd
POKRZYWINSKI Emory W dir com relations Ffld Pwr & Lgt 32 Polk Av
PRENTICE Linda M tchr Cheltenham Elem Schl 977 Jefferson Av
PROVIDENCE HOSPITAL Paul Nichol mgr 2000 Fairway Av

Q

QUICK Floyd R ptnr Quick Browne & Foxxe Ad Agcy 1280 Onyx Av
QUINCY Clark M (Beula lab tech) tchr North HS 1575 Carter Av

QUINCY Howard W (Jayne acct) mgr Sheraton Mtr Inn 776 E 7th St

R

RANNOW Christina W stdnt Carson Col 555 Westway Av #83
RANSOME J Henry (Yvonne) dir admissions Carson Col 2304 Ridge Dr
RAYMOND Elizabeth J (wid Herbert) rtrd 895 W Main St
RED BARON TRAVEL Maggie Matoba mgr 23 Twickenham Ln
REMINGTON Frederick J (Bonnie) Linc Co med examiner 332 Sandy Rd
RESTHAVEN FUNERAL HOME Herbert S Booth ownr 200 W 11th St
RICE Orville (Wanda trvl agt) engineer Acme Mfg Co 124 Oak Av
RICHARDSON George A (Meg piano tchr) mgr Sandy River Inn 11 Oak Av
RIVER AVENUE MKT Henry W Deerfield ownr 711 River Av
RIVER HOTEL & APTS Kaye E Zolotow mgr 222 River Av
RODRIGUEZ Frances L prin Cheltenham Elem Schl 880 W 6th St

S

SAKAMOTO Katsuyuki (Debbie L) prof Carson Col 2214 Carter Av
SALSTROM Helen L prof Carson Col 118 Harris Av
SANDY RIVER INN G A Richardson mgr 207 Fairway Av
SAVAGE Thomas K (Marsha) US Army retd 727 W 19th St
SCHOOLS Public (See Fairfield Public Schools)
SCOTT Fred W (Nancy librarian) reporter Telegram 1104 Potter Av
SCOTT Lars W (Heidi) mgr Fairway Hotel Suite 900 Fairway Hotel
SHERATON MOTOR INN H W Quincy mgr 800 McKinley Rd
SMITH Patrick L city police ofcr 107 W 7th #4
SMITH Victor A (Lori S med tech) Linc Co dist atty 2345 Monroe Av
SMITHE Roger S emp Overland Motor Freight 4323 W 1st St
SOURDOUGH JIM'S RESTR Jim Kusch ownr 777 Fairway Av
SOUTH HIGH SCHOOL Brian James prin 500 E 19th St
STAFFORD William R (Melanie A) phys & surg 4405 Nixon Av
STATE BANK W F Zbytovsky mgr 500 W 7th St
STEINHAUER Evelyn L prof Carson Col 3051 Market Ln
STEUBING Scott A (Brenda L clerk) dir city Parks & Rec 2609 Oak Av
STIRLING Tamara prin Cochin Elem Schl 4315 W 38th St
STONEROAD Charles D (Jacqueline) atty 3100 Lincoln Av
STOUT William A pstr First Presbyterian Church 1189 W 13th St
STUMBO James B (Alexis wght trainer) carpenter 2345 River Av
SUNDRAM MUSIC & SOUND S R Sundram ownr 55 Twickenham Ln
SUNDRAM Samuel R ownr Sundram Music & Sound 2167 E 6th St

T

TANNER Clyde E (Martha dietician) mgr Fairway Furniture 90 W 13th St
TAYLOR Gordon L (Diane) farmer & state senator Rt 1 Box 879

THISSEL Alan R (Alice) emp Acme Mfg Co 1607 W 17th St
THISSEL Delbert W 555 Westway Av #54
THOMPSON Anna Marie (wid Thomas) 100 Eisenhower Av #40
THOMPSON Ralph N (Susan) drvr Overland Motor Frt 3775 Monroe Av
TICHENOR Alan W (Sarah) mgr Fairview Manor 100 Eisenhower Av #1
TILLINGHAST Rebecca personnel mgr Acme Mfg Co 887 Ridge Dr
TIPPETS John A (Bethany) dir Ffld pub works 213 W 6th St
TREMAIN Timothy B mgr Agape Inn 745 E 10th St
TUBBS Henry W (Kathleen) farmer Rt 1 Box 555

U

UNDERWOOD Harvey A (Priscilla nurse) mgr Frederick & Frank 26074 Old Mill Rd
UPDEGRAVE Charles W (Sharmayne chef) mgr Metro Club 3487 W 1st St
UVERS Richard (Tammie) gov resrch bureau Carson Col 1911 Oak Av

V

VAIL Harold L prof Carson Col 888 Eisenhower Av
VALENTINE Walter (Erna E) VP Acme Mfg Co 3346 Ox Bow Way
VANDENBOSCH Ivan R (Ida) retd 104 Harris Av
VINTNER Robert W (Margaret tchr) ownr Vintner & Co CPA 11 Oak Av

W

WAFFLE Roscoe W (Edwina) cartoonist 3466 W 34th St
WALLING Karon W (wid Henry) teller State Bank 735 E 14th St
WALTON Kenneth L (Carol scty) pres Acme Mfg Co 2090 Eisenhower Av
WEAVER Hiram (Mary) pstr Friendly Av Church of God 1112 Friendly Av
WEBB Emily dir Linc Co dept of com relatns 1250 Detroit Av
WEBB James R (Lori) asst cmptrlr Acme Mfg Co 45666 Old Mill Rd
WEINBERGER John R MD (Sarah judge) phys 2240 Potter Av
WEMPLE J Richard (Arlene) ownr City Ambulance Ser 578 Lincoln Av
WESTERMAN Peter T (Janis) tchr North HS 11 Reagan Av
WESTSIDE MIDDLE SCHOOL John F Lowry prin 1700 River Av
WHEELOCK Kenneth J (Deana) CPA 448 E 18th St
WICKHAM Samuel B (Cheryl) ownr Wickham's Outdoor Store 789 Ridge Dr
WICKHAM's OUTDOOR STORE Sam Wickham ownr 77 Twickenham Ln
WILEN Myron K (Pauline tchr) ownr X-L Motel & Apts 1890 Oak Av
WILKINS Lyle C (Sally) tchr South HS 675 Eisenhower Av
WILLIAMS Dave city police ofcr 4598 Truman Av
WILLIAMS Eleanor M prin North HS 2344 Carter Av
WIILLIAMS Fred (Mariann Wood) mgr Downtown Motel 127 Arbor Dr
WILLIAMS Bill (Nancy tchr) dir Ch 3 News 1100 W 4th St
WIMBERLY Carl E (Caprice) circuit judge 3007 Eisenhower Av

WINNINGHAM Debra A hair stylist 118 Eisenhower Av
WOLFE Bruce D (Carmen) adm dir Providence Hosp 1899 Onyx Av
WORTHINGTON J Chesley Dr (Frances tchr) phys 3809 Monroe Av
WRZASZCZAK Konrad A (Aleksandre) plumber 1509 Harris Av
WYMAN Jerilee M sales Frederick and Frank 400 E 38th St #405

X,Y,Z

X-L MOTEL & APTS Myron K Wilen mgr 1598 Fairway Av
YAMASHITA Helen A circuit judge 1100 Potter Av
YAMATA David (Jane pharmacist) dir Dep Soc Ser Linc Co 910 Ridge
YAPUNCICH Richard O (Bev sales) sales Rt 1 Box 459
YOUNG Ellis T (Marje emp State Bank) VP Acme Mfg Co 600 Oak Av
YOUNGMAN Manfred A (Jo dental asst) district judge 4430 E 7th St
ZBYTOVSKY William F (Marylynn) mgr State Bank 1740 W 33rd St
ZENITH BAKERY Marsha Day mgr 1200 Fairway Av
ZIFF Jane W sales Frederick and Frank 400 E 38th St #405
ZOLOTOW Kaye E mgr River Hotel & Apts 222 River Av
ZWEIG Paul J mgr Hosanna Children's Cntr 1919 Truman Av

INDEX